THE MIND OF
ST. BERNARD
OF CLAIRVAUX

The Mind of
St. Bernard
of Clairvaux

G. R. EVANS

CLARENDON PRESS · OXFORD

1983

Oxford University Press, Walton Street, Oxford OX2 6DP

London Glasgow New York Toronto
Delhi Bombay Calcutta Madras Karachi
Kuala Lumpur Singapore Hong Kong Tokyo
Nairobi Dar es Salaam Cape Town
Melbourne Auckland

and associated companies in
Beirut Berlin Ibadan Mexico City Nicosia

Oxford is a trade mark of Oxford University Press

Published in the United States
by Oxford University Press, New York

British Library Cataloguing in Publication Data
Evans, G.R.
The mind of St. Bernard of Clairvaux.
1. Bernard, Saint, of Clairvaux
I. Title
271'.12'024   BX4700.B5
ISBN 0-19-826667-7

Library of Congress Cataloging in Publication Data
Evans, G.R.
The mind of St. Bernard of Clairvaux.
Bibliography: p.
Includes index.
1. Bernard, of Clairvaux, Saint, 1090 or 91–1153.
I. Title.   II. Title: Mind of Saint Bernard of Clairvaux.
BX4700.B5E9 1983   230'.2'0924   83-2239
ISBN 0-19-826667-7

Computerset by Promenade Graphics Limited, Cheltenham
and printed in Great Britain
at the University Press, Oxford
by Eric Buckley
Printer to the University

Preface

St. Bernard's first biographer, William of St. Thierry, presents his subject as a living paradox. He contrasts his spareness of frame, his habit of eating nursery food and little of it; and his limitless energy in working for the faith. What man within living memory, he asks, however robust his body and however sound his health, ever did as much as he, weak and near to death, to the honour of God and for the benefit of the Church? William speaks of the multitude of converts Bernard has won, the schisms in the Church he has healed, the heretics he has confounded, the peace he has brought to many contemporary communities and leaders in dispute. Beside these good deeds done for the Church in general, William sets the deeds done for innumerable individuals. A frail monk, a man of prayer, has turned the world upside down.

If we are to understand how this resolution of contradictions was brought about, we must look not only at the activity and the spirituality of the man, but at the working of his mind. The questions which presented themselves to him urgently were the paradoxes which arise when the spiritual and the temporal are brought together. May a monk take up arms in defence of the faith? How is a Pope to do his work effectively and remain at heart as humble and secluded as a cloistered monk? Bernard was formed intellectually by the abrasion of events and challenges. But he was trained academically, too, and he kept up with academic ideas. In this study I have tried to look at the ideas and assumptions which underlie his problem-solving and to allow the intellectual in Bernard to take its place beside the spiritual and practical in our picture of him.

Acknowledgements

I should like to thank Dr. Martin Brett, Professor C. N. L. Brooke, the Revd. Professor Henry Chadwick, Professor Christopher Holdsworth, Sir Richard Southern, Sister Benedicta Ward, and Dr. Rowan Williams for their friendly help and advice and for their kindness in reading parts of this study in draft, and Mrs. H. Chadwick for her invaluable help with the proofs.

Every student of Bernard owes an immense debt to the distinguished edition of his works by J. Leclercq, C. H. Talbot, and H. Rochais.

Contents

Abbreviations

AHDLMA	*Archives d'histoire doctrinale et littéraire du moyen âge.*
An. Cist.	*Analecta Cisterciensia.*
Anselmi Opera Omnia	*Anselmi Opera Omnia*, ed. F. S. Schmitt (Rome/ Edinburgh, 1938, 6 vols.).
BC	*Bernard de Clairvaux*, Preface by Thomas Merton, Commission d'histoire de l'ordre de Cîteaux (Paris, 1952).
Beiträge	*Beiträge zur Geschichte der Philosophie des Mittelalters.*
CCCM	*Corpus Christianorum Continuatio Medievalis.*
CF	Cistercian Fathers.
Coll. Cist.	*Collectanea Cisterciensia.*
Constable	*The Letters of Peter the Venerable*, ed. G. Constable (Harvard 1967), 2 vols.
Cousin	Peter Abelard, *Opera Omnia*, ed. V. Cousin (Paris, 1849–59), 2 vols.
CS	*Cistercian Studies.*
CSEL	*Corpus Scriptorum Ecclesiasticorum Latinorum*
Enquête	H. Rochais, 'Enquête sur les sermons divers et les sentences de S. Bernard', *An. Cist.*, 18 (1962).
LTR	*Sancti Bernardi Opera Omnia*, ed. J. Leclercq, C. H. Talbot, and H. M. Rochais (Rome, 1957–78), 8 vols.
MGH	*Monumenta Germaniae Historica.*
NMT	Nelson's Medieval Texts.
OMT	Oxford Medieval Texts.
PL	*Patrologia Latina.*
Recueil	J. Leclercq, *Recueil d'études sur S. Bernard* (Rome, 1962–9), 3 vols.
R. Bén	*Revue Bénédictine.*
S	*Anselmi Opera Omnia*, ed. F. S. Schmitt (Rome/ Edinburgh 1938–68), 6 vols.
SJ	*The Letters of Bernard of Clairvaux*, tr. B. Scott James (London, 1953).
VP	*Vita Prima.*

ABBREVIATIONS OF BERNARD'S WORKS

Apo	*Apologia ad Guillelmum abbatem*
Csi	*De Consideratione*
Dil	*De Diligendo Deo*
Epp.	*Epistolae*
Gra	*De Gratia et Libero Arbitrio*
Hum	*De Gradibus Humilitatis*
In Laud. V. Mar.	*In Laudibus Virginis Mariae*
Mal.	*Sermon on the Death of Malachi*
Pre	*De Praecepto et Dispensatione*
Sent.	*Sententiae*
Serm. Div.	*Sermones Diversi*
SS	*Sermones in Cantica Canticorum*
Tpl	*Ad Milites Templi de Laude Novae Militiae*
V Mal	*Vita S. Malachiae*

Chronological Table
An outline of events

1090	Bernard is born.
1098	Robert of Molesme, his Prior Alberic and twenty other monks found Cîteaux, 21 March.
1098	(?) Bernard's mother Aleth gives her son to Canons of St. Vorles de Châtillon to be educated.
1100	Robert of Arbrissel founds Fontevrault.
1103	Death of Aleth.
1106	Pope Paschal celebrates Christmas at Cluny.
1108	William of Champeaux and some of his pupils retire to St. Victor, near Paris, to live as Regular Canons.
1109	Death of Alberic, second abbot of Cîteaux, succeeded by Stephen Harding. Death of Hugh, Abbot of Cluny.
1113	Bernard enters Cîteaux with his thirty companions.
1115	Morimond and Clairvaux founded.
1118	Trois-Fontaines founded. William of St. Thierry visits Bernard in his retreat at Clairvaux, where he is recovering from illness.
1119	Foigny founded. Pope Gelasius II, who had taken refuge in France in 1118 in flight from the persecution of the emperor Henry V, dies at Cluny. Morimond founds Bellevaux. Stephen Harding presents the *Carta Caritatis* for the approbation of the abbots of the Order assembled at Cîteaux. Foundation of Fontenay by Clairvaux. Bernard's father Tescelin joins his sons at Cîteaux shortly before his death. Pope Calixtus II confirms *Carta Caritatis*. William, monk of St. Niçaise of Reims, is made abbot of St. Thierry. (?) Robert of Châtillon leaves Clairvaux for Cluny, under the influence of the Grand Prior of Cluny, who visited Clairvaux and talked to him.
1120–1	Several canons of St. Victor enter Clairvaux. Pope Calixtus II makes a solemn entry into Rome. Foundation of Trois-Fontaines. Norbert of Xanten founds a house of Regular Canons at Prémontré. Death of William of Champeaux, founder of the Victorine canons, bishop of Chalons and protector of Clairvaux.
1122	Peter the Venerable becomes abbot of Cluny.

	The Concordat of Worms brings some measure of settlement to the Investiture contest.
1123	First Lateran Council.
1124	Flight of Arnold, abbot of Morimond and Bernard's intervention.

Death of Calixtus II; Honorius II becomes Pope.

(or 1127?) William, abbot of St. Thierry, asks Bernard if he may come as a monk to Clairvaux; Bernard refuses.

1125   Death of Emperor Henry V; accession of Lothar.

Clairvaux becomes financially sound at last.

Before 1125 Bernard composes his homilies on the Annunciation, the *De Gradibus* and the *Apologia*.

Hugh of Champagne becomes a Templar. He is succeeded as Count of Champagne by Thibaut, who is more warmly disposed to Clairvaux.

1126   Norbert becomes archbishop of Magdeburg. Hugh of Fosses succeeds him as abbot of Prémontré.

Igny founded.

1127   Bernard sends *De Gratia et Libero Arbitrio* to William of St. Thierry.

Bernard writes to dissuade Artaud, abbot of Preuilly, from making a foundation beyond the Pyrenees. (But the Order does expand thus in time.)

Conrad (III-to be) proclaims himself (anti-) King.

1128   Council of Troyes. Bernard acts as secretary. The first rules of the Order of Templars are established (under Bernard's inspiration?).

c. 1129 Bernard refuses to make a foundation in the Holy Land when invited to do so by Baldwin II of Jerusalem. He uses his influence to see that the Premonstratenisians were able to do so instead.

1129   Death of Rupert of Deutz.

1130   Death at Rome of Pope Honorius II.

Double election of Innocent II and Anacletus II. Louis VI convokes a Council at Étampes to take up a position on the matter. Bernard is invited to speak and declares for Innocent. Innocent takes refuge in France.

Diet of Würzburg; the German clergy and king Lothar pronounce themselves in favour of Innocent II. Innocent stays at Cluny, where he receives Suger, sent by Louis VI to bring the homage of the Capetian realm.

1131   Raynaud, founder-abbot of Foigny, obtains from Bernard the favour of being released from his charge and returning to Clairvaux.

1131   Innocent II stays at Chartres, where he receives Henry I, King of England, come to do homage to the Pope.

Pope Innocent, with Bernard and eleven cardinals, on itinerary until March, when he arrives at Liège, where King Lothar receives him in honour and twenty-five bishops or archbishops and fifty-three abbots. The itinerary continues, until at Rouen in May he meets Henry I of England again.
The pope and three cardinals visit Clairvaux and are struck by the fervour of the monks and their poverty.
Two Benedictine houses (Bonmont and Eberbach) are given to Bernard and made the seventh and eighth daughters of Clairvaux respectively.

1131   Innocent II concedes that no archbishop or bishop shall have the right to summon Cistercian abbots to his synod.

1132   Innocent II stays at Cluny and is entertained royally. The contrast between Clairvaux's poverty and Cluny's wealth leads him to waive the dues Clairvaux pays to Cluny. As a result a quarrel begins between Cluny and Clairvaux. Bernard visits Aquitaine.
Foundation of Rievaulx.
Innocent II returns to Italy.

1133   Bernard and Innocent enter Rome.
Lothar is crowned Emperor at Rome.
Assassination of Thomas, Prior of St. Victor, under the eyes of the bishop of Paris. Innocent flees from Rome to Pisa.

1134   Death of Stephen Harding, third abbot of Cîteaux.
Death of Norbert. Bernard's second visit to Aquitaine.

1135   The Benedictines who have left St. Mary York and installed themselves at Fountains are adopted by Bernard and become the seventeenth daughter of Clairvaux. After being in Germany and Italy, Bernard returns to Clairvaux in December, where he remains until the spring of 1137, when the schism re-opens and he has to return to Rome.
Bernard composes his first sermons on Song of Songs.
Aelred, the Englishman, aged 26, becomes monk of Rievaulx, under abbot William, Bernard's disciple.
Death of Henry I of England. Accession of Stephen.
Bernard permits William of St. Thierry to become a Cistercian monk at Signy.

1136   Lothar drives Roger of Sicily out of Italy.
Bernard sends his first essays on the Song of Songs to Bernard of Portes, the Carthusian.

1137   Bernard recalled to Italy by the Pope and the Cardinals.
Death of Louis VI of France.
Accession of Louis VII.
Death of Emperor Lothar, crossing the Alps.

1138   Humbert, abbot of Igny, retires to Clairvaux. Bernard chooses

Guerric as his successor. End of Schism. Banishment of Arnold of Brescia.

Bernard leaves Rome and returns to France, to find that the Langres election has taken place and not in accordance with the agreements reached at Rome. He protests. He passes through Lyons to win the support of the archbishop.

Dedication of the new Church of Clairvaux, constructed after the removal of the monastery to a new site.

1138–52 Conrad III (never crowned Emperor).

1139　Bernard gives his Sermons on the Psalm *Qui Habitat* for the first time. William of St. Thierry writes to Bernard about Abelard.

Malachi, bishop of Armagh, stops at Clairvaux on his way to Rome and is so struck by the life there that he asks papal permission to become a monk there. It is refused.

Malachi stops at Clairvaux on his way back from Rome, and leaves four Irishmen for Bernard to train as monks, so that a foundation might be made in Ireland. (The result was the house of Mellifont.)

Second Lateran Council.

1140　Bernard preaches to the students of Paris. Many conversions.

Opening of the Council of Sens (2 June) which condemns Abelard's errors by Bernard's action.

Stephen, monk of Clairvaux, becomes a cardinal.

1142　Aelred becomes abbot of Rievaulx.

1143　Peter the Venerable asks for translation of the Koran.

Peter the Venerable replies to Bernard's *Apologia*.

War—Louis VII and Thibaut count of Champagne.

Death of Innocent II.

Celestine II becomes pope.

1144　Death of Pope Celestine II.

1145　Eugene III Pope (Bernard Paganelli, former monk of Clairvaux, abbot of St. Vincent and St. Anastasius).

William of St. Thierry begins the *Vita Prima*.

Bernard spends the winter at Clairvaux.

1146　William of St. Thierry writes his *Golden Letter* to the Carthusians of Mont-Dieux.

Pope Eugenius is forced to flee from Rome.

December, Bernard is drawn into the plan for the Second Crusade.

1147　Bernard preaches the Second Crusade.

April Pope Eugenius III visits Clairvaux.

Pope Eugenius III in Paris, Bernard present. The affair of the deposition of William archbishop of York.

September General Chapter of Cîteaux presided over by Pope Eugenius III.

1148   *April* Eugenius III stays at Clairvaux.
Death of Malachi, bishop of Armagh, at Clairvaux.
Death of Humbert, former abbot of Igny, at Clairvaux. An old friend; Bernard is sorrowful.

1150   The affair of the monk Nicholas, Bernard's secretary, who proved to have been a thief and a deceiver.

1150   Bernard in Brittany and perhaps Normandy.
Election of a new abbot of Trois-Fontaines. Bernard presents a candidate for the choice of the electors. Discontent at Rome, where Bernard's initiative is disapproved of.

1152   Bernard very ill at the end of the year.
Death of Conrad III.
Accession of Frederick I Barbarossa.

1153   Death of Bernard, Thursday, 20 August.

Chapter I

The Soldier of Christ

I. CONVERSION

Conversio may mean no more than the decision to leave the world and enter a religious order in the usage of Bernard's day, but for Bernard himself it implied an inward change as well as a change in outward circumstances.[1] His mother had intended him for the religious life, but after her death when he was little more than a child, he had been uncertain. He had dreams in which his mother appeared to him, upbraiding him for his hesitation.[2] Conversion came at last in a chapel where Bernard stopped to rest on a journey to join the rest of his family.[3] It seems to have been an experience not unlike that of St. Paul or St. Augustine or John Henry Newman; a sudden shifting of perspectives, a release of tension, and he found himself decided upon a way of life from which he was never to turn aside, and full of joyful certainty.[4]

Neither Bernard himself nor his biographers tell us how he felt at the moment when he rode off from the wayside chapel to join his brothers and his father and announce a decision which was to draw all of them after him into monastic life; but he preached a famous sermon on conversion to the scholars of Paris thirty years later, in which he sets out the characteristics of the experience and its aftermath. He sees it as an indispensable preliminary to entry into eternal life: 'For without conversion no way of access to life lies open to us'. He explains that the conversion of souls is brought about not by human effort or by human agency, but by God himself. Men speak to the outward ear, but the voice of God is heard within. As he speaks, we are recalled to ourselves and we hear him. We bring

---

[1] See my article 'A Change of Mind in some Scholars of the Eleventh and Early Twelfth Centuries', *Studies in Church History*, 15 (1978), 27–38.

[2] *VP* I.iii, 9, *PL* 185. 232A.

[3] *VP* I.iii, 8–18, *PL* 185. 230–7.

[4] A. D. Nock, *Conversion* (Oxford, 1933), and see William James's classic, *The Varieties of Religious Experience* (Gifford Lectures: Edinburgh, 1901–2).

before our memories what we know of ourselves and we scrutinise it. Then, when we see clearly where the trouble lies, we begin a battle with the vices within us.[5] The converted soul dwells in perpetual communion with God, and hears his voice more and more clearly as it learns to attend better. It is engaged in a progressive elimination of sinfulness through the living of a life in which virtue triumphs over vice. Of this inwardness of Bernard's conversion we learn only superficially from his contemporary biography, the *Vita Prima*, but in his writing on the monastic life he himself amply develops the themes of obedience to the divine will and of spiritual warfare: the after-work of conversion.

Its first effect, however, was to prompt him to become a monk. The fervour of his commitment demanded a hard life which would engage all his energies. When in March or April 1112, thirty companions set off for Cîteaux, they were making the hardest possible choice. Bernard himself explains his reason for deciding upon Cîteaux, in his *Apologia*: 'I chose Cîteaux in preference to Cluny not because I was not aware that the life was excellent and lawful [there], but because . . . I was conscious that my weak character needed strong medicine.'[6] Rejected Cluny was head of a great Order of reformed Benedictines which had dominated the monastic world for more than a century. Cîteaux had been founded by a party of Benedictines, led by Robert of Molesme, who sought to return to a primitive observance of the Rule of St. Benedict. Robert of Molesme's leadership had provided the initial impetus, but little in the way of solid foundations for the reformed community. Robert had originally been a monk of Tonnere. Although he himself had founded the community at Molesme, as it grew richer and the need for manual work declined, so the life there became less demanding and Robert became disillusioned. He left to try the life of a hermit. Then he returned to Molesme, intending to reform it, and bring it back to simplicity of life. In 1098, disillusioned once more, he

---

[5] Conv. I, LTR IV. 70; see, too, a short version which brings out exactly these points on the essentials of conversion, ed. J. Leclercq, *Analecta Monastica: Studia Anselmiana*, 20 (1948), 124–35, from MS. Engelberg 34.

[6] LTR III. 87. 25–6, Apo, 4. vii.

set off to make the new foundation which became Cîteaux, taking with him his prior Alberic, the Englishman Stephen Harding, and nineteen others. The community settled on a piece of marshy land given to Robert by Renard of Beaune, and attempted to live a hard and simple life. After less than a year, Robert (in whom there was much that was unsatisfactory) was instructed to give up his new abbacy and was sent back to Molesme by the Pope.[7]

Prior Alberic was left in charge. He attempted to ensure that the community preserved its zeal for a hard and simple life by refusing all endowments. He wanted the monks to make a living entirely by their own labours. The Cistercian habit made of undyed wool was adopted at this time, to express the principle. He was able to obtain papal support from Paschal II and thus to strengthen the position of the house a little.

Stephen Harding proved to be an abbot of a different stamp, when he succeeded to the abbacy on Alberic's death in 1108. He was an administrator of some ability; he was prepared to accept endowments, but he was firm with the lay magnates who offered them. He would not, for example, allow Hugh II, Duke of Burgundy and a good friend to the community, to hold his court at Cîteaux. Stephen was also something of a scholar. He made a complete revision of the text of the Vulgate, eliminating from it all the superfluities and accretions which had found their way into it because of the habit of annotating the text.[8]

It was to this abbot that Bernard brought his party of thirty eager new recruits.[9] Under Stephen Harding, Bernard did his year's novitiate. So outstanding was he that it was not long before he was entrusted with an abbey of his own, the new foundation at Clairvaux which, with its twin at Morimond, was one of Cîteaux's first daughter-houses. For forty years he remained Clairvaux's abbot.

[7] See J. A. Lefèvre, 'Que savons-nous du Cîteaux Primitif?', *Revue d'histoire ecclésiastique*, 51 (1956), 8–9: *Exordium Parvum* VII, ed. J. Bouton and J. Van Damme, 'Les plus anciens textes de Cîteaux', *Cîteaux*, 2 (1974), 64–8, 74–5.

[8] D. Knowles, *Great Historical Enterprises* 2nd ed. (London, 1963), pp. 197–222 and pp. 752–3; for a bibliography and discussion, see J. R. Sommerfeldt (ed.) *Cistercian Ideals and Reality*, CS 60 (1978).

[9] Knowles, op. cit., pp. 197–222.

II. UNITY

In a letter written to congratulate Suger, abbot of St. Denis, on his new humility (he had been accustomed to travel in pomp, but had mended his ways), Bernard draws a contrast between the life which is now lived in the house of St. Denis, and the corrupt state of things before. The comparison brings out, he says, both the beauty of what is beautiful now and the ugliness of what was previously ugly. The vaults of the great abbey used to echo with the bustle and noise of worldly affairs because so much secular business went on there. Now only spiritual songs are heard. The house of God used to be full of idle gossip and the chatter of boys and girls as men of the world and curious passers-by wandered into it or came in on business.[1] Now there is seclusion. The monastery is, as it should be, a world apart.

By a similar literary device Bernard addressed himself to the task of winning back the young Robert of Châtillon, a kinsman of his who had been one of his monks at Clairvaux, but who had been won over to the Cluniacs by the prior of Cluny. Cluny had some claim to Robert, because he had been promised to them from boyhood, but he had chosen to enter Cîteaux when he was old enough; the prior of Cluny had paid him a visit in which, says Bernard, 'he commended feasting and condemned fasting'; he mocked at the idea that a monk should engage in fasts and vigils and silence and manual labour; 'he called sloth contemplation, gluttony talkativeness',[2] and stole the young man away with his 'sophistries'. He asked when God was pleased by human suffering; where the Scriptures say that we ought to kill ourselves; why God made food if it was not so that we should eat it; why God gave us bodies if it was not so that we might look after them.[3] Bernard identifies these misleading arguments for what they are and sharpens the contrast between the soft life of Cluny and the hard and rewarding life of Clairvaux at every point. The monastery, as it should be, is a world withdrawn from the secular world in every respect, without

---

[1] Letter 78, 5, LTR VII. 204. 15–58, SJ 80, 5.
[2] Letter 1, 4. LTR VII. 4. 15–17, SJ 1, 4.
[3] Letter 1, 5. LTR VII. 5. 3–15, SJ 1, 5.

the ordinary comforts of life, making no concession even to standards which are perfectly acceptable in the ordinary world. 'What can please the citizens of heaven more than this?' Bernard asks in his letter to abbot Suger. If we could see them, we should find the angels joyfully joining in our singing, standing beside us when we pray, watching over us while we sleep and guiding those in positions of authority. The monastery is the heavenly city on earth; it is Jerusalem.[4]

Bernard thought of man as a social animal (*sociale animal*), who is intended by his Creator to be free from the limitations of his individuality, to pass from what is within him to what is around him with ease, so that his inner peace diffuses into a peace with all men. 'This is the law of natural society' (*lex naturalis societatis*), he explains, 'that we do not do to others what we would not have them do to us; and that what we wish to be done to ourselves, we strive to do to others.'[5] The etymology with which Bernard was familiar derived the very name of 'monk' (*monachus*) from the monad (*monas*), the supreme One.[6]

In his homily on Psalm 132: 'Behold how good and how joyous it is for brothers to dwell together as one', Ernald abbot of Bonneval comments on the manifold nature of this unity. He lists the many ways in which something may be said to be 'one'; as a herd of many beasts is one; as many singers sing with one voice in unison; as many men are of one mind; as many parts make one body; as an atom is the ultimate 'one' in being indivisible; as a soul with all its faculties is one simple substance. In all these respects, in collectiveness, in likeness, in harmony, in composing a single whole, in indivisibility, in simplicity, the members of a monastic community are to be one with the citizens of heaven.[7]

The proliferation of religious orders of the late eleventh and early twelfth centuries had resulted in such a multiplicity of monks and canons and hermits by the middle of the century that one commentator saw a need to take stock of the position.

[4] Letter 78, 6. LTR VII. 205, 5–20, SJ 80, 6.
[5] Serm. de Div. 16. iii, LTR VI. 146. 1
[6] Isidore, *Etymologiae*, ed. W. M. Lindsay (Oxford, 1911), VII. xiii. l.
[7] *PL* 189. 1571–2.

His *Little Book on the Different Orders* (*Libellus de Diversis Ordinibus*) was written in the Liège region in the middle of the twelfth century.[8] He wanted to show that all these different ways of professing oneself in the religious life (*diversitates professionum*) were pleasing to God, that there was an underlying unity in the diversity; and he wanted to distinguish the purposes of the different callings.[9] He arranged his treatise in a way which reflects his preoccupation with unity, beginning with hermits who are few and who live alone, and then considering monks and canons, whose numbers are greater. He compares this system with the practice of beginning with one and going up to larger numbers in counting. The unity of monks is like that of numbers; they are rooted in singleness and solitude just as all numbers derive from 'one'; they are of one heart and mind, although they are many in body, just as all numbers proceed from one and are rooted in one.[10] This unity in diversity is like that of creation, where God makes the various 'one' in the harmonious arrangement of the universe.[11]

The author of the *Libellus* felt his task to be pressing, not only because there were now so many orders of religious, but because they disputed with one another acrimoniously about their respective claims to observe the Rule perfectly. 'I judge none of them to be transgressors of their Rule', he says equably.[12] He presses for mutual tolerance. 'There were many things which the holy author of the Rule was not able to mention, although without doubt he knew that they had to be done',[13] such practical details as the advisability of readers and servers having something to eat before they begin their duties at mealtimes. In such matters each order and even each monastery will have its customs. 'I praise all those who live according to the order of each monastery',[14] says the author of the *Libellus*. It is important that each religious should be faithful in keeping the Rule as he understands it, in such a way

---

[8] *Libellus de Diversis Ordinibus*, ed. G. Constable and B. Smith (Oxford, 1972), OMT. pp. xviii–xxiii.
[9] Ibid., pp. 2–3.
[10] Ibid.
[11] Ibid.
[12] Ibid.
[13] Ibid., p. 30 (II.16).
[14] Ibid., p. 29 (II.14).

that they who have vowed to observe the Rule, 'when asked about this, answer that they observe it well and believe in it'.[15] 'I wish to blame no one even if I know he believes in a different interpretation, provided it is not at variance with the Christian faith ... Though they live differently, they aspire from one beginning to the one end which is Christ.'[16]

The author of the *Libellus de Diversis Ordinibus* divides the orders of hermits, monks and canons according to whether they live close to towns and villages or at a distance, and he discusses the value of, for instance, the Victorine Canons' attempt to set an example[17] by living near to men, the work of the Premonstratensian Canons[18] who live far from men. Among the monks, the Cistercians remove themselves far from men[19]; the Benedictines of the Cluniac Order live close to men.[20]

The Cluniacs and Cistercians in particular were very far from enjoying the harmony and mutual respect which would have made them one in the way he approves. About 1125 William of St. Thierry, Bernard's first biographer and himself a Benedictine who wanted to become a Cistercian, brought to Bernard's attention certain abuses which he believed were being practised by the Cluniacs. Bernard understood from his letter that William wanted him to do two contradictory things: on the one hand to scotch the rumour that the Cistercians were spreading malicious accusations against the Cluniacs, and on the other, to make just such accusations as might justify such a rumour, by speaking against Cluniac excesses in matters of food and clothing. 'This task you give me of removing a scandal from the Kingdom of God I gladly undertake, but it is not yet clear to me how you want this to be done', Bernard replied.[21]

Relations between Cluniacs and Cistercians had been

---

[15] Ibid., p. 29.
[16] Ibid., p. 29.
[17] Ibid., pp. 73–4 (VI.42).
[18] Ibid., p. 57 (V).
[19] Ibid., pp. 45–55 (III.22–9).
[20] Ibid., pp. 18–45 (II.8–21).
[21] LTR VII. 219. 4–14, Letter 84 bis.

strained for some time.[22] Pons, a kinsman of Pope Paschal II, succeeded abbot Hugh of Cluny in 1109. His abbacy appears to have begun well and then standards began to slip. The Cluniac reforms of the late tenth and eleventh centuries had strengthened the liturgical life of Benedictine houses of the Cluniac family, but at the expense of time for reading and manual labour. More than one commentator speaks of the 'strictness' which hampered the monk and kept him from labour of mind or body and from quiet contemplation.[23]

In some houses formal observances appear gradually to have become a substitute for real austerity; the time-consuming ritual of the elaborate liturgy took the place of fasting and silence and the self-denial which was in the spirit of the Rule as Benedict envisaged it. So at least it appeared to the critics of the Cluniacs as they saw them well-fed and well-dressed and leading comfortable lives. These were not, it seemed, mere matters of a difference in the details of observance, but of the deeper purpose of monastic life being lost.

Peter the Venerable, Pons's successor, took the criticism, and what he himself had observed, seriously enough to call an assembly at Cluny in 1132 to draw up new Statutes. His proposal to restore certain fasts which were no longer observed, to reimpose the obligation of silence, to reinvoke the ancient austerity of the Rule, met with opposition from many of those present, and even in the modified form in which Peter was able to get the reforms accepted, they were not always fully implemented.[24]

The breaking away of a small group of monks from the

---

[22] For the background, see D. Knowles, *Cistercians and Cluniacs* (Oxford, 1955).

[23] Ibid., p. 6. See William of Malmesbury, *Gesta Regum Anglorum*, ed. W. Stubbs, *Rolls Series* (London, 1887), pp. 380–5, on the Cistercian beginnings. See, too, A. H. Bredero, 'Cluny et Cîteaux au xiie siècle: les origines de la controverse', *Studi Medievali*, xii (1971), 135–75, *Cistercians and Cluniacs*, CF, 33 (1977), H. E. J. Cowdrey, 'Abbot Pontius of Cluny', *Studi Gregoriani*, xi (1978), 177–276, A. H. Bredero, 'Une controverse sur Cluny au xii siècle', *Revue d'histoire ecclésiastique* (1981), 48–72. PL 166. 840–2. See Orderic Vitalis, *Historia Ecclesiastica*, xii. 30, ed. M. Chibnall (Oxford, 1978), VI. 310–16, and also Book xiii. 13, on the austerities of the Cistercians, and on the new monastic orders in general: Orderic Vitalis, *Historia Ecclesiastica*, viii, 26, ed. M. Chibnall (Oxford, 1973), IV. 310–34.

[24] Orderic, ed. cit., VI. 424–6 (Book xiii.13).

Cluniac pattern under the leadership of Robert of Molesme might have occasioned no more than a frisson of resentment had the Cistercians not proved so successful and so attractive, especially when they had Bernard to lead them. Wherever the Cistercians founded a house, they drew men who might otherwise have become monks in a Cluniac house (for both orders observed the Benedictine Rule), and sometimes they attracted fugitives from the Benedictines themselves. William of St. Thierry is a case in point. Jealousy and a certain amount of acrimony was perhaps inevitable.

The Cluniacs were bound to strike a contrast with the Cistercians if only because the Cistercians had consciously set out to be different. Their emphasis upon prayer and silence made it seem that the Cluniacs were given to idle talk and that they neglected private prayer for liturgical prayer. The Cistercians at their hard manual work made the Cluniacs seem idle and luxurious. The plain, sparse food, and the harsh cloth of the Cistercian habit made it appear that the Cluniacs ate delicately and dressed in fine clothes. These, at least, appear to have been the grounds of dispute and the focal points of bad feeling between them.

William had set Bernard a delicate task. Bernard clearly felt unsure of his ground at first,[25] but William was persistent. He evidently kept closely in touch with Bernard while he was writing his treatise against the Cluniacs. (Bernard wrote him a note about the preface to which he added a long letter of reassurance that he has not ceased to love William because he is too busy to write and tell him so.) When he had finished his first draft Bernard sent the book to a scholar he respected, Ogier, a regular canon of Mont-Saint-Eloi, with the request that he read it and send Bernard his comments. Ogier had a copy made for William.[26] Bernard re-wrote it at least once.[27] When it was finished and published, the *Apologia* made a considerable impact upon the contemporary monastic world.

It was a *tour-de-force* of polemical good manners, for Bernard felt throughout some awkwardness in carrying out the task

---

[25] LTR III. 81. 5–14.
[26] Letter 88, LTR VII. 234. 1–4.
[27] LTR III. 67–79.

which William had given him to perform. The problem is not an obvious one, Bernard thinks[28]; there are no ravening wolves destroying the flock, but rather fleas gnawing away under the fleeces of the sheep.[29] For that reason Bernard's reproaches must be most exactly and carefully judged. Besides, he has himself often been a guest in houses of the Cluniac Order, where he has been treated with great honour.[30] Common courtesy requires him to make his accusations with politeness and consideration.[31]

He has a further reservation: there are different ways of serving God. Martha and Mary are not alike; Noah and Daniel and Job can certainly not be said to come by a single road of justice or righteousness to the Kingdom of God. The whole Church is like the Queen of Psalm 44: 15, whose garment has a multicoloured border.[32] There should be peace and concord, so that the colours make one garment.[33] Yet there are many paths, and many mansions in heaven.[34] Above all, Bernard is anxious not to fall into the trap of the Pharisee,[35] and thank God that he is not like his fellows.

When he wrote to William agreeing to attempt the work, he asked for a clearer idea of what William had in mind and further instructions: *manda apertius*.[36] Perhaps as a result of their correspondence, perhaps out of his own reflections, he framed two or three principles which he puts forward as the main points to be borne in mind. These are the tests against which monastic reform must be measured. Is the Rule being properly kept? Is right order (*rectus ordo*)[37] being adhered to? Is unity being preserved? Is life stripped as it should be of superfluities and trivialities?

---

[28] LTR III. 63–108, text from p. 81.
[29] (I. 1), LTR III. 81. 15.
[30] (II. 4), LTR III. 84. 2–6.
[31] (II. 4), LTR III. 84. 2–3.
[32] (III. 5), LTR III. 84–5.
[33] (IV. 7), LTR III. 87. 8–9.
[34] LTR III. 89. 9.
[35] (V. 10), LTR III. 90. 11.
[36] LTR III. x–xi and Letter 84 bis, LTR VII. 219. 15.
[37] (IX. 19), LTR III. 97. 3–4.

Bernard's *Apologia* is only one of a series of polemical writings exchanged by Cluniac and Cistercian authors.[38] The controversy over correct observance of the Rule gave a certain dignity to what must often have been petty resentment. Peter the Venerable, abbot of Cluny, and, in time, a friend of Bernard,[39] describes scenes which he has himself witnessed. A group of white monks talking animatedly, suddenly falls silent when they notice that a black monk is approaching them, as though they feel themselves to be in the presence of an enemy from whom state secrets must be kept.[40] Black monks, meeting a white monk, laugh at him as though he were a monster from a distant country, and make mocking gestures of amazement at his appearance.[41]

In the letter in which he relates these stories, Peter tries to give an account from the Cluniac side, of the very difficulties Bernard describes in his *Apologia*. Neither work shows signs of having been influenced by the other, or of being in any way a reply to it, and it is probable that they were composed independently at about the same time.

They show admirably by contrast the differences of approach of the two protagonists. Peter was a scholarly, quiet, thoughtful man. He wrote against the heretics[42] and he took an active interest in the effect Islam was having upon Christendom,[43] but he was not a polemicist of Bernard's persuasive power. He writes a calmly reasoned account, without acrimony, of the differences between the Cluniacs and the Cistercians, in which he tries systematically to get to the heart of their disagreement over the observance of the Rule, and to show that, at root, there is no disagreement at all.

Certain persons, he says, have engaged in deadly warfare with their rivals. Some of them are Cistercians, but some come

---

[38] See A. P. Lang, 'The Friendship between Peter the Venerable and Bernard of Clairvaux', *St. Bernard: Studies Presented to J. Leclercq* (Washington, 1973), 35–53, lists twelve.

[39] Ibid.

[40] Constable, Letter 28, paragraph 20.

[41] Ibid.

[42] Peter the Venerable, *Contra Petrobrusianos*, ed. J. Fearns, *CCCM*, 10 (1968).

[43] P. Kritzeck, *Peter the Venerable and Islam* (Princeton, 1964), and see Appendix.

from Peter's own Cluniac fold. Those who ought to live in the house of the Lord as friends have utterly failed in charity towards one another. They are of the same family; they serve the same Lord; they are soldiers of the same King; they all call themselves Christians; they are all monks. The difference they feel to exist between them is, nevertheless, lurking beneath these similarities.[44]

Peter briskly eliminates a number of possibilities. The quarrel cannot be over goods or money or possessions, for, as monks, both Cluniac and Cistercian brothers have given up possessions. If it is over differences of observance of points of detail in the Rule, then the quarrel is silly and childish. No difference in customs ought to rob the servants of Christ of their mutual charity.[45] Peter dwells on the problem of the observance of the Rule at some length.[46] He concludes, in the same spirit as the author of the *Libellus*, that what matters is the common intention of those who follow the Rule, not their identical observance. 'You ask me to show how a monk can safely travel by different paths when he is under the same Rule.'[47] The 'single eye', Peter argues, the common intention, confers unity on variety of observances; they all become acts of charity designed to save souls, and in that supreme purpose they are utterly at one. This principle makes the quarrel over the Rule seem not only foolish, but quite unnecessary. Peter's answer to Bernard would be that indeed the Rule is being properly kept and *rectus ordo* preserved, and that there is no danger of disunity if monks of both colours understand how alike they are in all that matters.[48]

The problem was not, of course, in reality so simple, if only because the good will necessary for such a view of things to iron out all differences was the one thing most spectacularly

---

[44] Letter 28, para. 6.
[45] Letter 28, para. 7.
[46] Letter 28, para. 8–19.
[47] Letter 28, para. 12.
[48] There is no internal evidence that the letter is in fact an answer to Bernard's *Apologia*. cf. *Libellus de Diversis Ordinibus*, ed. and tr. G. Constable and B. Smith (Oxford, 1972), p. 34, quoting Augustine *Ep.* 54, v. 6, *CSEL*, xxxiv. 165–6.

lacking from relations between Cluniacs and Cistercians. But Peter, like Bernard, sees unity as the supreme good and end of monastic life.

In the past a good proportion of monks and nuns had been given to the religious life as child oblates. They had never lived in the world; they were educated in their houses and remained there all their lives, as William of Malmesbury did at Malmesbury in Wiltshire. In the middle decades of the eleventh century communities of clerks arose in north Italy and the South of France, living a common life of poverty, celibacy, and obedience after the example of the early Christians. The way of life of these 'canons' was officially approved at the Lateran synods of 1059 and 1063. It was widely adopted in western Europe in the twelfth century. It demanded an adult vocation, a commitment which would ensure a high standard of asceticism, of adherence to the Rule, of observance of the vows of poverty, chastity, and obedience, in the house to which the novice came.[49]

The common desire of those who chose the religious life in full knowledge of the opportunities which lay open to them in the world, was to live as the apostles had done. 'What did the holy Apostles teach us?' Bernard was to ask in a sermon for the Feast of St. Peter and St. Paul. 'These are our masters, who . . . teach us even today . . . They do not teach the art of fishing . . . of the reading of Plato, nor to tangle in arguments with Aristotle, nor to be always learning and never come to the knowledge of the truth. They have taught me to live.' The search for the way of living which was the *vita apostolica* led some to try to live more perfectly by the Rule of St. Benedict, and others to look for an alternative rule of life, closer, as they believed, to the apostolic model. When in due course a Rule was adopted by some of those involved in such experiments, the Rule which was attributed to St. Augustine of Hippo

---

[49] J. Leclercq, 'Textes sur la vocation et la formation des moines au moyen âge', *Corona Gratiarum Miscellanea . . . Eligio Dekkers . . . oblata* II (Bruges/ The Hague, 1975), pp. 169–94, and J. Leclercq, 'Noviziato' in *Dizionario degli Istituti di Perfezione* VI (Rome, 1979).

allowed exactly the scope which was needed;[50] it better fitted the needs of those who were living a life, not strictly contemplative, but involving some active element, as was the case, for example, with canons who belonged to Cathedral Chapters. That they should live under a Rule was in every way desirable; that it should be the Benedictine Rule, properly observed, was practically speaking impossible.

From the early twelfth century many independent Augustinian congregations were established. Anselm of Havelberg, an admirer of St. Bernard, and himself a canon of the Praemonstratensian Order before he became bishop of Havelberg in 1129, describes how Norbert of Xanten founded his Order of Praemonstratensian canons. 'There arose in that same profession [the Augustinian] and in imitation of the apostolic life, a certain pious priest called Norbert, at the time of Pope Gelasius. He, on account of his piety, and the many enormities and schisms which were then to be observed in the Western Church, received the authority to preach from the Roman Pope Gelasius.'[51] The distinguishing marks of Norbert and his like[52] were their active ministry to ordinary people, while they themselves lived not an enclosed life, but under a Rule which separated them from the world. They were preachers;[53] they baptized, administered communion, absolved penitents.

The division between the Benedictine contemplative monk and the active Augustinian canon was not, however, a tidy one. Monks often took on the work normally done by parish clergy when they were sent by their Order to live in cells and priories and to keep an eye on their house's lands. They thus obtruded on the work of the canons. The Benedictine abbot Rupert of Deutz speaks of the *longa querela*, the lengthy complaint which

---

[50] Sermon for Peter and Paul, 2, 3, LTR II. x. On Augustine's Rule, and its adoption in the early Middle Ages, see C. Dereine, 'Vie commune, règle de Saint Augustin et Chanoines réguliers au xi siecle,' *Revue d'histoire ecclésiastique*, 41 [1946], 365–406.

[51] *PL* 188. 1155A, and see G. Salet's edition of the first book of Anselm of Havelberg's *Dialogus* (Paris, 1965).

[52] Janet Nelson, 'Society, Theodicy and the Origins of Heresy: towards a reassessment of the Mediaeval Evidence'. *Studies in Church History*, 9 [1972], 65–77.

[53] R. Brooke, *The Coming of the Friars* (London, 1975), pp. 92, 97, 108, *et alibi*, emphasizes how the Dominican and Franciscan preachers based their Rule on that of Augustine.

has been occasioned. Ought the monk who is dead to the world
(*cum sit saeculo mortuus*), and whose task, as Jerome describes
it, is to weep (*plangere*) and not to teach (*docere*), to be found
preaching and administering the sacraments? Rupert argues, in
a letter to Everard, abbot of Brunwilre, that Jerome was
speaking of the monk who was merely a monk, and not
ordained as a priest. If a monk is a priest, then it is his duty to
teach, says Rupert.[54] The point is developed at length in his
Altercatio between a monk and a clerk.[55]

The matter was of some importance to those who wished to
see themselves as true followers in the way of the apostles. The
apostles preached. It was difficult to contend that the monastic
life was truly the apostolic life if preaching was ruled out.
Some of the preaching clergy claimed superiority over the
monk, gloried in their clerisy, and were puffed up and swollen
with pride in their superior profession, Rupert reports.[56]

As a Benedictine, Rupert was bound to put the contemplative
life higher than the active. He is the author of a treatise *On the
True Apostolic Life* in which he weighs against one another the
claims of the four divisions of the faithful: monks, regular
canons, clergy, and laity, to be following Christ's way.[57] The
regular canons can, he concedes, be seen to be obeying the
instruction of Christ to the apostles themselves, to be 'the
light of the world'.[58] The monks are doing penance on behalf of
mankind, and they must, in order to succeed in this, hide their
light under a bushel; that is, they must live in the cloister. But
in truth, says Rupert, their life is hidden with Christ in God.
When he comes again they will be shown to have been living
Christ's life most perfectly.[59] Important though preaching is,
the contemplative life brings the soul closer to God. It is
directed inward and upward, while the preacher's duty is to
turn his thoughts outward to his listeners. In his long treatise
on Benedict's Rule, Rupert describes in a traditional image the

[54] *PL* 170. 543.
[55] *PL* 170. 537–42.
[56] *PL* 170. 539B.
[57] *PL* 170. 615.
[58] Matthew 5: 14, 15.
[59] *PL* 170. 616–17.

ultimate spiritual experience of standing upon a mountain-top, to which the monk may hope to attain through reading and contemplation.[60]

As a canon, Anselm of Havelberg felt bound to take issue with the notion that the monastic order is *dignior* than that of the Augustinian canons. He objects that it is false logic to argue from the novelty of the term 'regular canon' to the conclusion that the Order is contemptible, as though that were a necessary consequence.[61] Anselm's choice of this form of argument assumes in his correspondent, and indeed in all those who are likely to read this open letter, a level of education, and especially a familiarity with the technical terms of logic, which he would not have looked for a few decades earlier. Articulate men with trained minds are disputatious and Anselm conceives of the whole matter as a dispute.

He is aware of the difficulty which has prompted the attempt to emphasize the superiority of the monastic life: the overlapping of functions which takes place when monks behave like canons or work as parish priests, and when canons try to behave like monks.[62] Anselm would like to see two things: a clear recognition of the differences between the two, and an acceptance of their equal and complementary status. 'I would think it wholly right and good for all the clergy to live according to a rule [*regulariter vivere*], but for none of them to become monks', he advises.[63]

In his *Liber de Ordine Canonicorum Regularium* he sets out this principle at length, comparing and contrasting the two orders in a series of comparisons with the apostles Peter and John. Peter is the Augustinian canon, John the Benedictine monk. Peter and John, he explains, both ran to the tomb on the day of the Resurrection. John ran faster than Peter and came first to the tomb, but he did not enter. He stood outside. Then came Peter, and he entered into the tomb. Then John came in, too.[64] John, Anselm explains, was the disciple who was loved

---

[60] *PL* 170. 479D.

[61] *Epistola Apologetica, PL* 188. 1122D: 'Novum, ergo contemptibile . . . quasi necessaria sit illa consequentia.'

[62] *PL* 188. 1136.

[63] *PL* 188. 1136.

[64] John 20: 2–8, and *PL* 188. 1113–14, Chapter 34.

more than the others, and Peter the disciple who loved more than the others. John reclined on Jesus's breast and saw heavenly wonders; Peter walked on the water with Jesus and was made a wonder to the world. John was younger in body and quicker of mind; Peter was steady and of mature age. When John arrived at the tomb he waited out of respect to the elder disciple, to allow him to enter first; Peter took the lead as befitted the senior of the two. John's counterpart, the Benedictine monk, is better fitted for contemplation (*quietis ac theoriae assuetior*), for going apart and reading the Word of God (*videndo vacans verbo*). Peter's counterpart, the Augustinian canon, is better fitted for the ministry of the Word to others (*ministerio verbi paratior*).[65]

Anselm now turns to the task of showing why some ought to prefer the Petrine to the Johannine way. He explains that in order to be effective in the role of Peter, the canon must take John's way as his starting-point. Peter is active because the speculative vision (*visio theorica*) goes before him and leads him on. He has, as it were, the best of both worlds, the contemplative and the active. That is why, to change the comparison, Martha (Peter) is busy over many things and Mary (John) has only one thing to think about. The canon cannot, then, imitate Peter without the aid of the monk who is imitating John, but he has no reason to think his calling inferior. The two Orders are different, but not opposed, *diversi* but not *adversi*. They are like two cherubim who look upon one another with the friendly smiles of brothers (*semetipsos fraterna familiaritate respiciunt*). Sometimes the two callings come together in one person when men of proven knowledgeableness and good life in the monastic community are made priests or called to be in charge of churches. The supreme example to whom Anselm points in his own day, is the Cistercian monk who became Pope Eugenius III.[66]

III. OBEDIENCE

The *Libellus de Diversis Ordinibus* was written because the monastic world was deeply and painfully divided by these

---

[65] *PL* 188. 1114 and Luke 10: 42.
[66] *PL* 188. 1116.

differences. With a choice of several types or modes of monastic life both newly-converted religious and those of longer experience were attracted by what they heard of life in other houses. Bernard had sympathy for the desire to live a life in more perfect obedience to the Rule, but he could not countenance instability or the breaking of existing vows. He frequently found himself in a position of some awkwardness. He writes to the canons of Eaucourt about some brothers who wanted to transfer themselves from the Rule of St. Augustine to the Rule of St. Benedict. In so doing, he argues, they do not depart from the teaching of 'him who is the Master of us all'; nor do they break faith with their baptismal vows. He is inclined to approve their defection, with the proviso that if within the year of probation they must serve under the Benedictine Rule they wish to return to the canons' way of life, he will not prevent them.[1] He writes to a fellow abbot who has been having difficulties in imposing a stricter regime, and one of whose monks has run away and taken refuge with Bernard. He suggests that these Cluniac monks should be invited and not forced to adopt a stricter way of life. Those who want to live more strictly should be encouraged to accommodate themselves, as far as their consciences allow, to those who are weaker. Or perhaps they may be allowed to live a stricter life where they are. If that is not possible, they may perhaps be allowed to leave the house to find a life which suits them elsewhere, but that is a last resort.[2] As to the runaway, Bernard concedes that he has kept him for a time, although that is not his usual practice. But he has found from experience that a taste of a strict regime is often enough, and that the unsettled and restless monk may be content to return home afterwards.[3]

The theme of much of Bernard's advice in such situations is perseverance. To Adam, the monk who had followed abbot Arnold of Morimond on crusade, he suggests that Satan, having tried to seduce him in every other way from the time when he decided to become a monk, was irked by his perseverance and thought that if he could rob him of that he would overthrow

---

[1] Letter 3, 1. LTR VII. 23. 5–24. 9. SJ 3, 1.
[2] Letter 83, 1. LTR VII. 216. 16–217. 8. SJ 85.1.
[3] Letter 84, 1. LTR VII. 218. 8–22. SJ 86, 1.

him altogether. It was lack of perseverance that he showed when he left Morimond.[4] A young man called Fulk had been professed as an Augustinian canon and was then persuaded by a rich uncle to return to the world. Bernard does not blame the uncle, who was not bound by a vow of poverty; he was only seeking what was his own—the company of his nephew—and he had a right to do so. But Fulk himself was under no obligation to return to a world he had renounced. The leaving of his house of canons was an act of theft.[5] Fulk's obligation was to persevere in the state where he had placed himself.

Bernard was not unaware that he himself was open to the charge that he had abandoned his first commitment in leaving Cîteaux for Clairvaux. He answers any such accusation in his next letter to Adam. He was sent in peace, without scandal or disagreement, and according to the customs and usual practice of his Order; he was sent by his abbot. 'And so, as long as I persevere in the same peace and harmony in which I was sent, and as long as I stand fast in unity, I am not putting my personal judgement before the common observance', he claims. 'I am staying quietly and obediently where I was put.' He has not broken the bond of unity with his first brothers, and if he is absent 'in body' from Cîteaux he is there in spirit in a common devotion, living a life which is in every detail the same as the life at Cîteaux.[6] The unity of obedience is preserved. Bernard has persevered. It is in this spirit that he has sometimes received and kept monks who had run away from other monasteries when he believed that they could not keep their vows with perseverance in the houses they had left. He is aware that this confession will anger some, but he is sure that he is helping these monks in true perseverance in unity by allowing them to leave a situation which is impossible for them.[7]

Perseverance and stability were intimately connected in Bernard's mind with obedience. When the religious commits himself to God in the monastic life he gives up the use of his own will. The unity of the brothers consists supremely in the

---

[4] Letter 5, 2. LTR VII. 29. 6, SJ 6, 2.
[5] Letter 2, 2. LTR VII. 14. 5–6. SJ 2. 2.
[6] Letter 7, 16. LTR VII. 43. 5–21. SJ 8, 16.
[7] Letter 7, 18. LTR VII. 44. 18–45. 17.

absence of the discords which arise when the wills of individuals are set against one another. Thus Bernard writes to Adam, the monk of Morimond: 'Be reconciled, not with one brother only, but with the whole multitude who had this against you . . . that you have wounded their peace and unity by your desertion as if with a sword.'[8] But in giving up their wills monks swear to obey their superior. Adam had obeyed his abbot when instructed by him to go crusading, and his case raises some fine points about obedience which Bernard explores for him in his letter. He brings out the essential principle which he puts in brief in another letter (to Bruno of Cologne), written at the time of the affair of Adam and the abbot of Morimond. Bernard asked Bruno to talk to the crusading party as they passed through his area, and to try to make them understand that no one is bound by obedience to a superior who is himself disobedient; no one is bound by the Rule to obey someone who is going against the Gospel. A wandering monk ought to be rejected utterly.[9]

He comes to this point more gradually in his letter to Adam himself. He anticipates Adam's defences. Perhaps Adam will say that he was merely obeying his abbot, but abbot Arnold is now dead. Bernard compares the bond between abbot and monk with the marriage bond; surely it is no stronger than that? Yet the wife is not bound to her husband once he is dead. How can Adam think himself still bound to obey his dead abbot's wishes?[10]

This argument is no more than a preliminary skirmish. Even if abbot Arnold was still alive, says Bernard, Adam ought not to obey him. 'It is very perverse', he insists, 'to claim to be obedient by disobeying a higher authority so as to obey a lower one, that is, by disobeying the commandments of God for the sake of the commands of a man.'[11] In those things where there is nothing but evil no obedience can be due to anyone. No one can rightly order another to do wrong. Faith, hope, love are wholly good and it can never be wrong to order a man to show them; it can never be right to forbid them. Theft, sacrilege,

---

[8]   Letter 7, 1. LTR VII. 32. 1–2, SJ 8, 1.
[9]   Letter 6, 1. LTR VII. 30. 1–14. SJ 7, 1.
[10]   Letter 7, 2. LTR VII. 32. 10–33. 2. SJ 8, 2.
[11]   Letter 7, 3. LTR VII. 33. 11–14. SJ 8, 3.

adultery are always wrong; no one can rightly order them to be done, and it is always right to forbid them. But there is a large class of morally neutral things. Marriage is neither good nor evil until it is entered into, and then there can be no turning back; it becomes a matter of absolute obligation to continue in it.[12] Bernard now brings Adam to see that his act in leaving his monastery was neither good nor neutral but wholly evil; even if he might be excused for leaving on the grounds that he thought he was being obedient (which he was not), the delay in returning now cannot be excused.[13] Adam is confronted with the enormity of his deed.

Bernard ends his letter by catching Adam in a series of illogical positions. If he wants to obey his superior, ought he not to obey the head of the Order, the abbot of Cîteaux, who wants him at Morimond, rather than his own abbot who did not?[14] He has preferred his private judgement to the collective view of his brothers.[15] If he set out willingly, he was not being obedient; if he set out unwillingly it would seem he was in some doubt about the order he was following, and in that case he should have enquired about it.[16] 'I do not say that subjects should question the orders of their superiors when it is clear they do not conflict with divine ordinances, but I say that prudence is necessary in order to understand whether they do so conflict'.[17]

Some time before 1144[18] Bernard wrote a treatise on the observance of the Rule for two monks who had sent him some questions and were pressing him for a reply. Bernard addressed his answer to the abbot of another monastery in the diocese of Chartres because the two monks had put him in a delicate position. They had written without their abbot's consent and Bernard was obliged by propriety to adopt this roundabout

---

[12] Letter 7, 4. LTR VII. 34. 14–17, SJ 8, 4.
[13] Letter 7, 5. LTR VII. 35. 6–7. SJ 8, 5.
[14] Letter 7, 7. LTR VII. 36. 5–8, SJ 8, 7.
[15] Letter 7, 8. LTR VII. 37. 10–12, SJ 8, 8.
[16] Letter 7, 11. LTR VII. 39. 5–8, SJ 8, 11.
[17] Letter 7, 12. LTR VII. 40. 14–17. SJ 8, 12.
[18] See LTR III. 244 on the date of Pre.

method of furnishing them with an answer; he asks the abbot to send it on to their abbot if he thinks fit.[19]

The treatise, *De Praecepto et Dispensatione*, takes Benedict's Rule to be the base for all other rules; 'Unless I am mistaken', says Bernard, 'all the others or nearly all arise from it.'[20] Bernard had been asked in what way the notion of a 'rule' was to be understood; are all the precepts of the Rule to be regarded as carrying the penalty of damnation if they are broken, or are some to be thought of as merely advice or counsel (*consilia* or *monita*), and thus of comparatively small account if they are broken?[21] The question raises fundamental problems about the purpose and value of monastic life, and Bernard was anxious to answer it not by listing the more or less important parts of the Rule, but by looking at the larger implications. He gives clear guiding principles on which any precept can be assessed, but he encourages his questioners to take a larger view of the Rule as a whole rather than to occupy themselves with petty distinctions. He encourages them to look for the divine within the human law just as he had urged them to look for a higher obedience within their obedience to their abbot.

If the Rule as a whole is to be regarded as having such force that not to keep its precepts is to consign oneself to Hell, it is clearly of the first importance to establish whether this holds for all men or only for those who have vowed to keep the Rule. This is where Bernard begins. He himself thinks, he says, that the Rule is set before every man but imposed on no one: *omni homini proponitur, imponitur nulli*. If it is devoutly kept by those who have sworn to obey it, it is helpful (*prodest*); if a man does not take the vow, the Rule will not, on the other hand, form a stumbling-block to him.[22] At a stroke he has made the Rule at the same time no threat to those who choose not to commit themselves to it, and of incalculable benefit to those who do.

Within the Rule, Bernard suggests, there are spiritual laws such as the injunctions to love, humility, and gentleness,

[19] LTR III. 253. 6–254. 6.
[20] LTR III. 254. 23.
[21] LTR III. 254. 26–9.
[22] LTR III. 255.

which were instituted not by Benedict but by God. They cannot be altered; they are binding on all men. It is the remainder of the Rule containing Benedict's own counsels, which a man may choose to obey or not. Its contents are profitable to those who follow them, but for those who have not taken a vow to obey them they are merely *consilia*, not absolute laws.[23] Again, without diminishing the force or importance of the Rule, Bernard has shown it to be woven out of strands of divine law and strands of human provision.

Bernard's approach throughout is to make divisions in this way so as to reveal the deep structure of the Rule. Observances are said to be voluntary for those not professed, necessary for those professed; for priests, those invented by man are voluntary, and those divinely instituted are necessary.[24] For the professed, there are three grades of 'necessity'. The rules made by Benedict, or Basil, or Augustine for their communities are not lightly to be departed from. Such a rule may be called: *stabilis*. Other rules are divinely-appointed, but may on occasion be broken by divine order. Samson broke the commandment: 'Thou shalt not kill' when he died killing the enemy; and it is to be believed beyond doubt, says Bernard, that he was privately instructed by God to do so, even though nothing in Scripture explicitly tells us that he was. Finally, there are rules which are divinely appointed but which God will never command anyone to break, such as the command to love, to be humble, to be gentle.[25]

Perfect obedience will need to take no account of such distinctions. It will fit naturally within any constrictions so that they will not chafe or bind.[26] Christ himself furnishes the perfect example. In making himself obedient to the Father's will to death he felt no constriction; he went gladly to the limit of obedience. He wants us to do the same, not measuring how far we ought to obey this rule or that, but gladly going beyond our vows and 'obeying in all things'.[27]

Even the abbot can be obedient in this spirit, not to his

---

[23] Ibid.
[24] LTR III. 256. 16–18.
[25] LTR III. 256. 25–9.
[26] LTR III. 261. 26–7.
[27] LTR III. 262. 12–15.

superior, for he is himself a superior, but according to the Rule. The religious promises not to obey the Rule, but to be obedient according to the Rule, and the abbot, too, is free to show such obedience.[28]

IV. WAR

Son of a soldier, Bernard took his soldier brothers with him into Cîteaux in a fighting spirit. The metaphors of war came naturally to his mind on many occasions when he wrote to exhort a fellow monk to greater efforts or to congratulate him on a spiritual victory. He tells Suger, abbot of St. Denis, that he has acted like a resolute soldier in reforming his way of life, 'or rather, like a faithful and brave captain who, when he sees his men fleeing and slaughtered all about him by the enemy swords, would think it shameful to survive them.'[1] Fulk, the Augustinian canon who had been persuaded by his uncle to return to the world, had lost his battle. 'Show yourself in the fight', urges Bernard. 'If Christ recognizes you in battle he will recognize you . . . on the last Day'. 'Where are your arms of war?' he asks. 'Where is your shield of faith, your helmet of salvation, your corselet of patience?'[2] To Robert of Châtillon he writes: 'Arise, soldier of Christ, I say arise! Shake off the dust and return to the battle.' He draws a picture for him of a multitude of armed men surrounding his house while he sleeps, scaling the defences, pouring in by every entrance. 'Would you be safer alone or with others?' he asks, urging him to return to his 'fellow-soldiers' at Clairvaux. If he finds the armour heavy, Bernard assures him that it will seem light enough in battle when he finds that he needs it.[3]

One contemporary Order united the virtues of monk and soldier in a literal as well as a metaphorical manner. The Knights of the Temple were encouraged in their ideals by Bernard despite the existence of a profound anomaly in their position. They were a contradiction in terms, a confusion of spiritual and secular estates. Bernard wrote angrily of a case known to him in another connection, a Stephen of Garland

---

[28] LTR III. 259–60.
[1] Letter 78, 1. LTR VII. 201. 15–18, SJ 80, 1.
[2] Letter 2, 12. LTR VII. 22. 17–19, SJ 2, 12.
[3] Letter 1, 13. LTR VII. 10. 17–18, SJ 1, 13.

who was a deacon, archdeacon of Notre Dame and Dean of Orléans and at the same time seneschal of the royal palace under Louis the Fat. 'It is an abuse of both conditions' in Bernard's view, that a man should serve both God and Mammon in this way, serving the King's table and the altar of God alike. It is a disgrace to the kingdom that a cleric should command soldiers just as it is a disgrace to his orders that a cleric should take money from the King in payment for fighting for him.[4]

Bernard did not apparently see the same objection to the existence of the Knights Templar. The reason lay, no doubt, in the special circumstances of their beginnings and the place in which they served. They were soldier-monks of the Holy Land, perpetually engaged in that holy war which began with the First Crusade and which Bernard saw as an acting out in the external world of the spiritual warfare in every Christian soul. They were a living image of the battle between good and evil, virtue and vice in which he wanted every monk to be consciously engaged.

The Holy Sepulchre captured the imagination of intending pilgrims more strongly than even Rome or Compostela in the early years of the twelfth century. Peter the Venerable preached a sermon on the subject, probably during his stay in Paris in the early summer of 1147 for Pope Eugenius' Council. He explained why the Sepulchre is worthy of a special veneration, and he proposes it as an image of the Christian soul, which should receive Christ within it as the Sepulchre received his body.[5] The pilgrim to the Holy Land visited half a dozen other holy places, too; Jerusalem, Nazareth, Mount Sion, the Mount of Olives, Bethlehem, Hebron, Bethany, the River Jordan, Tiberias.[6] But as he travelled the Holy Land, the

---

[4] Letter 78, 11–12. LTR VII. 208–9. SJ 80, 11–12.

[5] Peter the Venerable, 'Sermones Tres', *R. Bén.* lxiv (1954), 232–54 and *PL* 189. 973–92, and see V. Berry, 'Peter the Venerable and the Crusades', *Studia Anselmiana*, xl (Rome, 1956), 153.

[6] M. Barber, 'The Origins of the Order of the Temple', *Studia Monastica* xii (1970), 219–20, and see (c.1350) *Guide-Book to Palestine*, tr. J. H. Bernard, *Palestine Pilgrims Text Society*, vi (London, 1894) For a bibliography, see M. Bessubré, *Bibliographie de l'ordre des Templiers* (1978); H. Neu, *Bibliographie des Templar-Ordens*, (1927–65). See, too, H. de Curzon, *La Règle du Temple* (1886), L. Daillez, *La Règle des Templiers* (1977).

pilgrim ran a considerable risk of being attacked by bands of robbers.

It was in response to this danger to pilgrims and in the hope of protecting them, that the Order of the Templars began.[7] Hugh of Payens and Godfrey of Omer seem to have been the principals, although we do not know who hit upon the idea. Hugh was a connection of Bernard's and probably a relative of the Counts of Champagne. He had probably been to the Holy Land on more than one occasion, perhaps on the First Crusade, perhaps with Hugh of Champagne who went to the Holy Land in 1104, perhaps later.[8] He was certainly there in 1119, when a particularly vicious attack was made on a group of pilgrims on their way from Jerusalem to Jordan.[9] Hugh, Godfrey (a vassal of the Count of Boulogne), and a number of other knights, took a vow of poverty, chastity, and obedience before the Patriarch of Jerusalem. Their plan was to live as regular canons. They had two small grants of accommodation in the Temple area and they were instructed to 'keep the roads and highways safe from the menace of robbers and highwaymen, with particular care for the protection of pilgrims'.[10] They began modestly and they continued modestly. In 1128 there were still only nine Templars,[11] and there is little sign of their activity until then. They became established and influential partly at least as a result of the interest Bernard began to take in them. King Baldwin II of Jerusalem wrote to him some time between 1119 and 1126 commending two Knights of the Temple to him, Andrew and Gondemar, and asking him to request the Pope's approval of the Order.[12] What action Bernard took we do not

---

[7] On the rough conditions and danger faced by the pilgrims, see *An Account of the Pilgrimage of Sewulf of Jerusalem and the Holy Land in the Years 1102 and 1103*, tr. W. R. B. Brownlow (London, 1872), *Pal. Pil. Text Soc.* IV, pp. 8–9; *The Pilgrimage of the Russian Abbot Daniel in the Holy Land*, 1106–7 AD, tr. C. W. Wilson (London, 1888) *Pal. Pil. Text. Soc.* IV, and *Ekkehardi Hierosolymita*, ed. H. Hagemeyer (Tübingen, 1877), p. 309.

[8] Barber, op. cit., pp. 221–3.

[9] *Alberti Aquensis Historia Hierosolymitana, Recueil des historiens des Croisades, Historiens Occidentaux*, iv (Paris, 1879) Book XII, xxxiii, pp. 712–13.

[10] William of Tyre (*Recueil des Historiens des Croisades, Hist. Occid., I.i*) (Paris, 1844), XII. 7, p. 520, and see Barber, op. cit., pp. 224–5.

[11] William of Tyre, loc. cit..

[12] Barber, op. cit., p. 226.

know, but in 1129 at the Council of Troyes, Hugh of Payens and five of his brothers put their case and were granted recognition of the Order. Bernard's interest is attested by the fact that he came to Troyes although he had a fever, and that it was he who drew up the Rule for the Order in 1128 and wrote the *De Laude Novae Militiae* for them shortly afterwards.[13]

Anselm of Havelberg describes them warmly in his *Dialogus* as 'religious men' who 'call themselves the Knights of the Temple and, leaving their possessions ... fight under obedience to one master; they reject superfluity and richness of clothing, ready to defend the glorious sepulchre of the Lord against the assault of the Saracens.'[14] This military complexion of the new Order became steadily more marked as the twelfth century wore on.[15] Indeed the Templars came to prize their independent position, not fully subject to any Latin magnate secular or ecclesiastical, autonomous allies of the kings of Jerusalem, free to adopt what policies they chose in dealing with Muslim rulers and, above all, in a position to offer valuable assistance on their own terms to the Christian princes who had settled in the Holy Land after the First Crusade, and who were in need of good soldiers.[16]

The battle of the virtues and vices, the war in heaven which overflows upon the earth and involves every Christian soul in a struggle to defend the good, has recently been intensified, writes Bernard in his treatise for the Templars. A 'new kind of soldier' has joined the battle, a soldier pledged to fight a double fight, a war of the flesh and a war against spiritual wickedness. He wears the metal armour he needs to protect his body, and a shield of faith upon his soul.[17] Bernard was writing to Hugo de

[13] Ibid., p. 229. I am much indebted to Dr Barber for his help and interest.

[14] Anselm of Havelberg, *Dialogus* I, *PL* 188. 1156. 'Viri religiosi et vocant se Milites de Templo, qui relictis proprietatibus, ... sub obedientia unius magistri militant, superfluitatem et pretiositatem vestium sibi absciderunt, parati ad defendendum gloriosum Domini sepulchrum contra incursus Saracenorum.'

[15] On the militarization of the Templars, see R. C. Smail, *Crusading Warfare*, (Cambridge, 1956), pp. 95–6.

[16] Ibid., pp. 102–3.

[17] *Liber ad Milites Templi* I. i, LTR III. 214. 1–17. See, too, J. A. Brundage, 'A Transformed Angel: the Problem of the Crusading Monk', *Studies in Mediaeval Cistercian History* (Spencer, Mass., 1971), 55–62, and J. Leclercq, 'L'attitude spirituelle de S. Bernard devant la guerre', *Coll. Cist.* 36 (1974), 195–225.

Payens. Hugo had asked him to give an exhortatory address to his knights,[18] and after three requests,[19] Bernard set to work. He wanted to provide a handbook for the Templars which would give them a clear picture of their unique position and define their vocation for them.

Whether a man dies in bed or in battle, Bernard assures them, the death of the saints is always precious in the sight of God, but to die in battle for the faith is better, and this will be a possibility open to each of the Templars as he goes about his work of protecting the Holy Places. They must live with a pure conscience and without fear of death, and then their lives will be *secura*, secure in a way which transcends the safety of other men's lives.[20]

Bernard has, however, a difficulty to overcome in giving advice to the new Order. There would appear to be a fundamental conflict of purpose between the life of a soldier, which must on occasion involve killing, and the life of a monk, who ought to live at peace with his fellow men. It had been Bernard's habit to discourage monks from going on Crusade, as we have seen.

In an effort to show how the conflict may be reconciled in the case of these military monks, Bernard looks first at the cause for which they fight, and then at their purpose or intention. If, he says, the cause of the fight is good, the outcome cannot be bad; just as a good end cannot come from a bad cause, so a bad end cannot come from a good one. The intention of the killer makes a difference, too. The Templar must cast out of his mind the desire to kill, the wish to conquer or avenge, so that if by chance he slays his opponent while fighting for the right, he will not himself be a murderer. It would be an unhappy victory (*infelix victoria*) if he were to overcome his human enemy and be himself dominated by vice or anger or pride,[21] but the good and holy man who does his soldierly duty experiences no conflict of purpose.

Unlike the secular soldiery who fight for frivolous causes[22]

---

[18] PL 185. 320. 'Exhortatorius sermo.'
[19] LTR III. 213–16.
[20] I. ii. 6.
[21] I. ii, LTR III. 215. 16–20.
[22] II. iii, LTR III. 216. 19–20.

this new soldier need not fear that he is in any danger of sinning when he kills or is killed; he is not a sinner, but glorious.[23] To reassure the conscientious Templar fully, Bernard is able to support his argument from Scripture. If it is altogether and always wrong for a Christian to kill, why did Christ tell soldiers to be content with their pay and not rather forbid them outright to be soldiers (Luke 3: 14)?[24]

Bernard wants the Templars to regard themselves as set apart in every way from common soldiers. He draws up a table of comparisons and contrasts for them, so that they can see clearly where the differences lie. The Templars and the ordinary soldiers alike ought to be under discipline and to be obedient. Both ought to avoid all superfluity in their lives and in their dress, and make do with necessities only. The common soldiery are notoriously breakers of all these rules, but the Templars must keep them faithfully, living together *in commune*, in one house and in the bonds of peace, undistracted by wives and children. They must never sit idle or wander about exploring their surroundings, for *curiositas* ought to be alien to the religious. When they are not marching or fighting, they must spend their time mending their armour and equipment, so that they do not eat the bread of idleness, but earn their keep. They should not defer to men who merely happen to be well-born, but rather to good men, without respect to their position. There should be no loud laughter, no hunting, no wearing of long hair, nor singing of ribald songs.[25]

The Templars are to see their lives as a pilgrimage to the Holy Places. Bernard takes them, one by one, to the Temple itself, to Bethlehem, to Nazareth, to Mount Olivet, to the Vale of Josaphat, to Jordan, to Calvary, to the Sepulchre, to Bethphage, describing the spiritual significance of each, so that when they visit these places in the flesh, the Templars will be able to look on them with spiritual eyes.

Bernard does not discuss here in any detail the practical difficulties of making the Rule of monastic life fit the life of a soldier. His purpose is to raise high expectations in the hearts of the Templars, so that they will set themselves high

[23] III. iv, LTR III. 217. 4.
[24] III. v, LTR III. 218. The argument is common in Augustine.
[25] III. vii, LTR III. 219.

standards. Some of these matters are, however, dealt with in the Rule the Templars followed. Calling on all those who have, until now, been ordinary soldiers looking to human favour alone, to make Christ their 'cause' and fight for him, the Rule sets out a few simple principles. The Templars are to live like monks, except that when they are on active service three Lord's Prayers may be substituted for Matins, seven for each of the canonical hours, and nine for Vespers. Arrangements are made for honouring those brothers who are killed, for the taking of communal meals, for reading aloud to the community at meals, for diet, and clothing. No children are to enter the Order.[26] As far as possible the community is to live in the unity proper to monks. The Templars are, then, first and foremost monks. Their knightly tasks are to be fitted into their monastic lives. To put it in Bernard's terms, they are to see themselves first as spiritual soldiers and only secondarily as soldiers with battles to fight with bodily arms.

The fall of Edessa to the Muslims in 1144 came as a shattering surprise to the West. The achievement of the first crusaders in recapturing the Holy Places for Christ had seemed a solid one, not perhaps in a military sense, but in its rightness. The crusaders had felt that sweat of their labour for God upon them which was so welcome a sensation to the contemporary monk in his active and effortful living of the religious life. Ralph of Caen speaks of the 'glorious sweat' of the pilgrimage 'which restored her heritage to our mother Jerusalem, extinguished idolatry, repaired the faith'.[27]

Now it seemed that God had stretched out his arm to drive out the infidel by means of his Christian soldiers and then withdrawn it. Anselm of Havelberg devoted the first book of his *Dialogus* to an attempt to resolve the question why God should permit unbelievers to appear on earth and to remain there.[28] Here was the problem in a new and acute form.

Bernard saw a great danger in letting aberrant Christians go

[26] Rule of the Templars. PL 166. 853–76.

[27] S. Runciman, *The Crusades* (Cambridge, 1952) II. 248. E. O. Blake, 'The formation of the Crusade Idea', *Journal of Ecclesiastical History*, 21 (1970), 11–31; G. Constable, 'The Second Crusade as seen by Contemporaries', *Traditio*, 9 (1953) 213–79. Ralph of Caen, *Gesta Tancredi*, PL 155. 491.

[28] Anselm of Havelberg, *Dialogus* I, ed. G. Salet (Paris, 1965).

on unimpeded, but the existence of unbelievers outside the Christian fold had not until now roused him to action. In the year of the Fall of Edessa, Peter the Venerable of Cluny urged Bernard to write against the Muslims: 'It is your duty and that of all learned men to attack, destroy, and crush underfoot with all zeal, by word and in writing, every teaching which raises itself up against the mountain of God.' He reminds Bernard of Augustine, who wrote volumes against the Pelagian Julian of Eclanum and the Manichee Faustus, and spared himself no pains.[29] Peter the Venerable himself went to a great deal of trouble to find out about Muslim beliefs and teaching.

Why was Bernard not stirred by what Peter had told him to take up his own pen or to preach against the infidel? The needs of existing Christians were always uppermost in Bernard's mind, and there were as yet more pressing claims on his energies, to do with the protection of his sheep from wolves who had got in amongst the flock. Bernard was much more in sympathy with Peter the Venerable in his campaign against the followers of Peter de Bruys, the popular preacher who encouraged the view that the people of God needed neither priest nor sacrament.[30] When Henry, a wandering monk who had gone back to the world, began to spread this teaching by his own preaching,[31] Bernard was strongly moved at the news. In a letter to Hildefonsus, Count of St. Giles and Toulouse about 1145, he expresses his anxiety that men are dying in their sins as a result of his teaching, and souls everywhere are being snatched away to judgement.[32] The people are listening to the voice of this one heretic more readily than to the voices of all the prophets and apostles.[33] This was a circumstance which roused Bernard at once; these were Christian souls at risk.

---

[29] Letter 3, Constable I. 298, 2 Cor. 10: 5. P. Kritzeck, *Peter the Venerable and Islam* (Princeton, 1964).

[30] Peter the Venerable, *Contra Petrobrusianos*, ed. J. Fearns, *CCCM*, 10 (1968).

[31] *VP* III. vi. 16. See R. Manselli, 'Il monacho Enrico e la sua eresia', *Bollettino dell'Istituto storico italiano per il Medio Evo*, 65 (1953) 1–63, and H. Grundmann, *Bibliographie zur Ketzergeschichte des Mittelalters*, 1900–66 (Rome, 1967).

[32] Letter 241. LTR VIII. 125. 12–13. 'Moriuntur homines in peccatis suis, rapiuntur passim animae ad tribunal terrificum.'

[33] Letter 241. LTR VIII. 126. 5–7. 'Ad vocem unius haeretici soluerunt in eo omnes propheticae et apostolicae voces.'

So fiercely did Bernard concentrate his missionary energies upon the threat to the faithful from renegade Christians that the Jews regarded him as no enemy to their beliefs, but as a valued friend and protector of their race. In *The Book of Remembrance*, Rabbi Ephraim of Bonn speaks of Bernard as 'a decent priest, one honoured and respected by all the clergy in France', one who said 'whosoever touches a Jew to take his life, is like one who harms Jesus Himself'. 'Were it not for the mercy of our creator in sending the aforementioned Abbot no remnant or vestige would have remained of Israel', he continues.[34] Unlike Rupert, abbot of Deutz in the period when Bernard was first building up Clairvaux, and the instrument of the conversion of Hermannus Judaeus, Bernard seems to have taken no special pains to try to convert Jews; nor did he engage, as Abelard did, in the exercise of trying to reason them into Christianity.[35]

A war of arms proved in the end more attractive than a war of words as a means of approach to the problem of the presence of the infidel in the Holy Land. Slow though he was to be won over to the idea that a second Crusade might be necessary and that it was his duty to try to raise support for it, when once he was convinced, Bernard gave all his energies to the task. Odo of Deuil, a monk of St. Denis, describes in his account of *The Expedition of Louis VII to the East*[36] how Bernard campaigned without doubt or hesitation.

Bernard was not the only churchman to have mixed feelings about the projected Crusade, but Eugenius III was in favour of the idea when Louis put it to him, and he supported his scheme when, at Christmas 1145, he first made a public statement of his intention at his coronation at Bourges. The Bishop of Langres, Bernard's kinsman and former prior, Godfrey de la Roche, supported Louis at once. Others held back, notably

[34] *The Jews and the Crusaders: the Hebrew Chronicles of the First and Second Crusades*, ed. and tr. S. Eidelberg (Wisconsin, 1977), p. 122.

[35] In his dialogue with a Jew, Rupert compares the Jew's and Christian's positions, *PL* 170. 561. See, too, Hermannus Judaeus, *De Conversione Sua*, ed. G. Niemeyer, *MGH* (1963), and Abelard, *Dialogus inter Philosophum, Judaeum et Christianum*, ed. R. Thomas (Stuttgart, 1970).

[36] Odo of Deuil, *De Profectione Ludovici VII in Orientem*, ed. and tr. V. G. Berry (Columbia, 1948).

Suger, abbot of St. Denis.[37] Peter the Venerable was present at
the Curia for several weeks on abbey business while the
launching of the Crusade was in progress early in 1145.[38]
Several of his letters indicate a strong admiration for the first
Crusaders at least.[39] Bernard may have been present at
Bourges,[40] but whether he was there or not it seems that he
had, up to this point, not declared himself ready to commit
himself to the plan.[41] It was perhaps the Pope who persuaded
him. Bernard gave his support in the first instance at Eugenius'
instigation. The Pope issued two Bulls, one in December 1145,
addressed to Louis and the princes, and another in March 1146,
addressed to the faithful of Gaul, calling everyone to Crusade.

On Palm Sunday 1146, at a great assembly at Vézelay,
Bernard preached.[42] His words were overwhelming. The crowd
who came to hear him was too great to be accommodated in
the town, so a wooden platform was erected outside, from
which the abbot could speak. Bernard mounted the platform
with the King beside him, wearing the cross. His *caeleste
organum*, the heavenly organ of his voice, poured forth the
'dew of the divine word', and with loud cries the people began
to demand crosses. Those Bernard had prepared beforehand
were given out broadcast—Odo says that he 'sowed' them
rather than 'bestowed' them (*seminasset potius quam dedis-
set*). When the supply was exhausted, Bernard was obliged to
tear up his own clothing to make crosses. He did not stop with
the ending of the assembly. As long as he remained in the
town,[43] and afterwards everywhere he went,[44] he continued to
preach the Crusade. He involved Conrad of Germany,[45] and
other German supporters, at Speier about Christmas 1146. In
February at Étampes, a starting-point was fixed for the Crusade
in June.[46] The reasons for this change of heart on Bernard's part

[37] Odo of Deuil, p. 7.
[38] V. Berry, op. cit. (*Studia Anselmiana*) 143.
[39] Letters 75, 80, 172.
[40] Letter 247 and Odo of Deuil ed. cit. pp. 8–9.
[41] Otto of Freising, *Gesta Frid. Imp.* 1, 35, ed. F. J. Schmalc (Darmstadt,
1965).
[42] *VP* III. iv. 9.
[43] Odo of Deuil, p. 8.
[44] Odo of Deuil, p. 10.
[45] *VP* III. xiv. 378.
[46] N. M. Häring, *An. Cist.*, 22 (1966), 4–5.

are perhaps not far to seek. He came to see the Crusade as a Christian duty; from that point he would need no further encouragement.

Before the Crusade set off, the sight of the faithful soldiers of Christ assembling and marshalling themselves for war moved Peter the Venerable deeply. 'What Christian would not be moved?' he asks.[47] The expedition, however, was a disaster; it came nowhere near achieving the success of its predecessor, and after the failure of the Crusade, its initiators and supporters were faced with the difficulty of understanding and explaining to the baffled army why God had allowed their efforts to come to nothing. There could be no question but that the expedition was necessary.[48] Certainly Bernard had preached with God's help and support. The signs proved it, and what signs! And how many signs![49] They were so numerous that it was impossible to keep a full record of them.[50]

In his *Vita Prima* Geoffrey of Auxerre gives a face-saving explanation of what happened which was resorted to by many. God's intention, it seems, was not to save the bodies of the pagans of the East, but rather to save the souls of the Christians of the West from sin. The whole affair was a lesson to the Christians, who needed a shock to bring them to their senses. 'Who shall dare to say to God, "Why have you done this?",' Geoffrey comments.[51] Christ endured the *opprobrium* of having unbelievers in the world, for the sake of the greater good of saving so many souls of lapsed and apathetic Christians.[52] Geoffrey quotes a passage in Bernard's *De Consideratione* where Bernard makes the same point.[53] He sees the episode as a proof that God has not forgotten or cast off his people.[54]

---

[47] Constable I. 327, II. 185, Letter 130. 'Ad tantam tamque stupendam exercitus domini Sabaoth commotionem non moveatur?'

[48] *VP* III. iv. 9, *PL* 185. 308C. The need had been audible (audita necessitas) for many years.

[49] *VP* III. iv. 9, *PL* 185. 308C. 'Domino co-operante et sermonem confirmante, sequentibus signis.'

[50] Ibid.

[51] *VP* III. iv. 10, *PL* 185. 309A–B.

[52] *VP* III. iv. 10, *PL* 185. 309B.

[53] *VP* III. iv. 10, *PL* 185. 309B. On the *De Consideratione*, see Chap. IV.

[54] *VP* III. iv. 10, *PL* 185. 310A.

An *exemplum* which survives in a sermon of the late thirteenth century perhaps preserves the flavour of Bernard's sermons after the failure of the Crusade, in which he attempted to comfort and reassure the bewildered crusaders. Bernard heard that the soldiers had returned in despair at their failure, and he hastened to find them (*occurrit eis*), so that he could talk to them and show them where they had gone wrong. They had, he explained, gone out in confidence that they could defeat the infidel by their own powers; they trusted more in themselves than in the help of God, and God had punished their pride. God repulsed them on earth so that they might learn to seek heavenly things. This explanation brought a meaning to an apparently meaningless defeat, and the barons and their men were comforted.[55]

Bernard behaved characteristically enough when once he had been won over to the idea of the second Crusade. He gave himself up with all his heart to promoting the cause. But in allowing himself to be persuaded he moved away from his usual insistence that it was the welfare of the faithful which most deeply concerned the Church and was her primary responsibility. Shattered by the disastrous end of the Crusade he could only ask himself what God had intended to teach the faithful.

In preaching the Crusade, he modified his consistent view that the best way to fight for Christ was spiritually, as a monk, or, perhaps for some few individuals, as a monk-Templar Knight who bore arms as an extension of his spiritual warfare. The Crusade, like the work of the Templars, remained in an important sense an idea rather than a reality for him, an acting out in the world of the battle between good and evil, virtue and vice. He stirred up his recruits for it no doubt in much the terms he used to rouse a fighting spirit in the religious, with the difference that he sent the former to active service with real weapons and the latter to active service with the weapons of spiritual warfare. But it was all of a piece in Bernard's mind.

---

[55] G. Constable, 'A Report of a lost sermon by St. Bernard on the failure of the second Crusade', *Studies in Mediaeval Cistercian History*, Presented to J. F. O'Sullivan (Spencer, Mass., 1971), and see ibid., p. 50, for a bibliography of studies on Bernard's crusading thought.

The real soldier of Christ always remained the monk; the real battle always took place within the soul.

Chapter II
Bernard the Preacher

1. *A Classical Education*

I. GRAMMAR

William of St. Thierry describes how Bernard's pious mother dedicated each of her children to God. For Bernard she had, he says, special hopes, because of a dream she had had of his future greatness.[1] It was usual for the sons of noblemen and knights to be left in the hands of their mothers and the women of the household when they were small, but Bernard's mother's influence seems to have continued beyond his infancy. She made every effort to give this favourite son a good education. Bernard's father had to do military service at Châtillon-sur-Seine, where the canons of St. Vorles ran a school with an excellent reputation, and Bernard was sent there.[2] William tells us that Bernard distinguished himself, working hard and outstripping his fellows.[3]

William does not describe Bernard's studies in detail, however. We must look elsewhere for a description of the training he is likely to have received. Otloh of St. Emmeram had exactly Bernard's experience in outshining his fellows and obliging his master to find more advanced work for him, early in the eleventh century.[4] A generation earlier than Bernard, Guibert of Nogent found himself in a similar position. His mother, widowed when she was very young, was, like Bernard's mother, ambitious for this son in particular. She ensured that he had a good education, and in due course tried to obtain a benefice for him.[5] She, too, had some difficulty in finding a suitable school for her son. When he was a boy there

---

[1] *PL* 185. 227–8, *VP* I. i.2. The parents' dream is a commonplace which goes back to pre-Christian times.

[2] *PL* 185. 228B, *VP* I. i.3.

[3] Ibid. 'Supra aetatem et prae coaetanis suis proficiebat.' A hagiographical commonplace, but surely true in this case.

[4] *PL* 146. 56. *Liber de Tentationibus Suis*, II.

[5] *De Vita Sua*, ed. G. Bourgin (Paris, 1905), p. 19, I.vii.

were no grammar-masters to be had in the towns, and scarcely any in the cities, and those who could be discovered were ignorant and ill-qualified; they were not to be compared, says Guibert, with the wandering masters of the early twelfth century, when he is writing his account.[6] She hired the best master she could find, as a tutor. He kept Guibert under strict discipline, out of a *saevus amor*,[7] a harsh love. Indeed he beat him so hard that when his mother discovered the weals and bruises she promised him that if he wanted to give up his studies and become a knight like his brothers she would equip him with arms when he was old enough.[8] Guibert would not hear of it; he was determined to be a clerk.[9]

The studies in which he was so eager to persevere were chiefly grammatical it is clear, and of an elementary kind at that. His master was competent to teach him nothing else; Guibert says that he had no skill at all in prose or verse composition, and that even as a grammarian he was a poor scholar.[10] The remorseless regime to which he subjected Guibert made him so familiar with the texts he studied that his writing is full of echoes of the Roman poets; and he learned for himself only too well how to write verses,[11] as we shall see.

II. LOGIC

The basis of Bernard's education would have been the same as that of every educated man of his day. He would have begun with grammar, as Guibert did; but it was becoming possible in the last decades of the eleventh century and the first decades of the twelfth to pursue more advanced studies in at least two directions.

For centuries the study of the seven liberal arts had been a superficial business, except for a few scholars who had a particular interest in logic or occasionally arithmetic, and who

---

[6] *De Vita Sua*, ed. G. Bourgin, pp. 12–13, I. iv: 'ut in oppidis paene nullus, in urbibus vix aliquis reperiri potuisset, et quos inveniri contigerat, eorum scientia tenuis erat, nec etiam moderni temporis clericulis vagantibus comparari poterat.'

[7] Virgil, *Bucolica*, VIII. 47, Ovid, *Ars Amatoria*, I. 17–18.

[8] *De Vita Sua*, Bourgin, p. 18, I. vi.

[9] Ibid.

[10] *De Vita Sua*, Bourgin, p. 15, I. v.

[11] *De Vita Sua*, Bourgin, p. 64, I. xvii.

sought out textbooks and wrote commentaries. But as a result of their work logic had begun to develop, and, about the time when Bernard was born, Roscelin of Compiègne had been able to win himself some fame by conducting a campaign of defamation against Anselm of Canterbury over a logical technicality. There were a sufficient number of contemporary scholars who could understand the issue to ensure that a lively controversy ensued. The heat arose, not from the logic in itself, but from its application to the discussion of theological doctrine. Roscelin thought he had shown that Anselm was teaching that the Trinity is three Gods. Anselm wrote a fierce warning to such *dialectici haeretici*.[1]

As a student of grammar, Bernard would have learned something of the nature and structure of language; he would have been taught that a word is made up of letters and syllables, and a sentence of words connected by the rules of syntax. He would have been taught to observe not only the form of words, but also their function, the ways in which they affect one another, qualifying or modifying.[2] He would have learned that a word may have several meanings, according to its context.[3] In this way he would have begun to move into areas where grammar overlaps with dialectic, and towards those problems of signification which were to occupy twelfth-century dialecticians.[4] As he studied the elementary textbooks of logic, Porphyry's *Isagoge*, Aristotle's *Categories* with Boethius' commentary, and Aristotle's *De Interpretatione* with Boethius' two commentaries, the student would encounter discrepancies between the teaching of the grammar textbooks and that of the textbooks of logic.

One such difference is the subject of the little treatise Anselm wrote for his pupils at Bec in the late eleventh century, for 'the beginner in dialectic'. In this *De Grammatico* Anselm

[1] The *De Incarnatione Verbi* was written by Anselm in an effort to set the record straight. On the *dialectici haeretici*, see *Anselmi Opera Omnia* II. 9. 21–2.

[2] For a summary of the grammar syllabus, see Isidore, *Etymologiae*, ed. W. M. Lindsay (Oxford, 1911), Book I–II.

[3] Bede's *De Schematibus et Tropis* deals with some aspects of this difficulty (*PL* 90. 175–86) but see, too, John Scotus Erigena, *De Praedestinatione* ed. G. Madec, CCCM 50 (1978), Chapter 9.

[4] See my *Alan of Lille* (Cambridge, 1983), pp. 21 ff.

takes a problem to which the ancient grammarians and dialecticans give different answers, and he invites his pupil to use his new knowledge to arrive at a solution for himself.[5] Anselm poses the question: is 'literate' (*grammaticus*) a substance or a quality? When we speak of the *grammaticus* do we refer to the man who is literate, or to the quality of literacy he possesses? To answer the question, although it proves to be full of meat and by no means philosophically trivial, the pupil need know only his *Categories* and enough of Aristotle's *De Interpretatione* to be able to set out his premisses in simple syllogisms and to see what conclusions follow from them. But for those with a bent for such studies, technically more sophisticated possibilities were opening up, and these were being pursued in Bernard's time, for the most part not in monasteries, but in the schools of northern France such as those in which Peter Abelard taught, the cathedral schools and the sometimes ephemeral schools set up by such masters as Abelard himself.

Bernard was never a student in such a school. We do not know how far his education went in the logical textbooks. His knowledge of the more advanced work of the day on problems of logic and language seems to have remained that of an educated amateur, in comparison with a Peter Abelard. Nevertheless, he got from his grammar a grounding which enabled him to keep up an intelligent interest in such matters, and to avoid making a fool of himself in his encounters with those more expert than he, as we shall see when we come to Bernard the preacher and the trials of Peter Abelard at Sens and Gilbert of Poitiers at Reims in the 1140s. The use of simple dialectical principles came to him quite naturally when he was preaching. 'I am black but comely' suggests a contradiction, he says in one of his sermons on the Song of Songs. (*Nullane in his verbis repugnantia est?*) 'I mention this for the sake of the simple,' he comments, 'those who do not know how to distinguish between colour and form.' Blackness is a colour. Not all blackness is ugly. It is not inappropriate in the pupil of the eye; black stones are pretty in ornaments; black hair

---

[5] *Anselmi Opera Omnia* I. 173.3, and D. P. Henry, *The Logic of St. Anselm* (Oxford, 1967), p. 66.

frames white faces well.[6] Discussion of colour as a quality is elementary in dialectical studies of the day and Bernard could expect his listeners to appreciate his wry compliment to their superior knowledge. He teases them into understanding how the Bride may be both black and beautiful.

III. RHETORIC

The second direction in which the study of grammar might lead is likely to have been more attractive to Bernard—that is, towards the development of the higher literary skills which in the ancient world would have been called rhetorical. In Bernard's day rhetoric was not much studied as a formal art learned from the textbooks. Indeed the only textbooks available were the *De Inventione*, a little-used manual Cicero wrote when he was barely out of school himself, and the *Rhetorica ad Herennium*, another simple textbook which was then believed to be by Cicero, too. Some fragments of Quintilian's *Institutio Oratoria* were known, but rarely used.[1]

A new 'art of letter-writing' had, however, come into use late in the eleventh century as a result of a growing need for competent letter-writers in papal and royal chanceries. The authors of the first manuals of the art—notably Alberic of Monte Cassino before Bernard's time—had drawn upon rhetorical principles. Cicero describes the parts an oration ought to have, and the properly-composed letter has parts to correspond, including a preliminary salutation.[2] These manuals are concerned primarily with the rules of composition but they also pay attention to the *cursus*, the rules for bringing each clause to a rhythmically satisfying conclusion.

It was not from a textbook that Bernard learned to distinguish a plain style from an elaborate 'fine' style, and to identify and use figures of speech in composition.[3] These were the essentials of the rhetorician's skill in writing with grace and persuasiveness, and they undoubtedly came in Bernard's case

---

[6] *SS* 25. ii. 3, LTR II. 164. 12.

[1] See J. J. Murphy, *Rhetoric in the Middle Ages* (California, 1974), on the history of mediaeval rhetoric. On Quintilian, see, P. Boskoff, 'Quintilian in the Late Middle Ages'. *Speculum*, 27 (1952), 71–8.

[2] Cicero, *De Inventione*, I. xiv. 19.

[3] J. Leclercq remarks on Bernard's strong sense of compositional structure, *Recueil*, II. 14–32.

first through studying the Roman poets and learning to compose verses of his own, and later by his reading and imitation of Scripture and the best prose models among the Fathers. We need not postulate that he had studied the *Rhetorica ad Herennium* at school and knew the rhetorical principles behind the choice of a plain, middle, or high style which are described at the beginning of its fourth book. The *Ad Herennium* was still something of a rarity in monastic circles, although it was becoming more commonly studied in the schools outside as the art of rhetoric was revived.[4] Bernard had a good ear and a natural eloquence. If he wanted authority, Augustine would have told him that the style should be suited to the subject-matter;[5] and he could see for himself how it had been made so by generations of Christian writers.

Bernard could write with all the devices of Augustine's Christian *eloquentia*.[6] He was a master of climax:

> occurristis eis cum panibus, eduxistis eos in refrigerium, constituistis eos super excelsam terram,[7]

of assonance and consonance and alliteration:

> longe lateque satis dilatata est magnificentia vestra super terram,[8]

of repetition:

> nusquam fides, nusquam innocentia tuta,[9]

of making lists to bring a point home:

> audite attentius quod sapit suavius, et gustatur rarius, et intelligitur difficilius,[10]

of parallelism:

> habetis quod petistis, fecistis quod promisistis.[11]

There was no elaboration which he did not have at his fingertips, and yet he is rarely over-elaborate. On the contrary, he could write in a plain and businesslike manner (*Letters* 313 to Geoffrey, abbot of St. Mary, York, in the autumn of 1133,

---

[4]   See M. T. Gibson, *Lanfranc of Bec* (Oxford, 1978), pp. 11–14, and 49–50.
[5]   Augustine, *De Doctrina Christiana*, IV. xvii. 34.
[6]   On the *eloquentia* see the studies in C. Mohrmann, *Études sur le latin des Chrétiens* (Rome, 1961) 3 vols.
[7]   Letter 209, to Roger of Sicily, LTR VIII, p. 68, 15–16.
[8]   Letter 207, to Roger of Sicily, LTR VIII, p. 66. 4.
[9]   Letter 117, LTR VIII. 77. 14.
[10]   *SS* VIII, LTR I, p. 36. 14–15.
[11]   Letter 209 to Roger of Sicily, LTR VIII. 68. 14.

and 315 to Matilda of England, *c.* 1142), and even in sermons (where he often allowed himself a good deal of stylistic licence) he could be perfectly plain (Sermon V on the Song of Songs for example).

Whether 'high' or 'low', Bernard's style is always distinguished, never a mere pasting-together of devices and quotations. He makes his rules and breaks them, orchestrates his words so that even where perhaps five echoes of Scripture are woven together in two lines[12] the two lines are his own.

Something of his classical scholarship survived. He does not stand out among his contemporaries as a classical scholar, but then we should not expect him to do so, especially when his early education was so deeply overlaid by the 'holy reading' (*lectio divina*) of his first years as a monk. Bernard cites a number of Latin authors, not all of them necessarily from his own reading. Collections of tags or *florilegia* could have provided a number of the citations. Cicero's *Tusculan Orations*, Horace's *Epistulae* and *Carmina*, Juvenal's *Satires*, Ovid's *Metamorphoses*, Persius' *Satires*, Seneca's *Ad Lucilium*, Statius' *Thebaid*, Tacitus' *History*, several of Terence's works, Virgil's *Aeneid*, are all represented,[13] but they were, for the most part, commonplace enough in the monastic libraries of the day.[14] The debate about Bernard's stylistic debt to Cicero on the one hand and Augustine on the other[15] is not easily resolved, and perhaps it is better not to try. Bernard was not a stylistic eclectic, but a stylist in his own right, who left his individual touch upon everything he wrote. Like Anselm of Canterbury in an earlier generation, he stands out as a writer by virtue of his mastery of the language in which he wrote and his power of imprinting it with his own marks of style. There

---

[12] Letter 318, LTR VIII. 251, to Pope Innocent, lines 6–7: 'Vadit in interitum Remensis ecclesia, data est in opprobrium civitas gloriosa; clamat transeuntibus per viam, quod non sit dolor similis dolori eius.' Rev. 17: 11, Jer. 23: 40, Soph. 2: 15, Thren. 1: 12, II Cor. 7: 5.

[13] See *BC*, pp. 549–54, for a list.

[14] For a range of catalogues, see G. Becker, *Catalogi Bibliothecarum Antiqui* (Bonn, 1885).

[15] D. Knowles following E. Gilson, says that Bernard's style is Ciceronian, *The Historian and Character* (Cambridge, 1963), pp. 39–40. C. Mohrmann finds more of Augustine in him, *Études sur le latin des Chrétiens* (Rome, 1961), II. 347–67, 'Le style de S. Bernard'. See, too, 'Observations sur la langue et le style de S. Bernard', LTR II. ix–xxxiii.

is no evidence that he did very much reading once he became a busy abbot and preacher, except for the daily reading he would have heard in the course of community life. His style, once formed, was subject to no new influence, but only the reinforcement of hearing the familiar models day by day and reflecting on them in his words to the community.

IV. A NEW WAY OF READING

The forming of a young monk is a complex matter, of which the training of his mind in new ways of thinking is only one aspect, but it is here that we can follow Bernard into Cîteaux most closely.

Again, Guibert of Nogent is informative. He tells us that he was drawn to the notion of becoming a monk by the example of his mother and his tutor. Guibert's mother found the idea of becoming a nun increasingly attractive until, although her son was still a boy, she retired to Fly. She left him, he says, almost an orphan, although he was well-provided for in a great house and had kinsfolk to take care of him. At Fly she lived in a hut near the Church with an old woman of proven holiness, and passed her time in searching her heart for sins and confessing day by day all the misdeeds of former years. Guibert's tutor was so moved by her action that he himself became a monk at Fly. Family and household groups not uncommonly joined in conversion in this way, as Bernard's own family did, and Guibert's mother was able to see something of her son and keep an eye on his welfare.

Released from severe discipline, Guibert behaved badly, until his mother asked the abbot of Fly to allow his tutor to resume his duties. When Guibert was summoned to Fly to see him, he was struck at once by a desire to become a monk himself. His mother was anxious in case this might be no more than a boyish whim, but Guibert had his way and was admitted. As a monk and no longer his mother's employee, his tutor could not teach him as he had before, but he encouraged Guibert to read the books of holy learning to which he was himself now being directed, with the same thoroughness as he had trained him to parse and analyse the Latin poets. There seems to have been no renunciation of secular learning on Guibert's part at first. He lay under the bedclothes when he was supposed to be resting, at work upon a verse or reading in secret. It was at this time that his talent for versifying began to get out of hand. He was unhappy at Fly because the other boys mocked him for his studiousness;[1] he was troubled, he says, by 'fleshly longings' which gave him a pleasure in obscene verses. He thought nothing of the universal truths contained in Scripture; he admired Ovid and the pastoral poets; he wrote amorous letters and schoolboy verses in praise of the beauties of the human body.[2] There was certainly no simultaneous passing from the world into the life of the religious, and from secular to holy learning for Guibert.

Nevertheless, in time, Guibert did make a change in his habits of study. He discovered in himself a strong love of learning which was proof against the mockery of his fellows; indeed, it thrived on it. This he describes as the *discendi appetitus* which is the key of knowledge (*clavis scientiae*).[3] It was this which brought him at last to turn his mind to the study of the Bible, as he grew out of writing verses for amusement. He read the commentators, especially Gregory, whose works he thought contained the best keys to the art; he learned to distinguish the four senses of Scripture which had, since the early Christian centuries, been the key to the interpretation of difficult passages: the literal, the allegorical, the moral and the anagogical.

Like all new monks, Guibert came to understand the allegorical meanings of Scripture above all through the liturgy. Rupert of Deutz explains, for example, in his *De Divinis Officiis*, what is the significance of the celebration of two Masses on the night when Christ was born—(they celebrate the two natures of the incarnate Christ), and why the first chapter of Matthew's Gospel is read before the first Mass, with its account of the genealogy of Jesus, and why the Evangelist arranged the 'generation of Jesus Christ' in such a way that the table leads to Joseph rather than Mary.[4] Day by day the young

---

[1] *De Vita Sua*, I. xv, Bourgin, p. 60.
[2] Ibid., I. xvii, Bourgin, p. 64.
[3] Ibid., I. xvi, Bourgin, p. 60.
[4] Ibid., I. xvii, Bourgin, p. 66. On the history of the four senses, see H. de Lubac, *Exégèse médiévale* (Paris, 1959) 2 vols; and see p. 116; Rupert of Deutz, *De Divinis Officiis*, *PL* 170. 75. On the chant, see *BC* pp. 164–5.

monk would absorb such principles as he sang the services, until it seemed natural to think in such terms as he read or heard the Bible.

Bernard's experience in making the transition from secular to holy learning must have been in many respects much the same as Guibert's. First he was taught grammar and learned to study hard. Then, in his mid-teens, with the death of his mother, his circumstances changed abruptly.[5] He was free to live as he pleased. His family encouraged him to travel, to study and become a master, rather than to enter monastic life as his mother had planned. He hesitated; but he was haunted by the image of his mother complaining that she had not brought him up with such care to make him a trifler.[6] When he entered Cîteaux with the band of friends and members of his family he brought with him, he was consciously putting behind him a career in the schools, and giving up 'secular' learning for 'holy' learning. Bernard made the transition more abruptly than Guibert, but he, too, had to adjust his habits of work gradually and learn to study the Bible afresh. He had to learn to see it in a new light, quite different from that in which he is likely to have regarded it as a schoolboy, when he would have studied the Psalms as an elementary textbook to help him master Latin.[7]

The value placed upon holy reading (*lectio divina*) was not the same in all houses. The Benedictines had, throughout the eleventh century, been increasingly inclined to give their time to liturgy; prayer, manual labour, and reading began to take a subordinate place. It was one of the features of the Cistercian return to strict observance of the Rule that the Cistercians strove to give each of these its due place in the day. That is not to imply that reading was not important in the formation of Benedictine monks. Rupert of Deutz reveals the intensity of concentration and the fervour with which he himself read the

[5] *VP* I. ii. 5, *PL* 185. 230A.

[6] *VP* I. iii. 9, *PL* 185. 232A: 'ita ut saepius sibi occurrentem videre videretur, conquerentem et improperantem, quia non ad huiusmodi nugacitatem tam tenere educauerat.'

[7] P. Riché, 'Le Psautier, livre de lecture élémentaire', *Actes du Congrès merovingien de Poitiers*, 1952 (Études merovingiennes, 1953).

Bible, in his commentary on St. John's Gospel. He describes how he meditated during the night, and how he felt himself burning as he wrote his commentary.[8]

According to the early Customs of Cluny, the brothers are to sit down to read at certain times, except for those whose duties prevent them. These are to return and begin their reading as soon as they are free. The purpose of this period of reading is made clear in the *Usus Ordinis Cisterciensis*: it is to lead to prayer. The monk is free to go and pray in the church at any time during the period of reading.[9] He is to apply himself to his reading in much the same way as Anselm of Bec suggested that the reader of his prayers should do, using it as a starting-point for his ascent to God.[10] His reading should absorb him, so that he is silent and still.

We find worked out everywhere in the writings of Ailred, later abbot of the English Cistercian house at Rievaulx, the twofold process of education through *eruditio* and *disciplina* which goes on in the new monk as he reads and as he lives by the Rule. His learning from Scripture (*eruditio*) brings him gradually to wisdom; his obedience to the *disciplina ordinis* alters him, until he is both wise and good.[11] He will not be filled with curiosity. ('Fervour, not questions, are what you seek, not to sharpen your tongue but to awaken your soul.') Ailred hopes that his own exposition will help him by sowing seeds of meditation in his mind.[12] Ailred of Rievaulx describes an unsatisfactory monk he has observed sitting in the cloister, looking up from his book repeatedly, yawning, stretching his hands and feet, putting his book down and picking it up again, and then, as if goaded into restless movement, wandering about and talking.[13] The early Customs insist upon silence, except for those who are learning antiphons, hymns, or

---

[8]   Rupert of Deutz, *Commentaria in Evangelium S. Johannis*, ed. R. Haacke, *CCCM*, 9 (1969), p. 1. 1–6

[9]   *Usus Ordinis Cisterciensis*, III. 71, *PL* 166. 1446, and ed. P. Guignard, *Monuments primitifs de la Règle cistercienne* (Dijon, 1878) and see R. O'Brien 'Saint Aelred et la lectio divina', *Coll.Cist.*, 41 (1979), 281–93.

[10]   *Anselmi Opera Omnia*, III. 3; *PL* 184. 377A.

[11]   A. Hallier, *The Monastic Theology of Aelred of Rievaulx*, tr. C. Heaney (Shannon, 1969), p. 85.

[12]   Ailred of Rievaulx, *De Iesu Puero Duodenni*, III. 32, *CCCM*, 1 (Turnholt, 1971), p. 278. 396–401, *PL* 184. 856. (11.32).

[13]   Sermon for Advent *PL* 184. 823A–B.

graduals, who may ask one of the brothers to hear them as they practise reciting what they have been committing to memory. The brothers are not to keep asking one another questions, except about such matters as the length of syllables (*de productis et correptis accentibus*) and the point at which the reading should begin when they read aloud at meals; these questions should be asked as briefly as possible. There are to be as few distractions as can be contrived. Books are valuable (no one is to leave his book on his seat, he is to replace it in the chest or give it to the monk next to him for safe keeping), but they are to be left behind when the brother goes into the church. Thus prayer begins where reading leaves off. Reading is a means to a higher end, and all the rules of the early Customs are designed to ensure that it is kept in its place.[14]

William of St. Thierry, who had been a Benedictine and who at last, in 1135, became a Cistercian, wrote about holy reading in the *Golden Epistle* he composed for the Carthusian brothers of Mont-Dieu towards the end of his life. He insists upon the importance of the regular habit of reading, and of consistent reading of a single work until it is mastered. Casual and varied reading (*fortuita et varia lectio*) not only does not edify, but tends to make the mind unstable. A monk who reads in this way finds ideas flitting in and out of his head, but nothing remains in his memory for long. He must concentrate upon certain authors until their habits of expression are familiar, and he begins to enter into their minds. The words of the Holy Spirit must be read 'in' his spirit. St. Paul must be pondered over until his mind becomes the reader's own. David's Psalms must be read in such a way as to make the experiences out of which they were written the personal experiences of the reader himself. The words of the text should be committed to memory daily, so that even when the reader has no book before him he can, as it were, bring the *rumen* of Scripture to mind and chew it reflectively, as if he were a cow chewing the cud.[15] The book which is to be left behind when the reader goes to

---

[14] *Usus Ord. Cist.*, III. 71.
[15] *Ad Fratres de Monte Dei*, I. xxxi. 120–2, *PL* 184. 327D. Cf. *VP* I. iv. 23, *PL* 185. 41A–B. On contemplation and frequent meditation, see Cassiodorus, *Institutiones*, ed. R. A. B. Mynors (Oxford, 1937), I. i.2 and I. i.7.

pray is not, then, to be put out of his mind, but carried within it and digested in prayer. The same habit of thorough and reflective reading was to be carried over into reading of every kind. Bernard speaks in one of his letters of his reading and re-reading of his friend's letter, and his increasing pleasure in it every time he reads it.[16] This, then, is the quality of the habit of reading formed in the Cistercian monk who follows the Rule as he ought.

William of St. Thierry's account in the *Vita Prima* of the way in which Bernard went about his reading when he first became a monk was written at about the same time as the letter to the monks of Mont-Dieu, and William looks for and finds perfected in Bernard the very method he outlines in his *Epistle*. Bernard read frequently (*saepius*) and in order (*seriatim*) through the canonical Scriptures, and said that he had no intention beyond the straightforward one of understanding them: *nec ullis magis quam ipsarum verbis eas intelligere se dicebat.* He simply wanted to learn from them whatever he could about truth and virtue. To help him he turned to the Fathers, the holy and orthodox expositors, just as Guibert did, and read them humbly, following in their footsteps. He laid such a foundation of knowledge and understanding in this way, William tells us, that he has, ever since, been able to use Holy Scripture in teaching with confidence, and for the benefit of his listeners. 'And when he preaches the Word of God, whatever of the Bible he introduces into his talk, he brings in so clearly and appropriately (*sic patens et placens*), and so movingly, that everyone, those with the learning of this world and those with spiritual learning alike, is astonished at the words of grace which proceed from his mouth.'[17]

V. BERNARD THE WRITER

Bernard was above all a talker; almost everything he wrote arose out of his sermons or discourses. He began to develop

---

[16] Letter 84 bis, LTR VII. 219. 6–7: 'Illam tuam epistolam dulciter legens ac relegens—saepius quippe repetita placebat.'
[17] *PL* 185. 241 A–B, *VP* I. iv. 24.

some of his teaching in books and monographs when he was asked to put his words into a permanent form so that those who had heard him could read him at their leisure. Letters 17 and 18 are addressed in 1126 to Peter, a cardinal-deacon and legate of the Roman Church, who had asked Bernard to send him a copy of his *De Moralibus*.[1] Bernard tells him that he has written no book with that title. He suggests that one of his monks may have set down extracts from his discourses to the community[2] and that that may be the 'book' of which Peter has heard.

Peter was persistent. Bernard wrote to him again, to say that he has little to offer in the way of works of his own, and none of them, he believes, is worthy of Peter's attention. Nevertheless, he gives him a list, so that he can choose the book he wants. Bernard has written a little book on humility (the *De Gradibus Humilitatis et Superbiae*) four homilies on the Annunciation, (*In Laudibus Virginis Mariae*), an *Apologia* to one of his friends (William of St. Thierry) about the Cluniacs and the observances of the Cistercians, comparing the two; and he has dictated a few letters. In addition, certain brothers have, as he had mentioned, taken notes of his talks and kept them for themselves.[3] By about 1126 when these letters were written Bernard had comparatively little to show by way of 'published' works, but he had evidently already done a great deal of public speaking, and his reputation was spreading widely,[4] with the result that his works were in demand.

Ogier, the canon of Mont-Saint-Eloi near Arras had, some time before September 1126, been made head of the community of regular canons at Saint Médard. Ogier had written to Bernard to ask his advice on various matters, and he, too, had asked for one of his *libelli*. Bernard sent him the *In Laudibus*

---

[1] Letter 17, LTR VII. 65, 11–5.

[2] LTR VII. 65. 13–5. 'Suo stylo excepere; nonnulla ex his quae me coram audiere loquentem.'

[3] LTR VII. 69. 1–14.

[4] On these two letters, see P. D. Van den Eynde, 'Les débuts littéraires de Saint Bernard', *An.Cist.*, 19 (1963), 189–98. In an article shortly to be published C. Holdsworth examines the dates of composition of these early works.

Virginis Mariae, with instructions that he was not to lose it, for Bernard had only just finished it, and he had no copy.[5] Ogier went further. He had it copied.[6] This lack of control over the dissemination of uncompleted and unpolished writings was a source of anxiety to Bernard from the beginning, with justification, as we shall see.

Bernard was not stimulated into writing more merely to supply in a general way the growing demand for his works. Each of his treatises was composed for a specific occasion or at a specific prompting,[7] and most of them grew out of his sermons (*ex sermonis occasione*).[8] At the beginning of the *De Gradibus Humilitatis,* for example, he describes how Brother Godfrey had asked him to write down what he had been saying about the steps of humility, and to explore the subject at greater length.[9] The treatise *De Gratia et Libero Arbitrio* was begun, not perhaps strictly as a result of a sermon, but in much the same manner, when Bernard had been talking about the way in which the grace of God worked in his own soul, and one of the bystanders asked him how he could reconcile his teaching that everything was the work of God with his encouragement to his monks to work hard at the living of a better life.[10] The *Liber De Diligendo Deo* was written for Aimeric, cardinal deacon of the Church of Rome, evidently at his request. 'You wish to hear from me why and how God is to be loved', Bernard begins.[11] The *Apologia* was written at William of St. Thierry's instigation. These 'commissioned' pieces were asked for to meet a need, and Bernard responded to such requests much as he would have done if someone had asked him a question face to face. He wrote as a preacher and lecturer.

The putting together of the 'register' of his letters exemplifies perfectly the way in which writing came second to talk and action for Bernard. The majority of the letters are not, like those of Peter of Blois and to a lesser extent those of John of

---

[5] Letter 89 (88 and 89 are in reverse chronological order), LTR VII. 237. 1–3.
[6] Letter 88, LTR VII. 233. 19–234. 7.
[7] Letter 153, LTR VII. 359. 21–2.
[8] *PL* 186. 461.
[9] LTR III. 16. 2–3.
[10] LTR III. 165. 17–8.
[11] LTR III. 119. 18–19.

Salisbury, literary accompaniments to a messenger with a piece of business, or written because there happened to be someone at hand to convey a letter. Bernard's letters do the business themselves. And we have merely a selection from his total corpus of correspondence, made about 1145 by his secretary Geoffrey of Auxerre in the first instance, and added to thereafter. Those which were chosen have as a rule some larger implication than their immediate purport. In some cases (that of the letter to Robert of Châtillon, for example) the original letter has been turned into a formal treatise. The whole has been worked up into a letter-collection for publication. This was the usual way in the twelfth century, but in Bernard's case it has been done in a manner which underlines both the immediacy of the originals and the after-thought which has gone into preparing them for publication.[12]

Bernard himself tells us how arduous he found the actual work of writing in a letter to Ogier, the regular canon of Mont-Saint-Eloi near Arras. 'When we are apart we have to compose what we want to say to one another laboriously,' he says, wrily contrasting this effortful method of communication with the ease of conversation. There is no peace for Bernard when he is writing. 'Where is the leisure, where the quiet of silence when one is thinking, composing, writing?' he asks. He describes the mental turmoil when several phrases are jostling for expression at once and a number of different senses and ideas present themselves in a shifting pattern. Many words come to mind, but the exact word escapes capture. The sense, the best way to convey the sense clearly, the best order of presentation, the literary effect, all have to be considered at once[13] when a piece is being given its polished form for publication.

2. *Bernard's Talk*

Bernard won converts and fame from the first by his talk, informal discourses to anyone who would stand and hear him.

---

[12] See J. Leclercq, 'Lettres de S. Bernard: histoire ou littérature?', *Studi Medievali*, xii (1971), 1–74, especially pp. 2–4 on the forming of the register.
[13] Letter 89, 1. LTR VII. 235. 14–22, *SJ* 92, 1.

'God's fisherman', says William of St. Thierry, caught his fish
in Châlons, Reims, Paris, Mainz, Lyons, and other cities in
Flanders and Germany and Italy and Aquitaine.[1] More formal
addresses to the monks of his own and other houses might take
the form of a sermon for a feast-day or an exposition of a
reading just heard by the community. In every context Bernard
infused his talk with such life that those who listened to him
gave each other accounts of what he had said, and some hurried
to write it down. Bernard liked to tell stories to make a point,
and these were especially appreciated and savoured. They were
his way of communicating profundities to the simple and of
leading men's minds on to the path towards the knowledge of
God which he believed their reason was designed to follow.
Thus he taught his listeners in pictures how to defeat the vices
and live in love of God and neighbour. Here we can see him
responding, not to a friend's conversation, as he had done when
he and William talked about the Song of Songs, but to an
audience.

We cannot recapture the sound and gesture which made
Bernard's talk so memorable, but a vast number of 'sayings' of
Bernard survive, some spurious but many with the stamp of
having been said by Bernard himself, or something very like
them. There are stories too, preserved in the same way,
detached from his treatises and sermons.

In his study of the manuscript tradition of the sentence-
collections and parables of St. Bernard, H. Rochais finds
himself in some difficulty, not only about the problem of their
authenticity, but also about their standing as works of such a
writer. He points out that Bernard 'n'a pas dédaigné d'utiliser
des paraboles' to clarify a point or to make what he had to say
more palatable to his listeners in his 'grands sermons', but he
implies a lingering uncertainty about the worthiness of such
material to be included among his writings. A similar difficulty, he notes, arises in the case of St. Anselm's *similitudines*.[2]

---

[1] *VP* I. xiii. 61, *PL* 185. 261C.
[2] H. Rochais, 'Enquête sur les sermons divers et les sentences de S. Bernard',
on the distinction between a sermon and a Sentence. It is not simply one of
length; some of the Sentences are long. *An. Cist.*, 18 (1962). 29, n. 6., cf. ibid.,
p. 29, and see H. Rochais and I. Binont, 'La collection de textes divers dans
manuscrit Lincoln 201 et Saint Bernard', *Sacris Erudiri*, 15 (1964), 15–19.

Sentence-literature of this kind presents immense editorial difficulties; it is widely-diffused and the 'sayings' and *exempla* appear in numerous versions and in a variety of combinations. A great deal remains to be done before anything can be said definitively about its extent and its derivations, but the contributions St. Anselm and St. Bernard made to its increasing popularity in the first half of the twelfth century have something important to tell us about the light in which contemporaries regarded such fragments. The comparison with Anselm is instructive for several reasons, not least because Anselm and Bernard are figures of comparable stature as talkers; but also because while Anselm's talk seemed new, Bernard's did not. He appeared to his listeners to be doing exceptionally well something they had come to look for. Between Anselm's and Bernard's day, as so often, a significant change had come about which throws Bernard's work into high relief.

'Indignes' as they may seem to a modern editor, contemporary biographers speak of these 'sayings' with admiration. Eadmer several times remarks on Anselm's gift of finding the right story or image when someone came to him for advice, or when he was talking to the community.[3] Geoffrey of Auxerre describes enthusiastically a parable which Bernard used to illustrate his discourse on the ten days between Ascension and Pentecost.[4]

Monasticism had, from the beginning, fostered the development of a literature of proverbs and sentences. Gregory the Great speaks in the *Regula Pastoralis* of the way in which the preacher may play upon the attentive minds of his listeners so as to make them 'sing' in response to him; they are, he says, like the taut strings of an instrument, which sound when they are plucked by a player.[5] Anselm's sayings seemed new. Their novelty lay partly in the freshness of his invention, and partly

---

[3] *The Life of St. Anselm by Eadmer*, ed. R. W. Southern, NMT (London, 1962), repr. 1972, OMT. pp. 13–14, 20–1, 54–7, 70–1, 74–8, 80–1, 89–91, 93–7, 101n, 120n, 121, 123n, 133.

[4] J. Leclercq, 'Etudes sur S. Bernard et le texte de ses écrits', *An. Cist.*, 9 (1953), 68.

[5] Gregory, *Regula Pastoralis*, PL 77. 490. J. Leclercq has edited a number of 'monastic sentences' in *Collectanea Ordinis Cisterciensis Ref.*, 14 (1952), 117–24, and see p. 117 on the *verba seniorum* and the *apophthegmata patrum*.

in the way he used his stories in his talks. His biographer Eadmer says that when Anselm first visited Christ Church, Canterbury, in 1079, the monks heard 'things which had been unfamiliar before his time'.[6] As he travelled about England he captured the interest not only of the monks, nuns, and canons he spoke to in the houses he visited, says Eadmer, but also of the laity, because he was able to adapt his teaching so that it was equally helpful to everyone.[7] It is this capacity to find an apt illustration for each of his listeners and show him how it fitted his own circumstances[8] that Eadmer singles out as something different from the usual method of instruction.[9] Anselm combined reasoning with his 'familiar examples', so that the listener not only had a clear picture in his mind, but remembered what it was intended to teach him.[10]

Even when they were taken out of their context, these sayings and stories aroused such interest and admiration that they continued to be popular beyond the reach of Anselm's personal influence, the memory of his gesture or inflexion, and after his death. Copies of both Bernard's 'sentences' and 'parables',[11] and Anselm's 'sayings'[12] proliferated.

In the case of Anselm's *Dicta*, we know something of the circumstances in which they were preserved. Anselm's nephew,[13] the younger Anselm, asked Alexander, one of the Canterbury monks, to send him some extracts from Anselm's addresses *in commune*, given to the community either in the Chapter or in sermons.[14] Eadmer's account of a talk Anselm had given at Cluny on the blessings of eternal life was sent to

---

[6] *Life of St. Anselm* p. 50 and cf. R. W. Southern, *St. Anselm and his Biographer* (Cambridge 1963), pp. 217–18.

[7] *Life of St. Anselm*, p. 55, 'ad cuiusque propositum sua verba dispensabat', cf. *VP* III. iii. 6, *PL* 185. 306C on Bernard's power of adapting what he has to say to his listeners.

[8] Ibid., p. 56.

[9] Ibid., p. 56: 'non es ut aliis mos est docendi modo exercebat, sed longe aliter'.

[10] Ibid., p. 56: 'sub vulgaribus et notis exemplis proponens, solidae rationis testimonio fulciens'.

[11] On the parables, see *Enquête* pp. 31–3, and cf. H. Rochais, 'Remarques sur les sermons divers et les sentences de S. Bernard', *An. Cist.*, 21 (1965), 1–34.

[12] *Memorials of St. Anselm*, ed. R. W. Southern and F. S. Schmitt (London, 1969), p. 34.

[13] *St. Anselm and his Biographer*, pp. 10–11.

[14] *Memorials*, p. 107.

his friend William, who had asked him for it.[15] Other sayings circulated in a more fragmentary form, at a greater or lesser remove from Anselm himself, but the work of these two monks who knew him well and heard him often is a valuable witness to the impact as well as to the content of his live preaching and conversation.

For Bernard, too, there were devoted recorders. Nicholas of Clairvaux, Odo of Morimond, Geoffrey of Auxerre, Gebouin of Troyes, Drogo, Guerric of Igny, William of St. Thierry, preserved Bernard's sayings and made collections of them,[16] but in many instances it is by no means clear how a collection of sentences was put together. 'Sayings' of other preachers—especially Hugh of St. Victor—are often found mingled with those of Bernard, and even with extracts from Anselm.[17] Among the 'secretaries' and scribes of Bernard were some who felt free to adapt him.[18] Gebouin, the Precentor of Troyes, a close friend of both Bernard and Peter the Venerable, and an active participant in the Langres affair which put such strain on relations between Cluniacs and Cistercians, appears to have developed some of Bernard's themes for himself, and made his own versions of Bernard's sayings.[19]

The sayings could be taken down initially in two ways: from the live address, or (if notes were made in preparation) by the usual method of dictation to a scribe, who then normally submitted his text to the author for approval and correction. It is easy to understand how an enthusiastic listener, accustomed to taking dictation, might note down what was said in a talk or sermon, perhaps without his master's knowledge, or without any direct instruction to do so. There can be little doubt that we owe some of the 'sentences' of our authors to secretaries

---

[15] *Memorials*, p. 273.

[16] H. Rochais, 'A Literary Journey: the New Edition of the Works of St. Bernard', *Bernard of Clairvaux: Studies Presented to Dom. J. Leclercq* (Washington, 1973), and J. Leclercq, 'Gebouin des Troyes et S. Bernard', *Revue des sciences philosophiques et théologiques*, 41 (1957), 632–40.

[17] Hereford Cathedral Library, MS I. i. 6, contains Anselmian *dicta* and others, and see *Enquête*, p. 33, on the mixture of Hugh of St. Victor's sayings with those of St. Bernard.

[18] See 'Gebouin', p. 632, on the range of transmitters.

[19] p. 633 and 634ff., and cf. *The Letters of Peter the Venerable*, ed. G. Constable (Harvard, 1967), II. 144–6.

exceeding their duties, adapting and juxtaposing with a far freer hand than they would use in making copies of the same author's treatises.

However, it is not unusual to find editing going on, even of finished treatises, and even of works of the Fathers. There survives from Clairvaux itself an adaptation of the works of Augustine which has been quite freely edited, words added to make a point clear, a familiar phrase substituted for something less idiomatic, grammatical slips corrected, even the style amended.[20]

Anselm was more efficient than Bernard in preventing his works from circulating under what J. Leclercq calls 'une forme provisoire'.[21] Anselm was always careful to give exact instructions for the copying of his treatises, and as a result the early manuscript tradition of his works is exceptionally good,[22] but by Bernard's day it was, it seems, no longer possible to keep such a tight rein on copying and sending out. Bernard wrote an apologetic letter to Peter the Venerable because his secretary Nicolas had written him an unpleasant letter without his knowledge. (This was the Nicolas who was to prove Bernard's trust so disastrous a mistake and who stole money and seals when he left Clairvaux.) Bernard pleads pressure of business, and explains that his secretaries (*scriptores nostri*) do not always catch his meaning exactly, and write more fiercely than he intends; and Bernard himself does not always have time to look over what they have written.[23]

After Anselm's death, his sayings were at the mercy of his monks. Alexander's *Liber ex Dictis Beati Anselmi* was perhaps written in this way, if we may take the evidence of his choice of tense. He speaks of what Anselm 'used to say to the community'.[24] His notes certainly seem to have been made here and there when opportunity offered.[25] Alexander left

---

[20] W. M. Green, 'Mediaeval Recensions of Augustine', *Speculum* 29 (1954), 531–4.

[21] J. Leclercq, 'S. Bernard et ses secrétaires', *R. Bén.* 61 (1951), 208, Recueil I.

[22] *Memorials*, p. 1. Hereford Cathedral Library, MS I. i. 6, contains an abbreviation of the *Proslogion* which dates at the latest from the mid-twelfth century, but this is unusual. See my article 'Abbreviating Anselm', *Recherches de théologie ancienne et médiévale*, xlviii (1981), 78–108.

[23] Leclercq, *R. Bén.* (1951), pp. 211–12.

[24] *Memorials*, p. 107: 'cum loqueretur in commune'.

[25] Ibid.: 'diversis in locis ac temporibus excepi et litteris commendari.'

them lying where others could see them, and (*me nesciente*), unknown to him, parts of them were transcribed and parts scattered.[26]

In contrast to this instance of the uncontrolled diffusion of sayings even of so vigilant and exact an author as Anselm, stands Odo of Morimond's direct instruction that his *dicta* were to be collected. A preface states that the compilation was made: *ipso volente, immo iubente*.[27] The closeness of supervision given to those who transmitted sayings and *exempla* must have varied enormously, in ways which it is now impossible to detect except where we have a chance witness. Whatever the speaker's wishes, his words were out of his control once he had uttered them. It seems unlikely that we can, in general, usefully think in terms of the speaker's 'permitting' some of his sermons to circulate in a 'provisional' form.

The surviving collections pose a number of questions: where texts are altered and corrected, as is the case even with Bernard's most 'literary' sermons, on the *Song of Songs*,[28] it is not always possible to arrive at the author's original intention. The difficulty is compounded in the case of the far more informal collections of sentences. An editor might feel free to present his own version of a story,[29] or to make extracts from it,[30] or to take over an *exemplum* and tell it as his own,[31] or to arrange the items in any order he chooses,[32] or to mingle one author's sayings with those of another.[33] Such texts rapidly become common property, even where they continue to be attributed to their original author in a rubric.

If they have a common feature in their written form, it is that they are extracts, sometimes quite long extracts, telling a complete story in some detail, but nevertheless extracted from

---

[26]   Ibid.: 'pars eorum transcripta; pars vero distracta est.'

[27]   Prologue, ed. Leclercq, *R. Bén.* (1951), p. 210.

[28]   J. Leclercq, 'Les sermons sur les Cantiques de S. Bernard', *R. Bén.*, 66 (1956), 63–91.

[29]   Parable I, in MS Engelbert 33, f. 149–151ᵛ, and see *Enquête*, pp. 52–6.

[30]   Parable III, *Enquête*, pp. 40–1.

[31]   J. Leclercq, 'Drogon et S. Bernard' *R. Bén.*, 63 (1953), 116–31, on the attribution to Drogo and the use by him of fragments of St. Bernard.

[32]   *Enquête*, p. 32.

[33]   *Enquête*, p. 19 and H. Rochais 'Une Collection de textes divers de S. Bernard dans MS Tours 343' *Recherches de théologie ancienne et médiévale* 29 (1962), 77–158.

something longer in which they formed merely asides or illustrations. Rubrics speak of them as *exceptiones abbreviatae*[34] or as *collectae breviter et utiliter*.[35] On what principles was this 'extracting' carried out? J. Leclercq cites a series of texts which suggest that the scribe was likely to be anxious to preserve, not the master's exact words, but his 'meaning': *sensus enim in his est, sed non stylus*.[36] One compiler says that he has not rendered his source word for word (*verbum ex verbo*) but he has done his best to keep to the sequence of the subject-matter: *sed seriem materiei vix tenere potui*.[37] Another (*notarius Godefridus*) thought himself at liberty to put the text into his own words (*suo stylo propagare*),[38] so long as the sense was preserved. Anselm's monk Alexander confesses that he, too, has been able to do no more than make extracts (*ut potui excepi*) in putting together the *Dicta*. He wants his reader to understand that he is to blame Alexander if anything seems *minus bene dictum*, and to give the credit to Anselm for what is well said.[39] The content of our sentences, then, is likely to be substantially Anselm's or Bernard's own, the distilled essence of their talk, recorded precisely because it is so characteristic, but the text may have undergone reworking in a dozen ways, and we may be some way from the author's words.

What was it that the compilers of the sentence-collections thought they were preserving of the original authors' teaching? Odo of Morimond's Sentences begin with a clear statement of the way in which he, at least, regarded these scraps. He cites the occasion when Jesus told his disciples to gather up the fragments which remained after the feeding of the five thousand. In the same way, he says, when the preacher has 'fed' his flock, the fragments (*excepta*) of his discourse may be collected to feed others on a future occasion.[40] Then what he

---

[34] Leclercq, *R. Bén.* (1951). 217.
[35] Paris, MS. B. N. lat. 12323, ff. 104ᵛ–5.
[36] Leclercq, *R. Bén.* (1951), 217, in MSS Cambridge, Gonville and Caius College 94 and Aberdeen, University Library, 218.
[37] MS Vienna 951, f. 187ᵛ.
[38] MS Engelberg 34.
[39] *Memorials*, p. 107, 10–15.
[40] Ed. Leclercq, *R. Bén.* (1951), 21.

has said will not be lost. Seen in this light, such a collection does not seem *inanis* or *superfluus*, though we are reassured on this point; and put together, the little drops (*exiguae stillae*) make a goodly quantity.

The *excerptiuncula* was undoubtedly recognized as something of value in its own right. Alexander and Eadmer made more or less orderly collections of *exempla* which were meant to be read as they stood, not used for future talks by Anselm himself or others in imitation of Anselm's own. William of Malmesbury explains the purpose he had in mind in making *deflorationes* from Gregory the Great. If anyone is prevented from reading the whole of Gregory's works by illness, or because he is busy—or even if he is too idle—he can open William's volume at random and find something at a glance upon which his soul may feed.[41] In the preface to his Prayers Anselm himself recognized the need for something of the sort. He suggests that the reader begins where he likes and allows his thoughts to flow on into prayers of his own.[42] He has, he explains, divided his material into paragraphs for the purpose. In this respect the sentence-collections resemble the *florilegia* of the day; they consist of little 'flowers' of sayings, rather than writings, but they serve a similar purpose in meeting the needs of monks who, for one reason or another, cannot practise *lectio divina* as they should. The titles and rubrics found (apparently indiscriminately used) in the manuscripts,[43] suggest that this was the *genre* to which they appeared to contemporaries to belong.

All these texts have two things in common: their emphasis upon practical and pastoral rather than speculative theology, and their aptness for placing in sequences of argument. William of Malmesbury is again helpful in his preface to the

---

[41] H. Farmer, 'William of Malmesbury's Commentary on Lamentations' *Studia Monastica*, 4 (1962), 309. 'Si quis nostrum vel valetudine vel occupatione vel etiam desidia impediente multis legendis non vacat, his impromptu inveniat, quibus et animam pascat et vitam componat.'

[42] *Anselmi Opera Omnia*, III. 3.

[43] H. Rochais, 'Remarques sur les sermons divers et les sentences de S. Bernard' *An. Cist.*, 21 (1965), 19–21 lists: excerpta; diffinitiones sententiae; ex dictis; liber florum; rerum quarumdam numeralis distinctio; exceptiones; sermones.

florilegium of Gregory. He, too, has seen his collection as practical; he has deliberately avoided theological questions where they arise in Gregory's writings. Let others make extracts of that kind, he says. He has restricted himself to passages which will encourage the reader to live a better life (*ad emendationem vitae*).[44] Eadmer says that in his early years at Bec Anselm began to reflect about such matters, especially upon the virtues and vices and the way they spring from one another. These thoughts were the foundation of the talks which have come down to us as the *De Humanis Moribus*.[45] The result is in many respects a highly Anselmian handbook. The reader is made to use his reason, to understand the 'seeds' and 'roots' of all the vices as well as what proceeds from them, so that he can learn how to attain the virtues and avoid the vices, but the collection includes a number of miscellaneous stories, and the overall purpose is undoubtedly a practical and pastoral one.

In this connection, a striking feature of the *dicta* and sentences and parables of Anselm and Bernard is the use of the same examples again and again. Eadmer found, when he tried to recall the details of the address Anselm had given at Cluny, that scraps of other talks on the same theme came into his mind, and he could not be sure that he had given an exact account of that particular address.[46] It would be surprising if Anselm and Bernard had never used the same or similar examples when they spoke to different communities, but something more is involved here, something closer in spirit to the classical rhetorician's use of commonplaces which made their point by their very familiarity. They were memorable because they were recognized as old friends. Whether, as is probable, Anselm and Bernard followed this tradition unknowingly, and simply because commonsense told them it was helpful to their listeners, or whether they were consciously

---

[44] H. Farmer, op.cit., 309.
[45] *The Life of St. Anselm by Eadmer*, ed. R. W. Southern (Oxford, 1962), p. 13. 'Origines insuper et ipsa, ut ita dicam, semina atque radices necne processus omnium virtutum ac vitiorum detegebat, et quemadmodum vel haec adipisci vel haec devitari aut devinci possent luce clarius edocebat.'
[46] Or: *conflictus*, after the battle in the story. *Enquête*, 35, p. 36, p. 41.

imitating the ancient art of rhetoric,[47] these *exempla*[48] are recognizably *topoi*, and they foreshadow the use of *topoi* in the Art of Preaching a century later. Anselm's talk at Cluny of the blessings of heaven has its parallels elsewhere in his writings, in the culminating chapter of the *Proslogion*, for example, and in the fifth chapter of the *Dicta Anselmi*. Bernard's thoughts on the steps or stages of humility appear again in the *Sentences*, with much the variation which might be expected when an experienced speaker talked on a favourite subject.

The most typical of all Anselm's and Bernard's sayings are the stories which make their point by analogy. Both are confident that simple men and the more learned among their audiences alike will be edified by such comparisons. Anselm's sayings were commonly called *similitudines*; the copyists of Bernard's 'parables' often refer to them as *parabolae*, if they do not simply call them *sermones*. *Parabola* was a good Scriptural term, used for Solomon's sayings in the Old Testament, and for Jesus's parables in the New, but its usual medieval usage seems to have been similar to that of *similitudo*,[49] Anselm's analogies and those of Bernard differ in flavour but not in genre.

The *similitudo* makes its point by its aptness, that is, by the exactness with which the analogy matches point by point that with which it is compared. The heading of one of Bernard's stories refers to the *apta similitudo* he has told about a wounded man, who has had an arrow plunged into him, tip and shaft. A doctor comes with his instruments and fire and extracts both, for if he takes out only the shaft and leaves the tip the wound will not heal. The sick man is in pain and cries out. The doctor soothes his pain by putting on ointments and dressings. Then, while the wound is healing, the sick man gains strength from food and wine. Bernard's explanation of the analogy is lengthy and elaborate. The arrow is the sin which wounds the soul to death. The doctor is the Holy Spirit. The painful application of fire and instrument is like the pang of

[47] Alan of Lille remarks on the usefulness of the method in his *Art of Preaching* late in the twelfth century: 'debet uti exemplis ad probandum quod intendit, quia familiaris est doctrina exemplaris.' *PL* 210. 114.

[48] See M. T. Gibson, *Lanfranc of Bec* (Oxford, 1978), pp. 12–14 and 49–50, on the study of these textbooks.

[49] *Enquête*, p. 30.

conscience and remorse. The ointments and dressings are contrition and hope and the desire to obtain forgiveness. Prayer is the restoring food.[50]

The *similitudo* has arisen out of a Scriptural text: *Ego sum qui deleo iniquitates et peccata hominum* (Isa. 43: 25) and its purpose is exegetical. This is the case with many of Bernard's analogies. In a similar example, Bernard takes as his text: *Voluntarie sacrificabo tibi* (Ps. 53: 8).[51] A father has a sick son who cannot be healed without surgery and cautery. The father asks the son whether he wants to be tied down during the operation. The son, who wants to be healed, asks that he be bound and the operation performed. When the operation begins he cries out and begs to be released, but his father will not loose him until he is healed. He wishes to be cured, but not, at that moment, to be cut and burned. So it is with the monk who submits himself to monastic discipline of his own free will for his soul's health, and then complains that he does not like it. If his abbot lets him go free he will be doing him no kindness.

These are *aptae similitudines*,[52] fitting together characters and events so as to bring out comparisons with exactly the points Bernards wants to make plain. Their superiority in precision and in detail to the work of less able speakers is clear in a crude parable which survives in MS. Troyes 2012. This is the story of a king who has a beloved servant who proves unfaithful. When the king asks him why he has disobeyed him he answers him insolently. The king hands him over to four torturers. Christ is the king, Adam the unfaithful servant, and the four torturers are the four afflictions which fell upon Adam after he had sinned: labour, which makes him weary, sickness, death, and the worms which eat him after his death.[53] The parable is attributed to Bernard in the manuscript, and it may indeed derive ultimately from him, but in the form in which it has come down to us it is told abruptly and awkwardly. It gives the impression of retaining the skeleton of a fuller and more developed analogy, but even in such an inexpert re-telling the

---

[50] LTR VI², Sent. III. 97.
[51] *Sententie* III, p. 85.
[52] See my article 'St. Anselm's Analogies', *Vivarium* 14 (1976), 81–93.
[53] J. Leclercq, *Coll. Cist.*, 14 (1952), p. 123, MS. Troyes 2012, f. 21.

story has not lost its *aptitudo*. The analogy proved a tough and resilient survivor in transmission.

Bernard's first and second Parables tell different stories using many of the same characters and portions of the same plot. In both the hero in danger is saved by the action of certain characters, who intervene in the same order: Fear and Hope, Prudence and Temperance; in both stories the hero rides the horse of Desire and has the rein of Discretion; in both, Prayer is sent to help and Love intervenes at the last.[54] These two Parables exemplify a pattern in the *dicta* in general: a flexibility in the detailed working out of an analogy which makes it possible to adapt it to different purposes without its losing its aptness. The same story, or a variant, is sometimes retold by someone else, or told in a different style. A version of Parable II survives which is cast in a much tauter and more vigorous style than the more usual version, direct and immediate: 'Meanwhile the soldiers of Babylon come together in a group and, complaining among themselves, they say . . . '; 'While the others were hesitating, Hope urging Fear to hurry . . .', and so on.[55]

The analogy sometimes takes a more schematic form, with no development of characters or action. This is the case for most of Anselm's *similitudines*. Each is identified by its principal characters and what they stand for: Self-Will and the Spring; Self-Will and the Adulterous Queen; Self-Will and the Poisonous Herb; The Human Heart and the Mill; God and a Lord; God and a King; The Monk and the Angel; God and the Emperor; The Monk and the Tree; The Monk and the Penny. The *Similitudo inter monachum et denarium*[56] describes *a simili*—surely a reference to one of the Ciceronian *Topics*[57]— the qualities of a perfect monk. There are, says Anselm, three 'goods' appropriate to a penny, which ought to be present in every good monk. The good penny is made of sound metal, is of the correct weight, and is legal tender. If one of these is lacking, it cannot be used to buy or sell. The same is true of the monk:

[54] *Enquête*, p. 36–7.
[55] LTR V12, 38. 15 and 36.
[56] *Memorials*, p. 76–7.
[57] Cicero, *Topics*, X. 41–5.

unless he has all three good qualities, he is not a true monk. His good metal is obedience, with no impurity of disobedience in it. His proper 'weight' is his promise of stability, for he should not easily be blown off course, but keep his vow to the end. The indications that he is a true monk ('legal tender') are his habit, his tonsure, and other outward signs. Anselm goes on to develop the analogy further, but his method of making his main points shows clearly how his *similitidines* typically differ from those of Bernard without ceasing to be analogies of a similar sort, matched point by point and 'apt'. Anselm takes care to keep the story plain. The listener is not distracted by lively pictures of soldiers in a huddle, or anxious Virtues uncertain how best to carry out their plan. The characters are deliberately kept flat. They are no more than familiar hooks on which to hang a perhaps unfamiliar notion. When Anselm tells the monk he is like a penny he gives him a basis for comparison, no more. There is no personification, no theatricality in Anselm's analogies.

The considerable differences of treatment possible within the genre are nowhere more conspicuous than in Anselm's and Bernard's respective uses of the motif of the battle of virtues and vices. The theme was a popular one throughout the Middle Ages and was, no doubt, principally derived from Prudentius' *Psychomachia*.[58] In the hands of a skilful story-teller it had a range of possibilities. Into it could be woven the whole story of man, how Adam first sinned and what was the result, how God rescued him, and how ever since, with God's help, he has been fighting his own battle for virtue against vice. This is the tale Bernard tells in his first three parables.[59] Anselm's *De Humanis Moribus* contains a section where each virtue is pitted against its corresponding vice. The fourteen *partes* of blessedness are matched by the fourteen *partes* of wretchedness, beauty against ugliness, agility against clumsiness, strength against weakness, freedom against servitude, and so on.[60]

The appeal of the story lay not only in its universality, but

[58] Prudentius, *Psychomachia*, PL 60. 11–90.
[59] A composite version of these is edited in *Enquête*, pp. 57–66 and ends: 'Explicit de conflictu virtutum et vitiorum secundum B.'
[60] *Memorials*, pp. 57–61.

also in the scenes and characters portrayed, kings and queens and princes, warfare and captives and dungeons and rescues. Anselm tells how Self-Will, the adulterous Queen, had three sons by her lover, the adulterous King. These three begot so many sons and grandsons that it was impossible to count them. They all lived together in the household of the King and Queen, and at their bidding each acted in his own way. The King and Queen made war on another king with their array of sons and grandsons. Their army attacked in such a way that sometimes one attacked many, sometimes many attacked one, sometimes one attacked one, sometimes many attacked many. Those in the enemy army whom they could overcome, they took captive, and thrust into prison, demanding a ransom they were not able to pay.

Anselm now explains the meaning of the story. Self-Will is mistress of the disobedient and so she is rightly called a Queen. We say she is an adulteress because she is separated from God, to whom she ought to be joined, and joined to the Devil, from whom she ought to be separated. The Devil himself is said to be *Rex et Adulter* because he rules men through Self-Will and abuses their souls, God's brides. When this Queen joins herself to the Devil, three principal vices are born from his *semen* (*perversa suggestio*). They are: *delectatio, extollentia, curiositas*, and they come out into the world through the five senses. From them spring all the other numberless vices, to join the Devil's household. The King against whom they wage war is God, and we men are the members of his army, against whom the vices come singly and in groups. Those they are able to overcome, they bind with bad habits. (*mala consuetudine ligatum*) and thrust them into Hell, where each vice exacts its own penalty, and no man can pay for his freedom.[61]

Bernard tells a similar story at greater length, explaining the significance of the characters and their actions as he goes along. Omnipotent God, a rich and powerful King, had a son, Man, to whom he gave the Law and the Prophets as teachers, as one might a delicate boy, and provided him with guardians and defenders, until he should be grown up. He instructed him and gave him his advice, and placed him as lord over paradise;

---

[61] *Memorials*, p. 51.

he promised him all the treasures of his glory if he would not desert his Father; so that he should not be in any way forced, he gave him freedom of choice.

The young Prince grew bored with the good things he had been given, and went out of the paradise of a good conscience, seeking something new; he ate the fruit which gave him knowledge of good and evil, against his Father's instructions, and then he hid himself, a wretched fugitive before the face of God. He wandered through the mountains of pride, into the valleys of *curiositas*, through the fields of *licentia*, the forests of *luxuria*, until the Old Serpent, seeing him wandering, pressed the little apple of disobedience into his hand and won his free consent. Then he threw him headlong into the maelstrom of earthly desires.

Where now is the loving and liberal Father of the boy, asks Bernard? Can he forget his son? By no means. He tells his friends and servants to look for him. Fear finds him, in a deep dungeon, sitting in the filth of his sins and bound and chained by bad habits. Fear cannot bring him out, so Hope tries. Hope brings him the horse of Desire from his Father, on which he may ride out of his prison. Bernard describes his coming-forth graphically, Fear pushing the horse from behind, Hope pulling it from in front, Fortitude fortifying him, Temperance exerting a moderating influence, Prudence giving sensible orders, Justice leading.

The second and third of Bernard's parables concentrate upon the battle scene which now follows in the first. The story, as it runs in the third parable, describes the two armies drawn up between Jerusalem and Babylon. On one side is David with his army of virtues in an orderly formation; on the other side is Nebuchadnezzar with his *tumultuosus exercitus*, his disorderly rabble of vices. Out from David's camp rides a raw novice of a knight. David himself has armed him. He rides a wild horse (*fervidus*) which is his own body (*proprium corpus*). The knight has first to subdue his horse and gain control of it, so that he can ride it into battle and overcome the most prominent of his enemies, the spirit of Fornication. Prudence cries from behind, 'Spare him! Spare him!' and Discretion shouts 'Keep it up! Keep it up!' as he tries to master the prancing horse. But two sisters, Pride and Vain-Glory ride in from either side and encourage him to think that he is doing well. Believing them, he allows himself to be carried into battle.

The spirit of Fornication is an old hand at battles. He pretends to flee and draws on the wretched prince, deluded, to follow him, until he has him through the open gates of Babylon and he is captured. Greed and Fornication take his horse and allow its qwner no more control over it. Anger, envy, and other vices surge in and Fornication leaps upon him and pins him to the ground with his sword. Thus he is bound by bad habits, and lies in prison. King David rescues him by sending Fear and Obedience, and he is led out at length to peace and to heaven.

Although Anselm could evidently tell a good story, the more schematic accounts of his tales and their perhaps cooler atmosphere suggest that he was less gifted than Bernard at creating suspense and carrying the audience breathlessly with him. Bernard had a well-developed sense of theatre. The scene unfolds vividly before us in Bernard's story, the standard characters take on life; in the account of the virtues pushing and pulling to get the prisoner out of his dungeon something livelier than allégory is needed to make the point. Bernard makes God an anxious father and brings him close in that way. 'Well now, says God the Father' (*Ergone, inquit Deus Pater*) in one of the Sentences.[62] Bernard takes his listeners into the mind of God on a homely, friendly level, telling them what God thought and how he made his plans. He tells us who is who in his stories as he goes along, so that the immediacy of the events is what sticks in the mind, rather than their overall plan.

Anselm habitually places the emphasis upon the force of the analogy as a whole. He wants it to be seen as a pattern so that when he explains the correspondences the whole scheme will fall into place at once. In the story of Self-Will everything is there before the meaning is revealed. This is in keeping with the measured calm and the orderly progression of his ideas in his treatises. The difference between Anselm and Bernard as masters of the *similitudo* reflects the differences between their works as a whole: Bernard was first and foremost a preacher; Anselm a speculative theologian; Bernard concerned to

---

[62] *Sententie*, Series III, 70, p. 102, 24.

awaken and involve his listeners, Anselm to show them the beautiful reasonableness[63] of God's ordaining of the universe.

The analogy was not the only form of the *exemplum* to be developed by our authors. Bernard sometimes used the debate-topos, a favourite of those medieval authors who had read Martianus Capella's *De Nuptiis Philologiae et Mercurii*. (Anselm preferred to confine his dialogues to his treatises, where master and pupil or—in the *Cur Deus Homo*—two friends, Anselm and one of his monks, discuss a difficulty and resolve it.) In one of Bernard's Sentences we find a dramatised account of the recovery of fallen man which takes this form. By the work of mercy (*agente misericordia*) a council is called in heaven to discuss how fallen man is to be restored. Mercy and Truth meet there because they are complementary. Mercy without Truth is mere wretchedness; Truth without Mercy is nothing but severity. Their discussion is carried on with close reference to Scripture. Truth quotes Genesis 2: 17: *In qua hora comederis morte morieris*. Man must die because he has eaten the fruit he was forbidden to eat. Mercy points out that he who lies down to sleep does so only in order to rise again: *Numquid qui dormit non adiciet ut resurgat*. That will not do, says Truth, for the earth was cursed by Adam's deed. Yes, replies Mercy, but, it is possible for man to be created *de humo* without sin. Truth gives a dreadful warning. Man and angel both fell. How can such a man, to whom is entrusted the responsibility of saving the whole world, not fail? As the discussion goes on, Justice and Peace join in, and the council becomes general.[64] In another debate, Reason and Will come to court to decide which of them should be master over the body. Reason wants to chastise the body and enslave it. The Will claims that it serves the body well and takes care of it. The body itself denies this. It complains to Reason of its bare breast, its thin hair, the ulcers with which it is covered because the Will neglects it.[65] In such passages Bernard's liveliness and sense of theatre is again apparent.

Equal in importance with the *exemplum* in the later

---

[63] *Rectus ordo* and *rationis pulchritudo* are notions fundamental to Anselm's argument in the *Cur Deus Homo*.

[64] *Sententie*, Series III, 23, p. 84.

[65] *Sententie*, Series III, 15, p. 73. 1.

development of the medieval art of preaching was the *divisio*. William of Malmesbury arranged his extracts from Gregory topically, according to a system. He divides the book into four parts. The first is concerned with faith, hope, charity, and their handmaids: compassion, almsgiving, hospitality, and so on, all the virtues which make a man behave lovingly towards his neighbour. The second deals with the virtues a man should cultivate so as to love himself as he should: custody of the heart, modesty of speech, circumspection of life, simplicity, chastity, patience, obedience, humility, discretion, perseverance. The third is concerned with the vices, the fourth with the ways in which the vices may be overcome, confession, penitence, prayer, compunction, fasting, with the death of the good man and his resurrection, and with the joys which await him in heaven.[66] William's reader remains free to choose his text as his eye lights upon it; but an orderly arrangement is there for him if he wants to use it.

The structure of Anselm's *De Humanis Moribus* reflects a similar concern for order, within which the reader may make his own selection of topics to concentrate on for a brief period of study. He begins by explaining that 'will' has three meanings. It is an instrument, a power, and an act.[67] Then he draws a picture. The instrument of the will is like a woman choosing between her husband and a lover. If she takes a lover she will give birth to the illegitimate children of the will we call vices. If she remains faithful to her husband she will give birth to legitimate children, the virtues. All the senses of body and soul, says Anselm, act upon the orders of the will. He explains how obedience works, and disobedience, which is self-will. He shows that self-will is pride, because it is will which has got above itself. Only in God is self-will a good. He tells a story to illustrate the likeness between self-will and a spring or fountain. Out of the spring flow three streams of vices, from which break out other vices. These three streams are *delectatio*, *exaltatio*, and *curiositas*. Anselm describes the permutations of the multitude of vices with a mathematical

---

[66] H. Farmer, op. cit., p. 310.
[67] *Memorials*, p. 40.

precision.[68] There are five simple kinds of *delectatio*, one for each of the five senses, ten double kinds, in which two senses at a time are involved, ten triple kinds, involving three senses at a time, five fourfold kinds, involving four senses at a time, and one fivefold kind, which involves all five senses. *Exaltatio* has four types (*opinio*, *voluntas*, *locutio*, *opus*) and, correspondingly, six double types, four triple types, and one fourfold type. *Curiositas* has five kinds, which are treated in the same way. Anselm gives an example for each possible combination. (A double *exaltatio* is involved when a man thinks himself worthy of ecclesiastical office and wishes for it, a triple *exaltatio* when he thinks himself worthy, wishes for it, and says so, a fourfold kind when he thinks himself worthy and wishes for it, and says so, and does all he can to obtain it.)

Divisions into twos and threes and fours are a conspicuous feature of Bernard's Sentences, too, and also of his sermons. One after another the Sentences begin: *tres sunt*; *tria sunt*; *sunt autem quatuor*. This device of dividing the theme so that the listener can concentrate upon one aspect of the subject at a time, was to become standard practice in the university-style sermons of the thirteenth century.

This sentence-literature is not, then, a trivial or unworthy by-product of the teaching of two great scholars. It forms a body of material of the first importance for the future development of the medieval art of preaching. It met a need in its own day which is amply attested by its popularity, and the consistency with which the 'sense' of the master is preserved even where his actual words are lost, speaks volumes for the effectiveness of the *topos* as a means of 'storing' a man's teaching and providing him, and others, with themes and arguments on many occasions. The method flourished first in a monastic context, where communities liked to be spoken to; but it proved equally helpful, as Anselm and Bernard found, in addressing the laity, and stripped of some of their more homely aspects, the *exemplum* and the *divisio* were useful to the university preachers of the later twelfth century and beyond.

Bernard undoubtedly thought well on his feet, and the

---

[68] See R. W. Southern, *St. Anselm and his Biographer* (Cambridge, 1963), p. 346 on Anselm's mathematical bent.

spontaneity of his asides must have contributed substantially
to his listeners' enjoyment, but he preached, too, according to a
plan, with certain intentions in mind, and here his capacity for
organizing his material and judging length and balance had an
opportunity to develop.

3. *Bernard's Preaching*

I. LECTIO

From the earliest Christian times preaching had been a form of
exegesis. Augustine's Homilies on the Psalms or on St. John's
Gospel are a running commentary. Bernard's preaching, too,
must be set in its context in the study of the Bible in his own
day. The *lectio* or lecture upon the text in the schoolroom was
a rather different matter from the *lectio divina* which had
helped to form Bernard as a monk, but the difference is as
much one of pace as one of approach. The slow, careful,
measured reading of *lectio divina* was often described by
comparing it with eating, chewing over the text, ruminating
upon it like a cow chewing the cud.[1] In the schools of northern
France where Anselm and his brother Ralph taught, and after
them Peter Abelard, pressure upon the syllabus demanded
something different, a more rapid ingestion and the provision
of aids to digestion.

Such an aid, on a grand scale, was evolving rapidly in
Bernard's lifetime. The *Glossa Ordinaria*, or standard commentary on the Bible, seems to have reached more or less its
final form by the decade or two after his death. There is
evidence that it may have been given its principal impetus in
the school of Anselm of Laon, who died in 1117. Anselm
himself was probably responsible for the Psalter, for the
Pauline Epistles and for John's Gospel; his brother Ralph
prepared the gloss on Matthew; Gilbert the Universal, Bishop
of London from 1228–34, had earlier taught at Auxerre, and he
appears to have covered the Pentateuch, Joshua, Judges, the

---

[1] Hermannus Judaeus, converted to Christianity partly by the efforts of
Rupert of Deutz, says that he formed the habit of ruminating upon what he had
learned in the stomach of his memory (*in ventrem memorie sepius mecum
ruminanda transmisi*), *De Conversione Sua*, ed. G. Niemeyer, *MGH* Quellen
(1963), p. 74. 15–6.

books of Kings, many of the Prophets; by the mid-twelfth century the whole Bible was provided with a Gloss in this way.[2]

The *Glossa* consisted mainly of brief explanations of difficulties, chiefly in the form of extracts from the Fathers. On 'Consider the Lilies' of Luke 12: 27, we have: 'This is an obvious comparison [*'aperta comparatio'*]. Lilies do not require any cultivation by farmers as the fruits of other plants do. It is usual, too, for heavenly blessedness to be signified by the lily.'[3] There is little attempt to develop any meaning further, or to explore its implications, although the Gloss will often indicate whether the interpretation proposed is literal or allegorical. It is likely that the lecturer would add reflections of his own as he read text and Gloss with his pupils, but the essence of the Gloss itself is its terseness and economy.

Anselm of Laon and his circle also produced 'Sentences' in which questions arising out of the text were examined and a fuller range of patristic material bearing on the topic in hand was assembled for the student.[4] But even here there is nothing of the slow reflectiveness of the *lectio divina*. The technique is more closely allied to that of the *disputatio*, the discussion of questions arising, which became popular in the later twelfth century. Peter Abelard applied his knowledge of the higher technicalities of grammar and logic to the exposition of Romans, and allowed himself to treat particular questions at length.[5] But again his intention is to make the point clear as economically as possible.[6]

Among the reforms carried out by the first abbots of Cîteaux was a revision of the text of the Bible designed to eliminate

---

[2] B. Smalley did much to unravel the history of the *Glossa Ordinaria* in a series of articles in *Recherches de théologie ancienne et médiévale* in the 1930s; the results are summarized in her classic study, *The Study of the Bible in the Middle Ages* (Oxford, 1952). For more recent work, see B. Smalley, 'Les commentaires bibliques de l'époque romane: glose ordinaire et gloses périmées' *Cahiers de civilisation médiévale*, 4, (1961), 23–46 and R. Wasselynck, 'L'influence de l'exégèse de S. Grégoire le Grand sur les commentaires bibliques médiévaux', *Recherches*, 32 (1965), 183–92.

[3] *PL* 114. 297A.

[4] O. Lottin edits the Sentences of the school of Anselm of Laon in *Psychologie et morale aux xiie et xiiie siècles*, vol. V (Gembloux, 1959).

[5] Peter Abelard, *Commentaria in Epistolam Pauli ad Romanos*, ed. M. Buytaert, CCCM xi (1969), pp. 113–7 contains one of his *quaestiones*.

[6] LTR VIII. 17. 17–8, Letter 190. 1.

accretions and corruptions which had crept in in the copying
(where it seems that in places portions of the gloss had become
incorporated into the text itself).[7] It may be that when Bernard
first came to the systematic study of the Bible as a novice it
was to a restored plain text. In any case, he became familiar
with the text of Scripture through readings to the community
and through the liturgy.

He would have been encouraged by the circumstances and
method of his reading to make his own applications of the
Fathers when he came to difficult passages, rather than draw
on whatever gloss may have been available to him. A good deal
of Augustine and Gregory and Origen and others evidently
went into the forming of his interpretations, but he applies
them in a less mechanical and broader way than was possible
for the user of a standard gloss. Peter Lombard's *Sentences*
published at about the time of Bernard's death, provided
exactly the aid later students needed to enable them to draw
what they wanted from the Fathers conveniently; Bernard had
a freedom in using the Fathers which was, for all practical
purposes, largely lost to later generations.

All Bernard's theological reflections, his sense of the divine,
his vision of God, his heightened perception of the beauty of
holiness, arises like a distillation from his study of the Bible.
When he talked about the Bible or wrote about it his purpose
was to communicate this grand view, of a text in which
nothing is ordinary or commonplace, and everything speaks of
God. He shared this vivid realization of Scripture with Gregory
the Great. Gregory thought it as absurd to ask who was the
author of the book of Job as if one were to hold a man's letter in
one's hand and ask what secretary had written it out. God was
the author of the book of Job, and his stamp was evident in
every word of it.[8] Scripture speaks of God with immediacy and
vigour and freshness and directness.

Not all those who expounded the Bible in Bernard's day took
so high a view, at least of the Latin text of the Scriptures. Some
were inclined to agree with Jerome that God's inspiration

[7] On the reform of the text of the Bible, see B. K. Lackner, 'The Liturgy of
Early Cîteaux', *Studies in Mediaeval Cistercian History*, CS 13 (1971), pp. 5–6.
[8] *Pref. in Job*, i. 2, PL 75. 517.

worked upon the minds of the human authors of Scripture in such a way that he supplied the content of what they were to say, but left the choice of words and imagery to them, with their various skills and their different educational attainments. Thus the surface texture of Scripture varies. Jerome himself, speaking of the translators, makes a similar point. He discusses the errors in some of the translations of the Pentateuch, making a distinction between prophet (*vates*) and translator (*interpretes*). Without such a distinction, he points out, we should have to say that Cicero, who translated some books of oratory from Greek to Latin, was inspired by the 'spirit' of rhetoric (*rhetorico afflatus spiritu*). If we insist that the translators of the Pentateuch were all inspired by the Holy Spirit there is an anomaly to be explained (*inconveniens*); if not, the difficulty disappears.[9] Peter Abelard pursues the same line of thought further still in his Prologue to the *Sic et Non*, arguing that allowance must be made for the different usages of different ages, and for copyists' errors, even in the earliest transmission of the text. Peter Abelard wrote Bernard a letter after a visit which he had made to the community of the Paraclete where Heloise was now abbess. Heloise had written to Abelard full of delight at the visit, but with some anxiety because Bernard had criticized a point of liturgical usage in the community. Abelard writes to Bernard to challenge him on the matter. In the two accounts of the Lord's Prayer given in Matthew 6: 9–13 and Luke 11: 1–4 respectively, we find that Matthew speaks of 'our supersubstantial bread' (*panem nostrum supersubstantialem*) and Luke of 'our daily bread' (*panem nostrum quotidianum*). Abelard argues that one Evangelist may be reckoned more reliable than the other in this instance, because Matthew was actually present when Jesus gave the disciples the text of the Lord's Prayer, whereas Luke was Paul's disciple, and had the text handed on to him.[10] This practical approach to Biblical criticism has force only if we set aside the assumption that the Holy Spirit's inspiration

[9] PL 28. 181A–182A, Preface to the *Pentateuch*, cf. Hugh of St. Victor, *PL* 175. 31C–32A.

[10] PL 178. 335–7, Letter 10. On this letter, see B. K. Lackner, 'The Liturgy of Early Cîteaux', *Studies in Mediaeval Cistercian History presented to J. F. O'Sullivan*, Cs, 13(1971), p. 17.

overrode all differences in the circumstances of the human authors of the Scriptures. On the Abelardian view, difficulties will disappear only if we are prepared to take the text apart and examine the construction and workmanship of its components for faults. On the higher inspirational view, difficulties will disappear readily enough if we simply look to the higher meanings above the literal and discover where amongst the allegories and tropologies and moralities the text makes sense as it stands. The fact that we are reading one of several translations will then be of no importance—although we must still be careful to treat the text with the utmost respect and to try hard to resolve anomalies in a straightforward way before we conclude that the literal sense will not allow us to reconcile contradictions.

These two methods of approach, those of Bernard and the *lectio divina*, and of some of the professional academics of the day, are so different as to run in opposite directions from entirely different starting-points. Bernard gives us no detailed account of his theory of interpretation. For a picture substantially in accord with his—although more pedestrian and combining something of the schoolroom with something of the monastic way of reading—we must turn to Hugh of St. Victor. In the Preface to his Homilies on Ecclesiastes Hugh—at once a regular canon and a Paris schoolmaster—says that: 'Every Scripture, expounded according to its proper interpretation, both shines out more clearly, and makes it easier for those who read it to find the way to understand it.'[11] The 'shining' Hugh has in mind is not unlike that of Cassiodorus' description of the Psalms as 'a heavenly sphere crowded with glittering stars, and, so to speak, a most beautiful peacock painted with circles like eyes and many colours and a lovely variety; it is also a paradise for souls, containing a myriad apples, on which the human mind, deliciously crammed, grows fat.'[12] Hugh teaches a method of exposition which will, in a simple and practical way, bring the student to this higher understanding.

---

[11] Hugh of St. Victor, *Hom. in Eccles.*, PL 175. 1140–5A: 'Omnis scriptura secundum propriam interpretationem exposita, et clarius elucescit, et ad intelligendam se faciliorem legentibus pandit accessum.'

[12] Cassiodorus, *Institutiones*, ed. A. C. Mynors (Oxford, 1937), I. iv. 3.

He describes how, when he was a boy, he used to make lists of words, so as to memorize them, and of different kinds of misleading arguments, so that he could learn the answers to them; he would set out counters and draw geometrical diagrams on the pavement with charcoal; he would stay up late at night to look at the stars. This was done with childish enthusiasm, 'but it was not useless,' he says. 'I do not repeat this to boast of my knowledge, which is little or nothing,' he tells his readers, 'but to encourage the right sort of intellectual curiosity'. It was the study of the Bible to which all these other studies were leading.[13] He wants his pupils to learn that nothing in the Bible is meaningless. 'There are many things in Scripture which, considered in themselves, seem to have nothing worth seeking out, but if they are brought together with other things and you put them side by side with them, and begin to weigh them as a whole, you will perceive them to be both necessary and in agreement.'[14] 'Learn everything; you will see afterwards that nothing is wasted',[15] he advises.

This process of careful scrutiny of every detail, of systematic juxtaposition of one passage with another, was designed to leave none of the Bible's meaning unnoticed. Every passage, Hugh goes on to explain, has a literal meaning (*littera*). Some have another obvious meaning too, the *sensus*, 'where . . . something is so clearly signified that nothing else is left to be understood'.[16] Other passages have a deeper meaning (*sententia*), which is not clear unless it is expounded.[17] Still other passages have both a plain meaning in addition to the literal one, and a hidden meaning.[18]

In the literal reading something may be left to be understood (*subaudiendum*) or there may be some repetition or superfluity (*superflua*).[19] There may be some grammatical anomaly such as the substitution of a noun in the nominative and a genitive pronoun for the genitive of a noun:

---

[13] *Didascalicon* VI. iii, *PL* 76. 800.
[14] Ibid.
[15] Ibid.
[16] Ibid., VI. viii, *PL* 176. 806–7.
[17] Ibid.
[18] Ibid.
[19] Ibid., VI. ix, *PL* 176. 807.

Dominus in coelo sedes eius,

for:

sedes Domini in coelo.[20]

In the *sensus*, too, some unusual way of speaking may get in the way of our understanding of the text, so much so that the meaning may appear to be incredible, impossible, absurd, or false. 'You will find many things of this kind in the Scriptures', Hugh warns, and especially in the Old Testament, according to the idioms of the language in which they are said, which, although they are clear enough there, seem to us to mean nothing'.[21] These difficulties of *littera* and *sensus* are the kind of problem with which Peter Abelard is normally concerned. They can be resolved, if at all, only with the aid of grammatical and logical expertise of a high order.

But when we turn to the *sententia* all such difficulties disappear. The inner and deeper meaning transcends the petty considerations of the surface operations of language. It is not restricted by the limitations of human language as it tries to talk about the divine. 'It can never be absurd; it can never be false . . . it admits no contradiction; it is always appropriate, always true',[22] Hugh claims. Thus it is that in its higher senses Scripture frees and enriches the understanding, and gives the reader an elevated perception of divine truth.

Hugh of St. Victor has a graphic image of the relationship between the literal and the higher senses, and of the possibility of contradictions and absurdities occurring in the literal sense which cannot arise in the higher senses. The foundations of a building rest upon, or rather within, the earth. Not all the stones which go into the foundations are cut and shaped, and there are therefore gaps between them and places where they do not fit together properly. The fabric of the building rises above the surface of the earth and is even and level, the stones cut to fit one another and allow for the unevenness of the foundation structure.[23] 'So the Divine Page contains many things according to the natural sense which seem to contradict one another and sometimes to bear some absurdity or impossi-

---

[20] Psalm 10: 5, *Didascalicon* VI. ix.
[21] Ibid.
[22] Ibid., VI. xi, *PL* 176. 808–9.
[23] *Didascalicon* VI. iv, *PL* 176. 802C.

bility. But the spiritual understanding admits no contradiction; in it there are many things which are diverse, but there can be nothing which is adverse.' Hugh has practical advice to help the student interpret a difficult passage. 'When you begin to read the book and you find many obscure, many clear and many ambiguous things, set upon its base what you find to be clear; ... interpret what is ambiguous so that it is not out of keeping; if you can, leave on one side what is obscure.'[24] Hugh's intention is to encourage the reader to be methodical, to build upon certainties, and never to allow himself to be led into pointless speculation about the meaning of difficult passages. This systematic, building-block approach is not Bernard's way, but it underlies Bernard's apparently freer movement from one sense to another in his own exegesis; and the two authors share a concern to reach the higher understanding by a safe and secure route.

The notion that the historical sense is lowlier than the spiritual is a commonplace in early medieval writers. 'The body of John [the Baptist] is buried; his head is set on a dish. The literal sense is hidden in the earth; the spiritual honoured and lifted up upon the altar', says an Irish commentator on Mark's Gospel in the seventh century.[25] Alcuin prefaced his 'Questions on Genesis' with the explanation that there are many difficult questions with which he does not propose to deal. Those he has included are mostly simple questions to which brief answers can be given and these are normally historical (*maxime historicae sunt*).[26] The respect for the higher meanings never, however, in Hugh of St. Victor or St. Bernard, led to a casting aside of the historical. It remained fundamental, but it was to be departed from where the text allowed, either in search of profounder understanding, or for the reason Augustine outlines in the *De Doctrina Christiana*: 'When the words taken literally give an absurd meaning, we ought forthwith to enquire whether they may not be used in this or that figurative sense with which we are unfamiliar; and in this way light has been thrown on many obscure passages.'[27]

---

[24] Ibid., *PL* 176, 804.
[25] *PL* 30. 608; see *Sacris Erudiri*, vi (1954), 199–202.
[26] Alcuin, *Quaestiones in Genesim*, Preface, *PL* 100. 517A.
[27] Augustine, *De Doctrina Christiana*, III. xxix. 41.

The greater part of Bernard's preaching was to monks, and those he wanted to encourage to be monks, rather than to students of the *artes* in the schools. His emphasis is, accordingly, often upon the practical lessons to be drawn from Scripture for the living of a good life. In a sermon for Epiphany, he promises to try to draw out this moral lesson.[28] The kind of lesson he has in mind is clear from a discussion in one of the *Sentences*, of a passage from the Song of Songs: 'Return, return, O Sulamite' (Cant. 6: 12). The 'return', says Bernard, is to be from foolish jollity, from useless sadness, from vainglory, from hidden pride. When the soul returns to Christ, having left all these vices behind, her husband will look upon her, for she will then be fit for his eyes.[29] In this way the 'seed' of the Word of God (which is the 'preacher's grain') falls into the 'earth' which is the soul, and having to all appearances died, springs up again.[30]

In a discourse on the story of Naaman the leper he explains his view of the relation between the literal and the moral sense. 'We are dealing, brothers, with the historical sense', he says. 'History is the doctrinal threshing-floor, on which the good threshers, that is, wise and learned masters, with the flails of diligence and the winnowing-fan of enquiry, separate the grain from the chaff.' Just as honey is to be found under the wax of the honeycomb and a kernel under the surface of the grain, so, under the *cortex historiae*, there lies the sweetness of the moral and allegorical senses.[31]

This, then, is the basis of *lectio* on which, as Peter the Chanter describes later in the century, the edifice of preaching is raised.

Peter the Chanter, Precentor of the Cathedral of Notre Dame in Paris, composed a manual for preachers, the *Verbum Abbreviatum*. He begins by dividing the study (*exercitium*) of Holy Scripture into three. He regards *lectio*, the reading of the text in the form of a lecture with a detailed gloss or commentary on each word or phrase, as the lowest form of exegesis. The *disputatio*, or discussion of difficult passages and

---

[28] LTR VI¹. 23–4.
[29] Sent. I. 10, LTR VIⁱⁱ. 9. 18–10. 6.
[30] Sent. III. 119, LTR VIⁱⁱ. 216. 1–4.
[31] Sent. III. 88, LTR VIⁱⁱ. 130. 4–7.

of questions which arise from the reading, is a more advanced exercise. In *lectio* the student draws upon the Fathers' commentaries and upon his knowledge of grammar to elucidate the sense of the passage. In *disputatio* he uses logic, too. Above these pedestrian schoolroom exercises stands *praedicatio*, the preaching of the Word.[32]

Lectio underlies the use of Scripture in Bernard's preaching at every point. Bernard encourages his reader to approach the text carefully, and to use all the skills he has acquired in this humble exercise. In a sermon on Romans 14: 17: 'The Kingdom of God is not food and drink', he discusses the characteristics of St. Paul's style. 'The apostle Paul is as a rule brief in words, full of meanings', he points out.[33] He cites, without naming him, Jerome's comment to this effect.[34] He relies upon his listeners' familiarity with both the style of St. Paul and the views of St. Jerome to capture their interest in his opening words. The liberty Bernard allows himself when he chooses, not exposition by gloss and commentary but preaching as the method of exegesis he prefers, is not, then, a freedom from the rules. On the contrary, it is a discipline of the highest order, in which grammatical, logical, and patristic aids to interpretation are used.

Again and again he refers to the Fathers in a way which indicates that he expects his listeners to recognize the context with the minimum of assistance. In a sermon on Epiphany he notes briefly that 'as we know', the Fathers teach that the Feast has a threefold significance.[35] Occasionally he quotes directly but often there is no more than a half-sentence summarizing a familiar opinion. 'Blessed Gregory expounds [that] love itself is knowledge.'[36]

So subtly interwoven are Bernard's references to the Latin

---

[32] Peter the Chanter, *Verbum Abbreviatum*, *PL* 205. 25. Bernard uses the expression *Verbum abbreviatum* in Sermon I. i *In Vig. Nat. Dom.*, LTR IV. 197. 15.

[33] *Serm. Div.* 19. 1 (Rom. 14: 17), LTR VI^i. 161. 3–7.

[34] Jerome *Epist*. 49. 13, *CSEL* 54. 370.

[35] LTR VI^i. 21. 2. 'Triplicem huius festivitatis rationem a sanctis patribus traditam esse cognovimus.'

[36] See, for example, LTR VI^i. 191. 5 and VI^i. 210. 10–11 for two quotations from Gregory.

Fathers that it is instructive to look at his handling of the less universally familiar and more controversial commentaries of Origen, who was sometimes difficult to reconcile with orthodoxy.

Not all even of the most learned of Bernard's contemporaries had read Origen. We have an account of the occasion when, at the trial of Gilbert of Poitiers at Rheims in 1148, his supporters and his opponents tried to confound one another by citing Greek authorities, whose names commanded general respect, even if the texts available were often obscure and of uncertain authorship. 'Athanasius' was quoted, and Theodoret.[37] Geoffrey of Auxerre, the reporter and Bernard's secretary at the time, speaks of the confusion caused by the citation of some unfamiliar 'letters of some Greeks', from a *corpus canonum*.[38] The Greek Fathers known to and used by the followers of Gilbert were necessarily few for they had little Greek amongst them; the canonical collections made a little material available.[39] Sometimes, as in the case of the 'Athanasius' citation, what purported to be a Greek source was in reality a Latin one, in this case Vigilius of Thapsus. The 'Origen' of the Porretani was John Scotus Eriugena's commentary on St. John's Gospel, which circulated under Origen's name.[40]

Nevertheless, Origen was known and quite widely read among the friends and disciples of Bernard of Clairvaux,[41] and not only for his writings on the Song of Songs. In one sermon Bernard found himself having to make an apology for Origen.

[37] Robert of Melun, *Quaestiones*, ed. R. Martin, *Spicilegium Sacrum Lovaniense*, 13 (1932), Question 19. Vigilius, *contra Ar.* II. 42, *PL* 62. 225A, and Theodoret, *Patrologia Graeca* 83. 1171B and 1167A. See *PL* 185. 605B for Geoffrey of Auxerre's account of the affair, and N. M. Häring, 'The Porretans and the Greek Fathers', *Mediaeval Studies*, 24 (1962), 181–209 on the general question of the knowledge of the Greek Fathers which was possible to Bernard's contemporaries.

[38] *Ep. ad Alb.*, *PL* 185. 591A.

[39] See Häring, op. cit., p. 185.

[40] Ibid., p. 207. See Sermon 7. iv on the Psalm 'Qui Habitat' for a reference to Ignatius, LTR IV. 414. 27. See, too, LTR I. 144. 20–2 on the Greek source of the phrase: 'know thyself'. (*SS* 23. iv. 9).

[41] On Bernard and Origen, see J. Leclercq, 'Saint Bernard théologien', *An. Cist.*, ix (1953), 46–51; J. M. Canal, 'La maternidad espiritual en San Bernardo', *Estudios marianos*, xiv (Madrid, 1954); H. de Lubac, *Exégèse médiévale*, i (Paris, 1959), 586–99 *et passim*; J. P. T. Deroy, *Bernardus en Origines* (Harlem, 1963), pp. 31–96; C. Dumont, *Coll. Cist.*, xxvi (1964), 145.

As he explains away a moment of embarrassment, he reveals some of the difficulties in which the reader of Origen might find himself if he cited him.

The community had had a reading from Origen's homilies on Leviticus, which implied that the Son suffers grief and distress because of our sins, as though he were mutable and passible like one of his creatures.[42] This had troubled some of his monks, and the next day Bernard preached on the passage he had chosen from Origen so that they should see better how to understand it. 'I fear that the words which were read to you yesterday from Origen's homily on that chapter of the Law where Aaron and his sons are forbidden to drink wine when they are to approach the altar, may perhaps do harm to some, if they receive them simply as they sound.'[43] He notes that there is much more in the passage in question along the same lines: *plurima quoque alia in hunc modum*,[44] and his explanation indicates that he is anxious to make the whole drift of Origen's argument plain, not solely to explain a difficult sentence or two.

Bernard's own view of Origen's words is that they are 'perhaps spoken *abundantius* rather than *circumspectius*';[45] 'Perhaps he spoke exaggeratedly; . . . that is not our concern',[46] he says. What is important is the effect his words may have if they are taken at their face value by the simple. 'I do not think I should be silent on this matter', says Bernard, 'for the authority of the Fathers warns us that he wrote some things which are clearly against the faith, and that he is therefore not to be read without caution.'[47] Bernard's concern was always the same when he encountered teaching which appeared unorthodox; his first anxiety was not whether there really was unorthodoxy in what was being said, but the damage which might be done to those unable to understand the subtleties of the argument, and

---

[42] *Origenes Werke* VI. i (Leipzig 1920), p. 374. 19–20: 'Salvator meus luget etiam nunc peccata mea', Ibid. p. 375. 5–6: 'tamdiu est in maerore, quamdiu nos persistimus in errore.'

[43] *Sermones de Diversis* xxxiv, LTR VI^i. 228. 11–14. *Leviticus* 10. 8–9: 'si recipiant ea simpliciter, sicut sonare videntur.'

[44] Ibid. p. 228. 16.

[45] Ibid. p. 228. 16–17.

[46] Ibid. p. 228. 20–229. 1.

[47] Ibid. p. 229. 1–3.

therefore likely to be misled into heresy by mistake. Here, he says, 'We do not ask what he himself thought, but we desire to bring it about that all of you, knowing what is sound doctrine, are unmoved by those words.[48] Now Bernard comes to the offence to orthodoxy contained in Origen's words. Origen implies that there is sadness in heaven. 'Perish the thought that it should be believed that there is a place of sadness in heaven!' Bernard exclaims.[49] On earth Jesus was troubled indeed, and he deigned to fear and to grow weary; on earth he truly wept and was sad, suffered, died, and was buried, but the emphasis is upon *dignatus est*. He 'deigned' to do these things, and at the resurrection he left suffering behind.[50]

In the course of his sermon Bernard quotes three further passages from Origen's homilies on Leviticus.[51] In the first of these Origen is comparing Paul's sorrow over sinners with that of him who is called the Son of Love. How can Christ not sorrow still, if even Paul does so? In the second, he is asking whether it can be possible that he who wept over Jerusalem no longer weeps or cares for us. In the third he draws his conclusion that it must be the case that if Paul grieves over sinners and weeps, the Lord does so, too. The argument is repetitive—even though Bernard has condensed Origen's full text somewhat—and it makes its appeal to the emotions more strongly perhaps than to the reason. Nevertheless, it is a powerful argument, and one to which Bernard seeks in vain for an equally compelling answer.[52] How can human frailty achieve a feeling like that of Christ? asks Bernard, to feel for

---

[48]   Ibid. p. 229. 3–5.
[49]   Ibid. p. 229. 6.
[50]   Ibid. p. 229. 15–17.
[51]   Ibid. p. 231. 22–3, Baehrens p. 375. 6–8: 'Si Apostolus ipsius luget quosdam qui ante peccaverunt nec paenitentiam egerunt in his quae gesserunt, quid dicam de ipso, qui filius dicitur caritatis?'
LTR VI^i. 231. 23–6, Baehrens p. 375. 11–14: 'Cum ergo quae nostra sunt quaesierit, nunc iam nos non quaerit, nec quae nostra sunt cogitat, nec de erroribus nostris maeret, nec perditiones nostras deflet et contritiones, qui flevit super Jerusalem?'
LTR VI^i. 232. 1–4, Baehrens p. 375. 25–376. 1: 'Nunc . . . quia misericors et miserator est Dominus, maiori affectu, quam Apostolus suus, flet cum flentibus et luget eos qui ante peccaverunt. Nec enim putandum est quod Paulus lugeat pro peccatoribus et fleat, Dominus autem meus abstineat a fletu.'
[52]   LTR VI^i. 232. 5–9.

wretchedness without being wretched, and so love—and passionately love—him who is in sorrow or danger without itself grieving or being disturbed? This is far beyond our experience, but nothing is impossible to God.[53]

God is able, Bernard insists, to rejoice with those who rejoice, without grieving with those who grieve. He develops the implications of this a little, but we hear no more of Origen. Bernard has concentrated, not upon Origen's words and their interpretation, but upon the point of doctrine they raise. He has not defended Origen directly, but on the other hand he has not condemned him.

Thus it is with Bernard's use of the Fathers in general. They are familiar supports for certain interpretations. Often it is unnecessary to mention them, but even where they appear to raise difficulties they are never to be dismissed out of hand. At every point their views are to be accommodated within the interpretation which is proposed.

A similar muted but efficient use of detailed scholarly knowledge is to be seen in Bernard's grammatical analysis of certain passages. In the course of systematic reading of the text of Scripture word by word the reader encounters a number of grammatical oddities. In the Sermon on the Song of Songs which deals with the text 'Thy name is an oil poured forth; therefore do the virgins love thee greatly' (*Oleum effusum nomen tuum, propterea adolescentulae dilexerunt te nimis*) Bernard's grammarian's eye (assisted by Augustine) is caught by *nimis*. 'What does *nimis* mean?' he asks. It surely cannot mean 'too much'? 'No, says Bernard, it means "wholeheartedly", "ardently": *Valde, vehementer, ardenter.*'[54]

This habit of looking for the special usages of Scripture and providing explanations for them in terms of something approaching a special 'grammar' of Holy Scripture, was to give rise to the development of a number of aids for the lecturer in the later twelfth century. One of these was the dictionary of theological terms, in which a given word was listed with all

---

[53] Ibid. p. 232. 9–15.
[54] *Cant.* 1. 2–3, *SS* 19.1, LTR I. 108. 19, cf. Augustine, *Enarrationes in Psalmos*, 118. iv. 1, CCSL 40. 1674.

the meanings which could be found for it in Scripture, and a context for each. These collections proved invaluable to preachers, who were able to use them as source-books for their sermons, and find in them in a moment a series of texts on their chosen theme.

In one of the earliest of these dictionaries composed a little after the middle of the century, Alan of Lille describes the peculiar qualities of Biblical language, the way in which it transcends the ordinary rules of grammar and signification.[55]

Bernard can be seen to be busy in a small way on the same task. In his discussion of the story of Naaman the leper, he comes to the point where Elijah sends his boy to tell Naaman to wash in the river. This 'boy', Bernard suggests, may be understood to be pure reason; or he may be thought of as the Holy Spirit, because the Holy Spirit makes men children in their simplicity (*quia pueros facit, id est pueros simplicitate*). Or the 'boy' may be understood to be Holy Scripture. In another *Sentence*, Bernard suggests that 'obedience' may mean the kiss of David because it opens God's secrets to us and brings us nearer God; it is a yoke, because he who is perfectly obedient pulls against his own desires, as though he were under a yoke; it is an altar under which there burns a perpetual fire (the hollow in which the fire burns is humility; the fire is love).[56]

It is easy to see how 'dictionary' entries of this sort lent themselves to the preacher's purpose. The words of Scripture are taken not only to possess more than one straightforward meaning, as in Bernard's example of *nimis*, but a number of figurative meanings, too. From the plain grammatical exercises of careful reading and analysis, it is a short step to the use of the technique of *lectio* in preaching.

II. DISPUTATIO

In the years immediately before Gilbert of Poitiers' trial at Rheims, Robert of Melun assembled a collection of *questiones*, short questions arising out of the lectures he gave on Holy

---

[55] Alan of Lille's *Dictionary of Theological Terms* is printed in *PL* 210. See Introduction, *PL* 210. 687–8.
[56] *Sent.* III. 10, LTR VI[ii]. 70.

Scripture, with their answers.[1] He had been one of Abelard's pupils, but by the time of Gilbert's trial he had attained a standing in his own right as a master of theology which made John of Salisbury (in his account of the trial) rate him the equal of Peter Lombard.[2] Such questions form perhaps the first stage of the development of the *disputatio* to which Peter the Chanter gives so important a place.[3]

Some of Robert's questions are concerned simply with difficulties over the meaning of the text. Someone had asked what is meant by saying that angels bear our prayers into the sight of God. Robert explains that our prayers are made more acceptable in the sight of God by the ministry of the angels towards us.[4] When, in Luke 16: 22, we read that souls are carried by the angels into Abraham's bosom, we are to understand, says Robert, that the angels rejoice to see their fellow-citizens admitted into their society, for they themselves are deputed to be their guardians in this life.[5] Questions such as these are so near to the close textual analysis of *lectio* itself that they scarcely constitute 'questions' for disputation.

Other questions raise problems of orthodoxy and require something more 'disputatious' to answer them. It is asked, says Robert, what is meant by the saying of the glossators that when Jesus rode into Jerusalem to the praises of the people, he did so in order to incite the hatred of the Jews against him. If that is what he did, he caused them to sin, and in that case the Jews are to be excused for what they did. Robert explains that this is like the hardening of Pharaoh's heart. Jesus did not make the Jews hate him; he merely caused the hatred in their hearts to show: *invidiam eorum mente conceptam manifestare*.[6] In another question, Matthew's words: 'Unless those days were shortened, all flesh should not be saved', are explained. This, says Robert, is a way of speaking (*modus*

[1] Robert of Melun, *Quaestiones*, ed. R. Martin, *Spicilegium Sacrum Lovaniense*, 13 (1932), p. lii dates the collection.
[2] Ibid., p. viii–ix.
[3] Ibid., p. xxxiv.
[4] Ibid., p. 14, 5–7, Question 20; cf. *Glossa ordinaria* on Phil. 4: 6, *PL* 114. 607, Tob. xii. 12.
[5] Robert, ed. cit., p. 25. 14, Question 43.
[6] Ibid., p. 21. 3–4, Question 34, Matt. 21: 10, *PL* 114. 153A. Invidiam eorum mente conceptam manifestare.

loquendi) as when we say 'I would have died if he had not come to my aid'.[7] Even in instances where something approaching a real disputation is involved, Robert's *Quaestiones* are, however, always brief. His students appear to have been content simply to have their difficulties removed for them.

Peter Abelard's *Quaestiones* are far lengthier. He preferred to deal with difficulties as he went along, rather than to make a separate list of questions and answers. His commentary on Romans contains a number of long digressions.[8] When, later in the century, such long disputations became more numerous, the *Quaestiones* seem to have been given a separate time, so that they could be discussed at leisure. Simon of Tournai set aside a regular period in the day when two or three questions were considered.[9]

Bernard cannot be expected, then, to have had in mind anything quite like Peter the Chanter's notion of *disputatio* in his own teaching on Holy Scripture. Nevertheless, he did, on occasion, have to pause to answer a question at some length—as in the example of the sermon he preached on Origen. In one treatise, the *De Gradibus Humilitatis et Superbiae*, he himself engages in a *disputatio*. The outcome was unfortunate. He did not pause to verify the quotation on which he based his argument. When he discovered his mistake he wrote a *Retractatio* which was to be placed in front of the work in all future copies.[10] To this apology we owe an account of Bernard's idea of a *disputatio*'s method and purpose.

Before we look at this striking instance, we must pause again for a moment over the question of Bernard's knowledge of logic. I have suggested that Bernard's dialectical competence is perhaps best measured against that which Anselm encouraged his pupils to attain in the generation before Abelard. Guibert of Nogent is again a help here, in giving us a preliminary picture of the way in which Anselm thought a monk might properly employ his dialectical skills. Without, it seems, any grounding

---

[7] Ibid., p. 21. 11–17, Question 35, Matt. 24: 22.

[8] Peter Abelard, *Commentaria in Epistolam Pauli ad Romanos* ed. M. Buytaert, CCCM, XI (Turnhoult 1969).

[9] Simon of Tournai, *Disputationes* ed. J. Warichez, *Spicilegium Sacrum Lovaniense*, 12 (1932).

[10] LTR III. 15. 9–13.

in dialectic, Guibert tried to resolve questions which arose in the course of his reading. He found himself in some difficulties at first, until Anselm, then prior of Bec, and a frequent visitor to Fly, gave him the help he needed. Anselm taught him to distinguish between the faculties of appetite (or desire or longing), will, reason and understanding (*affectus, voluntas, ratio, intellectus*) within him. Guibert objected that he could see no difference between will, and appetite or desire, and Anselm showed him that, although when they are governed by reason and intellect they do indeed appear the same, when they are not so governed, appetite may outrun the will. By discussing certain passages in the Gospels in detail with Guibert, Anselm was able to show him how this may be. Guibert himself then set about searching the Scriptures in this way, with renewed interest and a sense that he now understood the method by which he was to work.[11]

The method Anselm taught Guibert was his own invention; it is set out in some detail in the 'three treatises pertaining to the study of Holy Scripture' which he wrote for the monks of Bec, the *De Veritate*, the *De Libertate Arbitrii* and the *De Casu Diaboli*.[12] Anselm began by posing a problem for his readers: 'What is truth?' 'What is freedom of choice?' then some preliminary definition and discussion, drawing upon simple principles of grammar and dialectic, brings him to the point where he can introduce one or two texts of Scripture. In John's Gospel we find: 'He who does evil hates the light' and 'He who does good comes to the light.'[13] Working with the principles already established by reason, Anselm asks what 'truth' may be said to be in this context. Anselm expects his readers to be familiar with the notions of definition and division and with simple syllogisms.

Anselm's method involved the asking of questions. It was not in the spirit of the Cistercian customs or of the Benedictine Rule that there should be inquisitiveness or contentiousness, but questions arose none the less. We saw how Guibert of Nogent found himself so troubled by the endless questions of his fellows that he felt his own thinking impeded, until the

---

[11] *De Vita Sua*, I. xvii.
[12] *Anselmi Opera Omnia* I. 172. 2–3.
[13] Ibid. I. 181. 12–13 (John 3: 20–1).

stimulus roused him to fresh efforts. Then, he says, the questions by which they thought to trip him up sharpened his wits; he thought hard and turned over the pages of many books, and found answers.[14] Anselm encouraged his monks to ask questions sensibly, not out of rivalry or mockery. But it is inconceivable that in houses such as that of the canons of St. Victor in Paris, where William of Champeaux retired for a time from the hurly-burly of the schools, and Hugh of St. Victor later taught the liberal arts as well as lecturing on the Bible, that the *lectio divina* of quiet reflection can have been the only method of studying the Bible. William of St. Thierry opens his own *Expositio* of Romans with a remark on the 'many and varied and difficult questions' which the text raises.[15]

William did his best to avoid becoming entangled in such questions. He describes his commentary as a patchwork of the words of the Fathers. It is like a little bird dressed in the borrowed plumes of many more brightly coloured birds. 'If they were to come and take back their own feathers', he says, 'our little adornment would be naked'.[16] But Bernard did not avoid questions. Whatever training in dialectic he had received as a boy, or had picked up from his friends among scholars, he had, by the time he composed his treatises, acquired a smattering of technical vocabulary[17] and a good grasp of the essentials, so that he was able to answer questions by reasoning as well as by quoting authorities.

In his treatise *On Grace and Freedom of Choice* (*De Gratia et Libero Arbitrio*) Bernard makes almost exactly the distinction Anselm explained to Guibert of Nogent, between will and appetite. Like Anselm, he went on to apply it to a number of Scriptural passages so as to show how they are to be read, and he builds up a reasoned argument in a manner Anselm would

---

[14] *De Vita Sua*, I. xvi, Bourgin, p. 60: 'Noverint tamen qui me tamquam de otiosa et non necessaria explanatione suggillant, non tam intendisse exponere Evangelium, quam ex Evangelio sumere occasionem loquendi quod loqui delectabat.'

[15] *PL* 180. 547A.

[16] *PL* 180. 547B: 'Secundum poeticam fabulam, aviculam nostram diversarum plumis avium, et coloribus solemniter vestivimus; quae si venerint, et abstulerint singulae, quae recognoverint sua, nuda vel nulla remanebit nostra cornicula.'

[17] Much of which was clearly commonly in use among educated men.

have approved,[18] making use of simple principles of grammar and dialectic.

Bernard had been speaking one day of the way in which he had experienced God's grace working in him,[19] so that he felt himself to be making progress and hoped one day to be made perfect. One of the bystanders challenged him. 'What is your part, then, and what reward do you hope for, if God does everything?'[20] He suggested that Bernard ought to give glory to God for his grace, but at the same time live in such a way as to prove himself worthy to receive it. Bernard received his remarks with humour. 'It is not so easy to do the right thing as to know what is the right thing to do', he said; it is one thing to give a blind man a guide, and another to provide a vehicle for someone who is weary.[21] He himself is aware that he needs both to be taught and to be helped.[22] His critic persisted. 'What is the function of free choice?' he asked.[23] It is there, replied Bernard, in order to be saved. If free choice is taken away there is nothing to be saved; if grace is taken away, there is no means by which it can be saved. The work to be done requires both: one by which it is done, the other to which it is done.[24] Thus free choice is said to 'work together' (*cooperari*) with grace to bring about salvation, when it 'consents', that is, when it is saved, for to consent is to be saved. Bernard has been trying in this sequence of argument to make the bystander who had raised the difficulty define his terms and to see what they imply. Just as, in the *De Veritate* and the following treatises, Anselm demonstrates the relationships between 'truth' and 'rightness' and 'righteousness' (*veritas; rectitudo; iustitia*) by scrutinizing closely the meaning of each term, so Bernard subjects his terms to minute analysis.

He employs the dialectician's method of making a *divisio* or distinction between voluntary consent and natural appetite.

---

[18] *Csi*, I. vii. 8, LTR III. 403. 8. Bernard uses a variant of the Anselmian 'necessary reasons': *irrefragibiles rationes*. See *Theology*, p. 152 ff. for further discussion.

[19] LTR III. 165. 15–17.

[20] LTR III. 165. 17–19.

[21] LTR III. 166. 2–3.

[22] LTR III. 166. 5–6.

[23] LTR III. 166. 19.

[24] LTR III. 166. 21–2.

Here again there is an echo of Anselm in the characteristically Anselmian *aliud est . . . aliud est.*[25] Again he defines his terms. 'Voluntary consent' is a free habit of mind.[26] That shows us that it cannot be under any necessity, for if we were forced into consent against our will we could not speak of 'voluntary consent' (*Violentus est, non voluntarius*).[27] This voluntary aspect of *liberum arbitrium* is an essential element in its definition for Bernard.[28] He is anxious to make sure that this is quite clear, so he elaborates a little further.[29] He explains the difference between *sensus, naturalis appetitus, consensus,* and *voluntas.*[30]

Bernard has worked from what he believes to be first principles acceptable to every reader, by definition and analysis of the term *liberum arbitrium* and all that goes with it. Once or twice he draws a Scriptural parallel,[31] but for the most part he is concerned with reasoning, and with underlying philosophical problems such as that opposition between will and necessity which Anselm points to in the first pages of the *Cur Deus Homo.*[32] Bernard, then, although he was certainly not a natural logician of the order of Anselm, was in control of much the same basic technical skills.

To return to Bernard's mistake in his treatise on the *Steps of Humility and Pride*: he was distressed to find that he had tried to prove something true (*veram approbare*)[33] from a false beginning. He has allowed the whole sequence of disputation to follow from something which is not an exact quotation.[34] Although he had been able to provide a number of parallel examples, in which there was no mistake, he was anxious that the whole structure would be insecure: 'I put that which I later

---

25　LTR III. 167. 7. The formula often occurs in Augustine.
26　LTR III. 167. 12. 'Voluntarius consensus; habitus animi; liber.'
27　LTR III. 167. 16. 'Violentus est, non voluntarius.'
28　LTR III. 167. 16–19.
29　LTR III. 167. 21. 'Paulo altius aestimo repetendum.'
30　LTR III. 167. 25–168. 9.
31　LTR III. 168. 6. 'Unde est illud', (Luke 16: 8), for example.
32　*Anselmi Opera Omnia*, II. 49. 7–13.
33　LTR III. 15. 8–9.
34　Ibid. 'Totam ordiens sequentem disputationem, ex eo quod non veraciter posui.'

found not to be written in the Gospel in the middle, to confirm and strengthen an opinion', he confesses.[35]

Again we see Bernard's concern for scholarly exactness in the study of the Bible, admittedly a little late, but active enough once he realized his mistake. The danger of allowing inaccuracies to go uncorrected was great enough in the case of the plain reading of Holy Scripture, but it was perhaps even more considerable where a sequence of argumentation was to be based on it. His uneasiness about the *gigantes philosophi* of the day rested upon his suspicion that they were 'exulting to run' not the course God had laid down for them, but a course leading to vainglory,[36] that is, that they were allowing their skills in argument to run away with them until their thoughts became empty and foolish (*evanescentes in cogitationibus suis*).[37] Bernard had no love for 'philosophers' who tried to reason their way through mysteries. Nevertheless, he shows himself familiar with some of the most up-to-date techniques for resolving disputed questions arising out of the study of Holy Scripture.

A difficulty which had been apparent to the Fathers, and which Augustine had tried to solve in part in his *De Consensu Evangelistarum* and Bede in his *De Schematibus et Tropis*, was that of the apparent contradictions in Scripture. Peter the Chanter was to write a comprehensive handbook to enable his own students in Paris in the second half of the century to resolve contradictions of every kind. His *De Tropis Loquendi*[38] makes use of the latest work on fallacies, but it is also rooted in much older thinking on the subject.[39] Even if Bernard had wanted to employ highly technical aids, much of the material which was available to Peter the Chanter would not yet have been accessible to him. Nevertheless, he knows enough about

---

[35] LTR III. 15. 3–4.

[36] LTR VI^i. 235. 5–7.

[37] Ibid., and Cant. 2: 8; Rom. 1: 21.

[38] An edition of the preface to Peter's *De Tropis Loquendi* is shortly to be published. The editor was the late F. Giusberti. I should like to thank his widow for permission to examine his notes.

[39] *Logica Modernorum*, ed. L. M. de Rijk (Assen, 1967), 2 vols, contains several texts on fallacies. On the Carolingian version of Peter's approach, see John Scotus Eriugena, *De Praedestinatione*, ed. G. Madec, CCCM, 50 (1978), Chapter ix.

the approach required to confront the same difficulties in a very similar spirit to Peter's own. In one of his *Sententiae*, for example, he looks at the apparent contradiction between St. Paul's words in Philippians 1: 23–4: 'I long to be . . . with Christ' and Christ's own words in Matthew 28: 20: 'I am with you until the end of the world.' Bernard explains that in one sense we are with Christ in this world, through contemplation, but in the next we are to be with him in a different way, in his actual presence. Therefore both texts speak the truth.[40]

Bernard employs one of Peter the Chanter's more technical devices in the last of his homilies *In Laudibus Virginis Mariae*. When Jesus said 'my kingdom is not of this world' he appeared to be contradicting the statement of Luke 1: 32 that 'the Lord will give him the throne of his Father David', which is Jerusalem. Clearly the Jerusalem referred to is not the Jerusalem of this world, for Jesus never ruled in Jerusalem. 'You often find in Scripture', says Bernard, 'that the thing signifying is given instead of the thing signified': *significans ponitur pro significato.*[41] The technical application is not as precise or as clear as in Peter the Chanter's time, for in Bernard's day the theory of signification was still at the beginning of its twelfth-century development,[42] but in using it at all, Bernard shows himself familiar with at least one branch of the work of the schools in *disputatio* at a detailed technical level.

It would be overstating the case to suggest that Bernard had an up-to-date knowledge of fallacies. He speaks of the 'fallacy of life' (*fallacia vitae*), but he chooses rather to play with the word than to discuss the technical difficulties of resolving fallacies. It is deceptive; so that it may deceive men in a variety of ways, it alters its face and its voice; now it says yes; now it says no, and it does not blush to contradict itself; it gives different accounts of itself to everyone.[43] This habit of turning technical terms into practical illustrations in his preaching is a

---

[40] *Sent.* III. 31, LTR VI¹¹. 84. 13–19.
[41] *In Laud. V. Mar.* 4. 1, LTR IV. 47. 6–8, cf. Zachary of Besançon *In Unum et Quatuor, PL* 186. 21B.
[42] De Rijk op.cit. and Introduction to *Petrus Abaelardus Dialectica* (Assen, 1956) discusses the technical developments in signification theory of the day.
[43] *Serm. Div.* I, LTR VI¹. 73. 3–7.

marked feature of Bernard's borrowing from the technicalities of contemporary *disputatio*. A little later in the same sermon on the *fallacia vitae* he introduces a geometrical pun on the words of the Psalm: *Erraverunt in solitudine, in inaquoso; viam civitatis habitaculi non invenerunt*. There can indeed be no 'wandering' *in via*, says Bernard, for the road has no width. We may correctly speak of the *rectitudo* of the road, its straightness in a linear way, but not of its *latitudo* or *planities*.[44] He avoids being drawn into a technical discussion of the divine names in a sermon on the *varia nomina Christi*. 'He is called wonderful, counsellor, mighty God, Father of the world to come, Prince of Peace', says Bernard. All these can be appropriately attributed to him (*congrue assignari*) because of his work for our salvation.[45]

In another sermon he touches on one of the classic problems of the day: how two disparate things may be joined together. 'What participation, what union (*conventio*), has that which does not exist with that which exists? How can such *diversa* be conjoined (*coniungi*)?' Again, he avoids the discussion of disputatious technical principles, and simply explains that 'we cannot be joined to God immediately, but perhaps that conjunction could be brought about through some being who would act as a *medium*'.[46]

He makes use of a device found in Hugh of St. Victor and in other writers on the divisions of philosphy. The three branches of human knowledge, intellectual, practical, and ethical (*theorica, mechanica, moralis*) are said to be a threefold remedy provided by divine wisdom against *ignorantia, indigentia* or physical needs, and *vitia* (for by *moralis scientia* we learn to acquire virtues).[47] Bernard says in one of his sermons that the Son of God came to perform these functions for us, 'to help us and instruct us', which he is able to do, for he is the Power and Wisdom of the Father. Power aids, Wisdom

---

[44] *Serm. Div.* I, Ps. 106: 4, LTR VI¹. 74. 20–4.

[45] *Serm. Div.* 53, LTR VI¹. 277. 11–2, Isa. 9: 6.

[46] *Serm. Div.* 4, LTR VI¹. 95. 167. 'Immediate ei iungi non possumus, sed per medium aliquod poterit fieri fortassis ista conjunctio.'

[47] L. M. de Rijk, *Logica Modernorum* (Assen, 1967), II^ii. 459. 3–7, *Dialectica Monacensis*.

instructs and informs. The weak need help and blindness needs instruction and learning.[48]

These indications that Bernard was well-informed about some of the leading technical developments of the day—in so far as they were directly helpful to the student of Holy Scripture—show him to have been no enemy of the work of the schools. His only proviso was that the technical principles he made use of should be adopted only where they were needed. In the letter he wrote to the Curia before the trial of Peter Abelard, he speaks with scorching indignation against those who 'rashly' try to solve questions which are too high for them,[49] who are affronted by the Fathers, who are quibblers in trivia (*disputantes in triviis*).[50] Disputation for its own sake is to be discouraged, but sometimes questions arising out of Scripture need to be resolved for the sake of the simple.

Bernard is, then, a preacher with an impressive learning underlying his exposition of the Bible, not in the forefront of the work of the schools, but up-to-date nevertheless. He felt it necessary to defend his attempt to provide an exposition for his listeners: 'I have expounded the Gospel reading as far as I could', he says. 'I am not unaware that it will not please everyone, . . . and that I shall be judged either to have done something superfluous, or to be presumptuous.'[51]

He defends himself against the charge that he has 'dared' (*ausus fuerim*) to put his hand to a task which the Fathers have already fully accomplished. 'If something is said after the Fathers, which is not against the Fathers, I do not think it ought to displease the Fathers, or anyone.' If his words achieve their intended effect of rousing his listeners to devotion (*ut non esit fructus devotionis*), they are not wasted.[52] That is his purpose as a preacher, and it is different from that of the lecturer. His justification lies in the fact that he has not added to the expositions already available; he has merely taken the words of the Gospel as a starting-point for his sermon.[53]

---

[48]   *Serm. Div.* 54, LTR VI^1. 279. 3–5.
[49]   Letter 188, LTR VIII. 11. 2–4.
[50]   Ibid., p. 12. 2.
[51]   *In Laud. V.Mar.* 4. 1, LTR IV. 46. 18–19.
[52]   *In Laud. V.Mar.* 4. 11, LTR IV. 58. 5–9.
[53]   LTR IV. 58. 10–11.

Here, in a word, is the difference between *lectio-and-disputatio*; and *praedicatio*. The systematic reading of the text with a commentary is not Bernard's way; even in the series of sermons on the Song of Songs where he works his way through the text word by word, each word or phrase provides him with a point of departure for reflections more appropriate to the pulpit than the schoolroom. The listener is not only to understand the text better as a result, but to be moved by its teaching and by its beauty. Bernard speaks of the way in which he has taken 'the words of the saints' as adornments with which to make his preaching more beautiful to the reader or listener.[54] In the light of this higher purpose it is easy to understand why the close analysis and scholarship which underlies Bernard's preaching is kept so much in the background, but unless we look for it we shall miss much of what is most solid in Bernard's apparently airy creations, and which made them such excellent meat for his listeners.

III. PRAEDICATIO

The twelfth century was a time of revival of preaching, both in monasteries and abroad in the world. For centuries it had been the custom to read the homilies of the Fathers to the community rather than to attempt anything new. Anselm of Bec and Canterbury made free use of the permission allowed to the abbot in Chapter 28 of Benedict's Rule to address his community on occasion and Bernard did likewise. This was novel, but not something beyond what had been envisaged by Benedict and allowed for in the Rule. Moreover, there was some protection in this arrangement, for an abbot was likely to be a responsible person.

The preachers who began to arise among the rebel religious and the would-be leaders of new sects were another matter; unlicensed and without any guarantee of their learning or soundness of doctrine, they went about winning popular support for their ideas. The licence to preach which a bishop could give was a coveted acquisition because it gave the preacher a stamp of respectability and brought him and the converts he won securely within the bounds of the Church.

[54] *In Laud. V.Mar.*. 3. 1, LTR IV, 35. 22–3.

Thus it was that Norbert of Xanten came to be the founder of a great Order while the followers of his contemporaries, Henry the Monk, and Peter of Bruys[1] were regarded by responsible Churchmen as a rabble of heretics.

New preaching was not necessarily unsound preaching, but it was often the case that half-educated zealots presented unbalanced teaching, in which one leading idea predominated, and that an idea whose implications were unacceptable to the Church. Peter of Bruys, for example, saw no need for the Church's sacraments, and consequently no need for the priesthood and the whole apparatus of the established Church. He taught his followers to make their own confession and to approach God for themselves. These anti-Establishment views won ready support from simple men, and in various forms they were to spread widely in the course of the following century.

The rise of popular heresy created a fresh need for the preaching of orthodox doctrine and for an active campaign to win men back to the orthodox Church. The business of persuading the heretics that they were in error proved to be far from straightforward, and on the whole the Church's preachers seem to have fought a losing battle here for some decades. In time, Bernard, too, became involved in the struggle against heresy. When he heard of the outbreak of heresy at Cologne in 1143–4, he preached an impassioned sermon against the views of these 'hypocrites'.[2] But on the whole he seems to have devoted remarkably little of his power as a preacher to the problem, to judge from the surviving corpus of his sermons.

The twelfth century also saw the beginnings of an academic type of sermon, which, by about 1230, became the formal university-style sermon. Bernard's most notable contribution here was his sermon to the masters and students of Paris in 1140, at the time of Peter Abelard's trial, which won several

---

[1] See D. Lambert, *Mediaeval Heresy* (London, 1977), p. 51 and R. I. Moore, *Origins of European Dissent* (London, 1977), Chapter IV. On Peter of Bruys, see J. V. Fearns, 'The *Contra Petrobrusianos* of Peter the Venerable', Ph.D. thesis, University of Liverpool, 1963, and *Archiv für Kulturgeschichte*, xlviii (1966), 311–35. The *Contra Petrobrusianos* is edited by Fearns in CCCM, 10 (Turnhout, 1968).

[2] *SS* 66, LTR II. 178–88. On the episode at Cologne, see p. 138.

converts, among them his future secretary Geoffrey of Auxerre.[3]

Bernard's efforts as a preacher were always directed primarily towards the winning and above all the sustaining of souls. The form of sermon to which he gave most thought and care in composition was that which he delivered within the community, to his own monks or the monks of other houses and which was intended to be a vehicle of teaching. If the fragments and echoes of Bernard's talk show us something of his power of winning souls, the complete sermons which survive demonstrate something more: the capacity for sustained and closely-argued pleading.

Bernard wanted his listeners to be able to apply his teaching in practical and contemplative ways. He preached upon Biblical texts not, as a rule, in the way that a modern preacher may do, taking the text as a theme which he goes on to develop freely, but as an exercise in practical Bible-study.[4]

In one of his sermons St. Bernard describes the *multiplex efficacia* of the Word of God. It brings life, he says. It melts, warms, illuminates, cleanses; it is both food and sword; it is also medicine and strength and peace; it is resurrection and consummation.[5] When we read it in search of the divine wisdom, it alters our very thinking. We can judge how far by the double test to which James refers in his Epistle: every thought which is both pure and peaceable, *pudica* and *pacifica* is inspired by God. Both characteristics will always come together in that 'wisdom which comes from God'.[6] Bernard valued the importance of Holy Scripture in forming the minds of Christians highly; its 'manifold effectiveness' seemed to him to cover all the needs of the human soul in its acquisition of true wisdom.

Bernard approaches the study of the Bible through preaching with certain assumptions. He believes that everything in Scripture is there for a reason, even if it is not immediately apparent. The preacher's task is to make it apparent. In the first

---

[3] *De Conversione*, LTR IV. 61–116.
[4] See B. Smalley, *The Study of the Bible in the Middle Ages* (Oxford, 1952), p. 27, on preaching as a method of exegesis in patristic times.
[5] Serm. Div. 24, LTR VI[i]. 183. 17–184. 1.
[6] Ibid., p. 184. 13–15.

of his four homilies *In Laudibus Virginis Matris* he asks what the Evangelist intended when he gave so many proper names in the text: 'The angel Gabriel was sent from God to a city of Galilee, whose name was Nazareth, to a Virgin espoused to a man whose name was Joseph; and the Virgin's name was Mary.' Bernard insists that we must not listen carelessly (*negligenter*) to what the writer of the Gospel strove with such care (*diligenter*) to narrate. He names the messenger who is sent, the Virgin to whom he was sent, the Virgin's Bridegroom, the race, the city, the region of both. None of this can be said lightly (*supervacue*). The Holy Spirit pays infinite attention to detail in inspiring the sacred text, and so the Christian reader must scrutinize the Scriptures (*scrutare Scripturas*) with due care.[7]

Bernard believes with Ambrose that it is only when we struggle to understand that God will illuminate the text for us. When we reflect on something in the Scriptures, and cannot find the explanation of it: while we hesitate, while we search, suddenly it seems to arise upon us as if above the mountains. Then, appearing like the sun above the hills, that which seemed difficult to find floods upon us; our minds are filled with light; the Word who seemed to be absent is present in our hearts.[8] This description of Ambrose's occurs in his commentaries on the *Song of Songs* where Bernard is likely to have found it and recognized it with delight. It expresses exactly the way in which he himself thought Scripture should be read, and the experience he believed that he himself had had of God's help over his difficulties.

Bernard preached a sermon on the Fool of the Psalms, who said in his heart that there is no God—the Fool to whom Anselm addresses himself in his *Proslogion*. This Fool, as Bernard presents him, is the man who does not allow God to work upon his understanding in this way. 'God, although he is one, has different "tastes" for us, because of our own differences of mind. To the fearful he tastes of justice and power. To the loving he tastes of goodness and mercy.' This is

---

[7] Homily I.i, Luke 1: 26–7.
[8] *Commentarius in Cantica Canticorum e Scriptis S. Ambrosii Collectus.* PL 15. 1851–1962, col. 1880, paragraph 35.

like the text of the Psalm 'God spoke once; I heard two'. The 'two' things heard of God are his power and his mercy. The Fool is he to whom God tastes neither of fear nor of love. He therefore thinks that God does not exist because his sense of taste cannot perceive either of the 'flavours' God has for men.[9] The Fool is incapable of responding to the preaching of the Word, which, if he makes an effort on his own account, will help the believer to receive the divine illumination.

Perhaps the best example of Bernard's exegetical preaching in miniature is the series of seventeen sermons he preached for Lent in 1139 on the Psalm *Qui Habitat*.[10] These sermons constitute the longest extended sequence of exegesis in Bernard's works apart from the eighty-six sermons on the Song of Songs. Bernard does not claim that his commentary is comprehensive; he has taken 'some things' from the Psalm he has chosen, and he proposes to discuss and explain (*disserere et explanare*);[11] his term for the exercise is *tractare*.[12]

He prefaced the first sermon with an introduction, in which he explains that he is undertaking this exposition because his brothers have asked for it, but his chief reason is to bring them consolation: *sit vobis in verbo Domini consolatio*. This is to be more than an exegetical exercise. It is to change men's hearts. Bernard says that he has chosen the Psalm expressly because it is concerned with the battle with temptation which is fought especially hard in Lent.[13]

The first verse of the Psalm speaks of the man who dwells *in adiutorio Altissimi*, in the help of the Most High. Who are these 'dwellers', Bernard asks, and what does it mean to be 'in the help' of God? He proceeds, as he does in the *De Gradibus Humilitatis*, by opposites. There, he explains the degrees of pride; here, he tells us who does *not* dwell *in adiutorio Altissimi*. It is a most effective way of clearing the listener's mind so that he can see before him exactly what he ought to see, without clutter. There are three sorts of these non-

---

[9] LTR VI^i. 311. 9–312. 4. Ps. 13: 1.

[10] LTR IV. 119 discusses this series of sermons, which was written in 1139.

[11] LTR IV. 384. 25–6.

[12] LTR IV. 384. 16, cf. Hugh of St. Victor, *De Assumptione Beatae Mariae*, PL 177. 1209 on his method of *expositio*.

[13] LTR IV. 384. 16–17.

dwellers: those who do not hope; those who despair; those who hope in vain.[14]

The first is the man who does not make God his helper but trusts in his own power and the multitude of his riches.[15] No doubt watching the faces before him conscious of their own virtue in this respect, Bernard turns upon his listeners. 'I fear, brothers, that perhaps there may be among you some one who does not dwell in the help of the Most High, but trusts in his own power and the multitude of his riches.' Such a man would be full of fervour, assiduous in keeping vigils, in fasting, in labour, and so on.[16] But these are precisely the things he has come to think of as his riches, acquired over a long period. Trusting in them, he is likely to fail in the fear of God.[17] If he truly dwelt *in adiutorio Dei* he would realize his need of God and be fearful of offending him.[18] The more of such 'riches' one has, Bernard argues, the more one should be fearful and anxious[19] for without God's help we cannot keep and hold what we have from him.[20]

The second category of those who do not dwell *in adiutorio altissimi* is that of those who despair. They go too far the other way and, reflecting on their own *imbecillitas*, they flag in their efforts out of feebleness of spirit.[21] Those who hope in vain reassure themselves that God will not take their sins seriously.[22]

Bernard now gives a series of threefold comparisons to drive his point home: 'The first "dwells" in his merits, the second in his punishments, the third in his vices'; 'the habitation of the third is unclean, of the second anxious, of the first foolish and dangerous'.[23]

The sermon ends with the man who does indeed dwell 'in the help of the Most High'; he realizes that he needs not only

[14] LTR IV. 385. 1–2.
[15] LTR IV. 385. 7–8.
[16] LTR IV. 385. 13–14.
[17] LTR IV. 385. 15–19.
[18] LTR IV. 385. 20–386. 1.
[19] LTR IV. 386. 1–3.
[20] LTR IV. 386. 3–4.
[21] LTR IV. 386. 14–15.
[22] LTR IV. 386. 19–25.
[23] LTR IV. 387. 3–5.

divine help in order to do good, but also divine protection which will release him from evil.[24]

In the sermons which follow, Bernard systematically whets the listeners' appetite for more by promising at the end of each sermon that he will tell them something further in his next. In his second sermon he looks at the words: *Susceptor meus es tu et refugium meum*. What does *susceptor* mean? When a just man stumbles and falls God's hand catches him; the unjust man does not have God's help in rising when he falls.[25] We must be aware that God's attention is always upon us. How then can we become negligent?[26] Bernard asks, if we are conscious that God is watching us. The very tense of the verb tells us so: *sperabo in eum*, it says, 'I will hope in him', not 'I have hoped', or 'I hope'. This is a reference to the intention and purpose, the very vow we take, to hope in God (*votum, propositum, intentio cordis*).[27] Sermon III is concerned with the 'hunter's snare' of verse three of the Psalm. Bernard explores the hunters and the snare, drawing out of each all that he can by way of illustration and food for thought. The pattern goes on throughout the series: a word or phrase is brought forward for scrutiny. There is a minimum of gloss in the usual sense of the day; even where a grammatical point, for example, is made, it has a place in a close-knit argument, as we saw in the case of the discussion of the tense of *sperabo*.

In evoking their failure and the consolation which awaits those who dwell in God's protection as they should, Bernard attends meticulously to the details of the text. He notes that 'in Holy Scripture adversity is commonly designated by night',[28] in an attempt to place what he is saying in a familiar context. It is, he says in another sermon in the series, ordinary and common (*usitatus sermo, communis sermo*) to say 'For God's sake', but where it is not said vainly (*vacue*) it is a most profound saying. 'It often sounds in men's mouths, even those from whose hearts it is proved to be far away', but when it is said with its true meaning, then it is a 'lively and effective

---

24 LTR IV. 388.
25 LTR IV. 390. 14–15.
26 LTR IV. 391. 10–11.
27 LTR IV. 391. 17–18.
28 LTR IV. 404. 5, Serm. 6. 1.

saying': *vivus plane et efficax sermo.*[29] A little later Bernard coaxes his listeners to listen to a further exposition of a verse he has already expounded. 'What has been said would seem to be sufficient for the exposition of this verse, if the prophet had said "For I have hoped in thee", as is found in certain other Psalms,' but he adds more: 'Lord, you are my hope', and so we must examine his reasons for adding these words, and so he goes on discovering to his listeners more and more of interest and importance in the text.[30]

One of Bernard's gifts as a preacher was his ability to vary his approach to suit the needs of the audience before him. The two surviving versions of his prefatory remarks to the first sermon on the *Psalm Qui Habitat* show how he could work a passage up so that it would do its job more effectively:

A (LTR IV. 383 text)

Considero laborem vestrum, fratres, non sine multo miserationis affectu. Quaero consolationem quam exhibere possim, et corporalis occurrit; sed ea non prodest quidquam, magis et obesse plurimum potest. Siquidem modica sementis detractio, non modicum messis est detrimentum, et si paenitentia vestra minuatur miseratione crudeli, paulatim gemmis corona vestra privatur. Quid tamen agimus? Ubi Prophetae farinula? Siquidem 'mors in olla' est, et mortificamini tota die in ieiuniis multis, in laboribus frequenter, in vigiliis supra modum, praeter ea quae intrinsecus sunt: contritio cordium et multitudo tentationum. Mortificamini, sed propter eum qui mortuus est pro vobis. Quod si abundat tribulatio vestra pro eo, abundabit consolatio vestra per eum, ut in eo delectetur anima, quae in aliis renuit consolari.

B (LTR IV. 383 apparatus)

Scio, fratres, scio, in quanta afflictione sitis, quomodo mortificemini tota die in ieiuniis multis, in laboribus frequenter, in vigiliis supra modum, in fame et siti, in frigore et nuditate; praeter ea qua extrinsecus sunt, contritio cordium et multitudo tentationis; quantum ergo compatiar, et si quid solatii possem impendere, quam libenter id facerem novit ille quem nihil latet. Verum si de poenarum diminutione solatium praebere voluero, crudelis ero et non misericora. Quantum enim sub traham de poena, tantum de corona furabor. Tantum minus erit de fructu quantum de semente subtraxero. Renuat igitur consolari anima vestra consolatione huiusmodi, sed memor sit Dei et consoletur in eo.[31]

[29] LTR IV. 436. 16–24, Serm. 9. 2.
[30] LTR IV. 441.
[31] LTR IV. 119–20, contains a discussion of the second version in the manuscripts.

In both versions, Bernard begins by addressing himself directly to the struggles of his monks:

Considero laborem vestrum, fratres . . .

Scio, fratres, scio in quanta afflictione sitis . . .

From here he pursues his argument by different routes in the two versions. In A he says that he is seeking a way of consoling them. His urge is to help them, to spare them bodily suffering. But he runs at once into a paradox as his heart goes out to them. To help them in that way would be not to help but to hinder. Bernard explains himself in an image in which patterns of alliteration, assonance, repeated syllables do a good deal to make the point:

Siquidem modica sementis detractio,

non modicum messis est detrimentum,

modica matches *modicum; detr-actio* matches *detr-imentum; se-ment-is* matches *detri-ment-um*, and the alliterative repetition of m, s, d, draws all together.

A similar subtle patterning occurs in what follows:

si paenitentia vestra minuatur miseratione crudeli,

paulatim gemmis corona vestra privatur.

The initial *p* of *paenitentia* is picked up by *paulatim* and *privatur*. *Minuatur* strengthens *miseratione; crudeli* contrasts with *corona*.

What, then, are we to do?, asks Bernard. 'Where is the "meal" of the Prophet which, when it is thrown into the pot renders it no longer poisonous but harmless?' These abrupt questions are answered with: 'We die all the day long, in many fastings, in frequent labours, in endless vigils' (II Cor. 11: 27–8), apart from those inward deaths of contrition of heart and a multitude of temptations. 'We die, but for the sake of him who died for us.' Here is the 'meal':

Quod si abundat tribulatio vestra pro eo,

abundabit consolatio vestra per eum,

ut in eo delectetus anima, quae in aliis renuit consolari

The parallelism of *abundat/abundabit; tribulatio/consolatio; pro eo/per eum* again makes the contrast.

B is probably a version tried out and finally rejected. In it, Bernard brings in the citation of 2 Corinthians 11: 27–8 at the beginning and follows it at once with the 'inward' deaths of contrition and the multitude of temptations. Bernard has not, in this version, made the most of the notion of 'death'. His own declaration of his willingness to help ('How much I suffer with you and how freely I would comfort you if I could, He knows from whom nothing is hidden') is surely weaker for being in its now secondary position. And when Bernard moves on to his paradox, that it would be cruelty not mercy to relieve his brothers of their trials, the point is made neatly, but without the elegance of version A:

> Quantum enim subtraham de poena
> tantum de corona furabot.
> Tantum minus erit de fructu
> quantum de semente subtraxero.

'Let your soul refuse to be consoled in this way, then, but let it be mindful of God and consoled in him'. The status of B—whether it was in fact a discarded draft, or a version Bernard actually used when he preached and thought better of later, or even a reworking by one of his secretaries—remains obscure. But if it was indeed an early draft it has much to tell us of the way in which Bernard could look over an argument, see how to reconstruct it and reorder it to better effect, and then enhance that effect by his devices of style.

But to speak of stylistic 'devices' is perhaps to misrepresent B, and seriously. Deliberate though his patterns of antithesis and parallelism, climax and paradox, undoubtedly are, and careful though he was to reinforce these figures of thought with appropriate figures of diction, this method of writing undoubtedly came very easily and readily to him: in his reading he would have found plentiful models. He simply gave the stylistic method his own imprint.

No one who had heard Bernard expound the text of the Bible could read it afterwards without perceiving new depths in it. That is what Bernard intended—to form habits of perceptive and reflective reading in his monks which they could use in their own private *lectio divina*.

In all the display of brilliant imagery, the subtlety of distinction, the clarity of explanation Bernard is able to marshal when he preaches on a Biblical text, he has then, a single purpose in mind. He wants to concentrate the mind of his listener or reader so that he will understand the words of

Scripture as he has never understood them before. He wants him to grow sharper-minded, more profound in understanding.

4. *The Song of Songs*

I. CONVERSATIONS IN THE INFIRMARY

Bernard evidently made an impression upon his abbot during his year's novitiate. When, in 1113, the two daughter-houses of Cîteaux at Morimond and Clairvaux were founded, Stephen Harding chose Bernard as abbot for the latter. From this time onwards Bernard began to be confronted with the difficulties of reconciling monastic ideals and practical necessities. There was no doubt a practical reason for Stephen's choice which made such pressures a likely consequence. Clairvaux was to be in the territory of Josbert la Ferté, and Bernard was connected with his family. It was to be Bernard's responsibility to maintain goodwill.

Bernard and his party eventually chose a site about seventy miles from Cîteaux, near Bar-sur-Aube. It was felt to be wise to get confirmation of the donation from the Count of Champagne and an abbatial blessing from Joceran, bishop of Langres, as soon as possible and Bernard set out in person to obtain the latter. Joceran was away when Bernard arrived in Langres, and, anxious not to allow time to elapse before he could obtain the blessing, he went to the nearest bishop, William of Champeaux, newly consecrated bishop of Châlons-sur-Marne. Bernard came into William's presence accompanied by a monk called Ebald, an older man, of some physical presence. William of St. Thierry tells us that the bishop did not hesitate for a moment, but instantly recognized the slight young figure of Bernard to be that of the abbot.[1]

The community struggled at first to survive financially. It was to be over a decade before its economy was reasonably secure. Bernard's uncle Gaudrey, a good businessman, acted as cellarer or bursar. On one occasion he came to Bernard to tell him that the community had no money left, and that unless a

---

[1] *VP* I. vii. 31, *PL* 185. 245C; the Cistercian foundations were readily approved by bishops because, unlike Cluniac houses, they did not as a rule seek exemption from episcopal jurisdiction.

certain sum could be found, there was no possibility of carrying on. Bernard prayed, and we are told that almost at once a pious woman arrived with a gift of exactly the amount needed. In such hand-to-mouth ways, and by prayerful hopes fulfilled, the community carried on.

Perhaps as a result of his own experiences in the early days of his abbacy, Bernard was later to place an emphasis upon the abbot's responsibility to comfort and support his monks in times of difficulty. 'You must understand,' he wrote to the future abbot of Foigny, 'that you are especially the abbot of the sad, fainthearted, and discontented amongst your flock. You were given to them as abbot not to be comforted but to comfort, because you were the strongest of them all, and, by God's grace, able to comfort them all without needing to be comforted by any.'[2]

William of St. Thierry describes how under Bernard's influence the dry and barren abbey of the Cistercians began to 'drop sweetness'. 'What had been empty and barren of all good began to abound in spiritual fruit', he says. The effects of Bernard's influence were also visible and tangible. The Order grew. The mother house at Cîteaux bore daughters, and Clairvaux in her turn, like her twin sister Morimond, was prolific in her progeny.[3]

---

[2] Bernard wrote a series of letters to Raynald (72, 73, 74), to fortify him in his abbacy.

[3] *V.P* I. xiii. 61, *PL* 185. 260D–261A.

The foundations of both Cîteaux and Clairvaux multiplied steadily. The first daughter of Clairvaux was established at Trois-Fontaines. William of Champeaux, once Peter Abelard's master, then a canon of St. Victor in Paris, and now Bishop of Châlons-sur-Marne, invited Bernard to found a Cistercian house in his diocese. He got a grant of land for the purpose from Hugh, Count of Vitry, and over a period of two years from 1116 to 1118 Bernard was busy with preparations. He was a frequent visitor to Châlons at this time and he won a large number of converts, both clerical and lay, whom he brought to the new house under Roger the abbot.

After Trois-Fontaines in 1118 came Fontenay in 1119, Foigny in 1121. There was a severe winter in 1124–5, followed by a lean year, but a gift of Raynald, Archbishop of Rheims, made it possible for Igny to be founded in 1126. In 1128 came Reigny, in the diocese of Auxerre and in 1129 Ourscamp, in the diocese of Noyon. 1131 saw three foundations, and an extension of Cistercian influence to Geneva (Bonmont) and Mainz (Eberbach). In 1132 four new houses were founded, and although in 1133 Bernard was absent on his first visit to Rome, and no foundations were attempted, two more were made in 1134 and five in 1135.

During the planning and building of Clairvaux's daughter-house at Trois-Fontaines Bernard himself became ill.[4] By the time the house was launched, Bernard was exhausted. William of Champeaux, the Bishop of Châlons and patron of the enterprise came to see him, so as to judge for himself how ill Bernard was, and gave instructions for him to be removed to a little cell outside the abbey precincts. He remained in this *domuncula* for a year, apart from the brethren, living in his 'infirmary' like a hermit.[5]

William of St. Thierry describes how he himself was often at Clairvaux at that time, and used to visit Bernard in his wooden hut, which was like the hovels built for lepers at crossroads.[6] William had first met Bernard a year earlier, when he was himself still a Benedictine monk at Saint-Nicaise. (It was not until 1119 or 1120 that he became abbot of St. Thierry.) He was strongly drawn to Bernard, and when he saw him frail and ill, living what seemed to him a life of extraordinary sweetness in the squalor of his surroundings, he was filled with a longing to live with him and be his servant.[7]

William's friendship with Bernard had almost as profound an influence upon Bernard as it did upon William himself. He was a considerable scholar; we shall see how he stirred Bernard to action over Peter Abelard's controversial teaching, and furnished him with texts and commentary for the campaign. He had pastoral gifts complementary to those of Bernard in his emphasis upon prayer, where Bernard made his mark as a preacher. Above all, he helped to form Bernard's vision of the monastic ideal by his talk and by drawing out Bernard himself on the subject.

William describes an occasion when he and Bernard were both ill, and lying side by side in the infirmary. *Infirmi ergo ambo*, he says, 'Both sick, we talked all day long . . . of the medicine of the virtues against the languors of the vices. And so

---

[4] *VP* I. xiii. 64–5, *PL* 185. 262–3.

[5] *VP* I. vii. 32, *PL* 185. 246B.

[6] *VP* I. vii. 32–3, *PL* 185, 246C: 'In suo illo tugurio, quale leprosis in compitis publicis fieri solent.'

[7] *VP* I. vii. 33, *PL* 185, 246D: 'Tantoque desiderio in paupertate illa et simplicitate cohabitandi ei, ut si optio illa die mihi data fuisset, nil tam optassem quam ibi cum eo semper maere et serviendum ei.'

he expounded the Song of Songs to me . . . just its moral sense,
leaving out the allegorical sense.' William listened to him day
after day, and wrote down all that he could remember in case
anything should be lost.[8] The effect on William himself was
deep and lasting. He collected Gregory the Great's sayings on
the Song of Songs, and those of St. Ambrose[9]; he wrote an
exposition of his own.[10] He collected Bernard's thoughts on the
subject.[11] Bernard himself came to love the Song of Songs so
much, finding in it a key to the life of faith and to monastic life
in particular, that he preached eighty-six sermons upon it,[12]
and was still at work upon the last when he died.[13]

William of St. Thierry was a little older than Bernard, and in
certain respects he had a more powerful mind. He was
certainly more than a humble admirer, and on occasion when
he wrote to urge Bernard to take action over some offence or to
write about it, he told him decisively what he wanted him to
say. It is likely that it was he, by his questions and comments,
who helped Bernard to see the possibilities of the Song of

---

[8] *VP* I. xi. 59, *PL* 185. 258–9. What William wrote down may have formed
the basis of his *Brevis Commentatio ex Sancti Bernardi Sermonibus Contexta*,
PL 184. 407–36. See J. Hourlier, 'Guillaume de Saint-Thierry et la "Brevis
Commentatio in Cantica" ', *An.Cist.*, 12 (1956), 105–14. For commentaries on
the Song of Songs in general up to this time, see F. Ohly, *Hohelied-Studien.
Grundzüge einer Geschichte der Hoheliedauslegung des Abendlandes bis um
1200* (Wiesbaden, 1958) and R. Herde, 'Das Hohelied in der lateinischen
Literatur des Mittelalters bis zum 12 Jahrhundert', *Studi Medievali*, 3 series,
viiii, 2 (1967), pp. 957–1073. J. Leclercq's *Monks and Love in Twelfth Century
France* (Oxford, 1979) is a not altogether successful attempt to examine its
subject in the light of 'psycho-history'; but it contains much learning and good
sense on Bernard and the Song of Songs.

[9] *PL* 180. 441–74, and *PL* 15. 1947–2060.

[10] *Expositio altera super Cantica Canticorum*, *PL* 180. 473–526. See
Déchanet, op.cit., p. 35 and p. 46.

[11] *PL* 184. 407–36.

[12] LTR I. xv–lxviii. Three principal recensions can be distinguished in the
surviving manuscripts. The first, which is probably closest to the talks Bernard
gave to the monks of Clairvaux in the chapter house, is preserved in a group of
manuscripts chiefly from Bavaria, Austria, and other areas under the influence
of Clairvaux's sister-house at Morimond. The second is chiefly confined to
English manuscripts, which derive perhaps from an interim version which was
sent across the Channel before Bernard had finished polishing the collection.
The last, which we may take to be Bernard's final version, survives in a group
of Clairvaux manuscripts; Bernard seems to have taken more trouble over
these sermons as a group than over anything else he wrote.

[13] Gilbert of Holland continues the series, *PL* 184. 9–252.

Songs. Although the two friends rarely met, the complementary qualities of their minds, William's forceful, logical, Bernard's excitable and responsive, meant that William did a great deal to encourage the development of Bernard's thinking and to give it an edge of hard argument and a purposefulness.

II. EARLIER COMMENTARIES

The Song of Songs had had an attraction for several commentators in the generation or so before Bernard. Robert of Tombelaine in the late eleventh century secretly found the older commentaries unsatisfactory; he mentions that of Bede in particular. This acquaintance of Anselm of Bec was an enterprising thinker in a small way; he worked privately on a commentary of his own.[1] One day some friends came upon him working at it alone in his cell. They took up what he had written and read it, and they were full of praise and encouragement, but they pointed out that he had not included *canonicorum exempla*, quotations from the authorities, by which what he said might be proved.[2] Robert defended himself in the covering letter he wrote to abbot Ansfrid with the finished commentary. He is aware that he himself is not a wise man, a man possessing the qualities of a Solomon (*qui de Salomone nihil habeo*).[3] He knows that Bede and others have expounded the *Cantica* and made its mysteries plain (*secreta patefecit*), but he has felt justified in attempting a fresh exposition, a brief one, in which he has said things which are not to be proved, but which he hopes will work inwardly upon the soul (*non probanda sed interius inserta*). It is this inwardness of the Song which has attracted him. According to the patristic commonplace, of the three books Solomon wrote, Proverbs is for children in the faith, and deals with good behaviour (ethics); Ecclesiastes is for adults, and deals with the created world (physics); the Song of Songs is for those perfected

---

[1] Anselm's letter to Robert of Tombelaine (Letter 3) mentions the scholar Anastasius, for whom Robert wrote the Commentary. *Anselmi Opera Omnia*, III. 102–3.

[2] *PL* 150. 1363. Robert's Commentary is in *PL* 150. 1361–70, and *PL* 70. 471 ff., under Gregory the Great.

[3] *PL* 150. 1363.

in the faith and it is concerned with speculative and intellectual truths, the *theoria* of true theology.[4]

The commentaries upon which Robert was thus turning his back were those of Origen (the most read of the early commentaries on the Song of Songs in the Middle Ages in Rufinus' Latin version, and perhaps the most often-studied of Origen's works),[5] Bede and Gregory.[6] In Carolingian times lengthy compilations were made of extracts from the Fathers by Alcuin, Angelôme of Luxeuil, Pseudo-Haimo, and others.[7] Robert of Tombelaine was sensible in seeing a need for something briefer. Among his fellow-Benedictines, Bruno of Segni[8] and Rupert of Deutz[9] also composed reinterpretations of the Song of Songs according to the principles to be found in the Fathers and the Carolingians.

Although, as we shall see, Bernard had a place for the interpretation of the Song of Songs which makes the Church the Bride, he preferred to see the Song of Songs as a dialogue between God and the human soul, a spiritual interpretation which owes a great deal to Origen, but more perhaps to Bernard's own reflections upon the inward workings of his own conversion. Bernard's vision communicated itself to his admirers and imitators.[10] Geoffrey of Auxerre wrote an *Expositio in Cantica Canticorum*, a sprawling construction, put together over many years and containing unrelated portions dedicated to various people who had asked him to write it.[11] It includes a preliminary book of notes and glosses, followed by a sequence of full commentary. He explains that he has begun briefly so as

---

[4] *PL* 150. 1364.

[5] On Origen in the twelfth century, see pp. 82–5.

[6] The authorities agree by the end of the patristic period in the West that the Song of Songs is a dialogue between two persons or groups of persons. See Justus of Urgel (*PL* 67. 963), Cassiodorus (*PL* 70. 1055), 'Isidore' (*PL* 83. 1119), Gregory the Great (*PL* 79. 471–548; on the authenticity of this, see B. Capelle, 'Les homélies de Saint Grégoire sur le Cantique', *R. Ben.*, 41 (1929), 204–217), Bede (*PL* 91. 1079).

[7] In Carolingian times lengthy commentaries were produced by Alcuin (*PL* 100. 639), Angelôme of Luxeuil (*PL* 115. 562); Pseudo-Haimo in *PL* 117. 296.

[8] *PL* 164. 1234–88.

[9] *PL* 168. 839–962C.

[10] For Gilbert of Stanford's commentary, see J. Leclercq, 'Le commentaire de Gilbert de Stanford sur le Cantique des cantiques', *Studia Anselmiana*, 20 (1948), 205–30.

[11] Ed. F. Gastaldelli, *Temi e Testi* (Rome, 1974), 2 vols.

to play, as it were, the melody of the Song in outline. When he reaches the place where Bernard left off in his own exposition, he intends to continue in more detail. (Origen he rates the *victor* among earlier commentators; Bernard is the best of the interpreters of recent generations.)[12] Geoffrey includes sermons and treatises in his commentary as he goes along, with the barest of apologies for the mixture of style and genre which results. 'It is my belief that the variety of the Song will excuse the variety of the exposition', he says comfortably.[13]

III. BERNARD'S SERMONS

Bernard began his sermons about 1135. In 1136, Bernard Desportes, a Carthusian monk, wrote to ask him to expound the Song of Songs for him. Bernard replied that he was under too much pressure of business to attempt a full commentary. In any case, he pleads, he is unworthy. He will, like the proverbial mountain, bring forth nothing but a 'ridiculous mouse' if he attempts it.[1] However, he sent Bernard Desportes copies of the sermons he had recently been giving on the Song of Songs, as they stood, not yet polished for publication. It is possible that the Carthusian's encouragement helped him form the plan of continuing with his series and turning his sermons into a commentary. He was evidently enthusiastic in his reception of the first few, for by the end of 1136 when the abbot of Clairvaux left for Italy, he had the first twenty-four completed, and he took up the series again when he returned in 1138, and again at intervals until his death.[2] The sermons on the Song of Songs became a vehicle for all sorts of aspects of Bernard's teaching and exegesis, his comments on current events; but above all, they were a journal of his own spiritual pilgrimage.

In his first sermon Bernard tries to show his listeners why the Song of Songs is unique, even among the works of Solomon. Can we not be content with Ecclesiastes and Proverbs, he asks? 'Is not your life and your behaviour

---

[12]   Gastaldelli, Book II, Vol. I. 99. 3–5.

[13]   Gastaldelli, Book V, Preface, Vol. II. 361. 9–10.

[1]   Letters 153 and 154, especially LTR VII. 359. 21–2. For the 'ridiculus mus', see Horace, *Ars Poetica*, 139.

[2]   *Recueil* I, 1–25 and 27–46.

sufficiently influenced and improved by the teaching which is found in these?' he enquires (1, 2). The Song of Songs has something more; it is not only a holy, but a *theoricus sermo*. It is more than practical; it is speculative; it looks upwards in contemplation of God. Bernard sees this as an extra dimension, complementing and completing the *activa* of the other works of Solomon. The Song of Songs has exactly that duality, that lively tension between this world and the next, which he found so stimulating in everything he did.

This liveness and immediacy strikes him so forcibly that it is the first thing he brings to the attention of his listeners. The Song begins: *Osculetur me osculo oris sui*; suddenly, in the middle of a conversation. We are not told who the speaker is. Our curiosity is aroused. Bernard pursues the point. Why, he asks, does the text read: *ore* and indeed: *ore suo*, as if a kiss could be given by anything else but a mouth, or by the mouth of anyone but he who gives the kiss? Even the grammatical form is odd; we read, not: *osculetur me ore suo*, which would be normal usage, but something else, most unusual (*profecto inusitatius*): that is, *osculo . . . oris sui*.[3] Everything about our first encounter with the Song of Songs awakens our interest. *Quam iucundum eloquium*; 'What a delightful way to begin!' exclaims Bernard.[4] The Song shows us a winning face to tempt us to read, and promises us the most delightful of rewards for the labour we must spend in reading. This opening which is not an opening, this *principium sine principio*, tells us who is our author. In this way, God calls us to read with a divine jest.

Bernard shows his listeners in this first sermon something of the range of the Song of Songs, its multiple senses, how it speaks of Christ and the Church, and at the same time of the longing of the holy soul (I. iv. 8), how it is a wedding-song (I. iv. 8) and also a battle-song (I. v. 9) to cheer the monk to victory in his battles with sin. More: it is a processional hymn, for monastic life is a series of steps, or stages, and each step is given here, in accordance with the stages by which each man walks forward in his heart. (I. v. 10). This song is not only a

---

[3] *Sermones in Cant.* I. iii. 5: 'ita subitaneum et factum repente de medio sermonis exordium.' LTR I. 5. 4–5.
[4] LTR I. 5. 12.

song about knowing God, but also a song about experiencing him. (I. vi. 11).[5] It is all things to all men, and yet exact and specific in its evocation of all these aspects of the Christian life.

William of St. Thierry, too, communicates the vitality of the Song of Songs which had so excited Bernard, and which we may suppose to have been one of the aspects which impressed them most vividly in their conversations in the infirmary. Like Origen, William sees the Song of Songs as a drama.[6] It has characters and events (*personae; actus*) and, just as in a comedy[7] the characters enact the events, so here we see the characters coming together for a wedding. There are four *personae*, the Bridegroom and his companions, and the Bride and the young girls who accompany her. The action of the play is mainly confined to the Bride and Groom; the other characters scarcely speak. The plot[8] is as follows: King Solomon takes the daughter of the King of Egypt as his bride; he shows her his riches and his glory; he kisses her, and makes her no longer black, but fit to be his bride. Then she is allowed to taste how sweet the Lord is; she is placed in the *domus conscientiae suae* so that she may learn (*erudienda*) and become chaste in the obedience of love (*castificanda in obedientia charitatis*) and at last she is perfectly cleansed of vices and adorned with all the virtues.[9] This story is re-enacted in William's *Golden Epistle*, not, this time, as a drama, but as a series of steps the reader may himself take, as though he were one of the characters in the play. The reader is brought within the drama and made to act it out for himself.

---

[5] LTR I. 6–8.

[6] *PL* 180. 476B–C. 'Scribitur autem Canticum hoc in modum dramatis et stylo comico.'

[7] The comedies of Terence in particular were commonly read in the monasteries of the day. On acting and live theatre, see J. Leclercq 'Joculator et saltator, Bernard et l'image du jongleur dans les manuscrits', *Translatio Studii in honorem O. L. Kapsner*, ed. J. G. Plante (Minnesota, 1973), pp. 124–48 and on Peter the Chanter's *Verbum Abbreviatum* on acting, J. W. Baldwin, *Masters, Princes and Merchants* (Princeton, 1970), II. 144, note 234. See, too, S. Gaselee, *The Transition from the Late Latin Lyric to the Mediaeval Love Poem* (Cambridge, 1931), p. 30 for: *Crebro da mihi*, a pastourelle on the Song of Songs, and J. Leclercq's discussion in *Pierre Abélard–Pierre le Vénérable*, ed. J. Jolivet and R. Louis (Paris, 1975), pp. 671–87.

[8] *Argumentum*, *PL* 180, 476D.

[9] *PL* 180. 477A.

IV. MANY MEANINGS

Much of this 'variety' of the Song of Songs arises from the richness of meaning which makes it possible for the Song to say all things to all men. 'There flow from it abundant springs of spiritual meanings', Gilbert of Stanford promises in his commentary.[1]

The habit of looking for several levels of meaning in every text of Scripture began in the first Christian centuries, with the work of the Alexandrians, the Jew Philo and the Christian apologists Clement and Origen, but it was Origen who laid the foundations of medieval exegesis,[2] with its fourfold distinction of the literal or historical sense, the moral sense, the allegorical sense and the tropological sense, which became familiar to every monk through the liturgy.

It is not easy now to enter into the spirit in which these interpretations were accepted by medieval readers. To draw out the moral or the allegorical teaching of a passage was not merely to use it as a starting-point for reflection, as a modern preacher might use it; the different senses were held to be, not read into the text, but present there by divine dictation, and waiting to be discovered by the attentive reader. They were put there by God out of a desire to make Scripture as helpful as possible to all spiritual conditions of men, so that there might be something for the new young Christian, and something for the experienced warrior in the faith, all in the same sentence.[3]

When he was abbot of Rievaulx, Ailred, the English Cistercian and master of spiritual friendship, preached one Palm Sunday in these terms:

Every day, spiritually speaking, the Lord approaches Jerusalem by Bethphage and Bethany and the Mount of Olives and sends two of his disciples into the village which is over against him, to loose the colt which is tied there upon which no man has ever sat. Jerusalem is the

---

[1] J. Leclercq, 'Gilbert of Stanford, Le commentaire de Gilbert de Stanford sur le cantique des cantiques', *Studia Anselmiana* 20 (1948), 205–30, especially p. 205. Cf. Alan of Lille. *PL* 210. 54: 'duo exemplaria bene vivendi: castitas et humilitas.'

[2] H. de Lubac, *Exégèse Médiévale*, 2 vols. (Paris, 1959), I. 586–99 and *passim*.

[3] Augustine discusses the ways in which figurative and literal are to be distinguished in the third book of his *De Doctrina Christiana*.

vision of peace; Bethany obedience, Mount Olivet mercy. The village is the sinful soul, fortified by a tower of pride and a wall of obstinacy. The two disciples are the fear and love of God, which lead out the colt, who has been bound with the chains of shame and paralysing fear. If we read Matthew instead of Mark, we find an ass tied, with her colt. These are humble simplicity and agile liberty, who have been thus confined within the soul, and are now led out to carry Christ into Jerusalem, as the soul which has Christ within is able to approach the vision of peace.[4]

Ailred has accounted for every element in the story and he is able to expand its implications by adding to this moral interpretation an account of the way in which the soul comes by a straight road to Jerusalem if it comes by purity of confession, humility of obedience, sublimity of mercy, and so on. In a not dissimilar spirit Bruno of Segni asks 'What do you see in the Sulamite, but the chorus which, ... according to custom, rejoices and sings and decorates the camp ... and exhorts the army to be virtuous and bold. In the Church indeed the praise of exultation and confession resounds ... '.[5] He, too, spares no detail in drawing parallels. The comparisons he makes are more than resemblances; they are real, if figurative, meanings of the text.

There was no reason to refrain from making figurative interpretations ever more elaborate; there could be no question of going beyond the bounds of the reasonable here. Anything the human mind could discover in Scripture by prayerful reflection could be only a small part of its potential complexity and richness. It is in this spirit that Bernard approaches the task of exposition when he preaches on the Song of Songs.

V. LOVE-SONG

William of St. Thierry says that in the infirmary where he and Bernard first discussed the Song of Songs, Bernard confined himself to the moral sense. This outward-looking and practical application fitted well with the interpretation of the dialogue of the Song as a conversation between Christ and the Church. The same emphasis is to be found elsewhere, in Bruno of

---

[4] Matthew 21: 1–2, Mark 2: 1–2. Ailred of Rievaulx, *Sermo De Ramis Palmarum*, PL 195. 264–71.
[5] Bruno of Segni, PL 164. 1276.

Signi,[1] in Rupert of Deutz[2] and, much later in the century, in Alan of Lille. Alan insists that the Song refers 'especially' to the Church,[3] but the 'moral' sense of the Song has a bearing too on the interpretation, which makes it also an account of the love between the individual soul and Christ, in which, as William of St. Thierry puts it, the Christian loves himself and his neighbour in Christ: 'This is a living and shining love, free and freeing from corruption, the sweeter as it is more pure.'[4] It is in accordance with this conception of love that monastic life exercises not only the monk's love for God, but also his love for his neighbour. The seventy-second chapter of the Rule of St. Benedict is concerned with the love monks ought to have for one another. It is to be the love of one's neighbour at its highest, a supreme brotherly love, in which each strives to obey the other in a loving contest and each thinks not of what is good for himself but of what is good for his brother. They are to love their abbot 'with a sincere and humble affection'.

Bernard draws a picture of the Song of Songs as a pattern for human love both in his *De Diligendo Deo*, written between 1126 and and 1141 for Aimeric, cardinal deacon of the Roman Church, with its letter at the end on charity,[5] and in his sermons on the Song of Songs. The *De Diligendo Deo* is much concerned with the way to the heights of the love of God; the sermons on the Song of Songs have, in addition, a good deal to say about the practical business of living the religious life in love, not only of God but also of one's neighbour.

Bernard himself points the contrast between the two works. He describes how he dealt with a text from the Song of Songs in one of his sermons. ('Stay me with raisin cakes, comfort me with apples: for I am sick of love. His left hand is under my head and his right hand embraces me.')[6] He now proposes to

---

[1] *PL* 164. 1234.

[2] *PL* 168. 839–962.

[3] *PL* 210. 53.

[4] William of St. Thierry, *Expositio altera super Cantica Canticorum, Praefatio Auctoris. PL* 180. 474C: 'Et hic est vivens et luminosus amor, liber et liberans a corruptione, quanto purior, tanto dulcior.'

[5] This appendix consists of a long section of Letter II, which Bernard wrote to Guigo I, and to the religious of La Grande Chartreuse shortly before 1125. See LTR III. 112.

[6] Cant. 2: 5–6.

give a different interpretation to it. In the *De Diligendo Deo*
Bernard shows how the soul is transfixed by the pain of love as
though by a sword when she beholds Christ crucified and cries
out that she is 'sick with love'.[7] In the Sermon on the Song of
Songs, he wanted to bring out a different point 'whether better
or worse, the reader shall decide if either of them pleases him'.[8]
Here, it seems that the Bride is speaking in the absence of the
Bridegroom, encouraging her handmaidens to make progress in
faith and in good works until he comes, knowing that she will
be both well-pleasing to her Husband and the saviour of her
handmaidens if she does so. The experience is of love for God
at its height in the first case; in the second it is a more ordinary
emotion, a steady sensible preparation for the joy of heaven to
come, undertaken in the company of others and involving
practical daily love for one's fellow-men.

The *De Diligendo Deo* shares with all the writings on love of
Bernard and William of St. Thierry, and much else that was
written on the subject in the twelfth century,[9] a sense of the
progressiveness of its development in the soul. Like the ladder
of humility, the ladder of love is a step-by-step progression to a
perfection to be realized only in the life to come. Love is a
mountain to be climbed.[10] It takes its beginnings from the
divine communication of good things to man, which God gives
for the sake of his own merit (*merito suo*), and for our benefit
(*commodo nostro*). Natural goods are easy to love; all rational
creatures love them. God himself, their author, deserves to be
loved for his own sake, and not to love him is inexcusable. The
artefact ought in any case to love its creator.[11] There is a *rectus
ordo* in this which Bernard—in Anselmian spirit—finds intellectually satisfying.[12]

Thus man begins by loving himself for his own sake. Then
he moves on to the point where he loves God, but for his own
sake, not for God's sake. Then he learns to love God not for

---

[7] *Dil.* III. 7, LTR III. 124. 23–5.

[8] *SS* 51. 4, LTR II. 86. 19. 20.

[9] For a basic list, see E. Gilson, *The Mystical Theology of St. Bernard*
(London, 1940), pp. 3–4.

[10] *Dil.* x. 27, LTR III. 142. 5; cf. *Dil.* xv. 39, LTR III. 152–3.

[11] *Dil.* ii. 6, LTR III. 123. 18–19; *Dil.* v. 15, LTR III. 131. 12.

[12] *Dil.* xv. 39, LTR III. 152. 19–20; cf. *Dil.* viii. 23, LTR. III. 138. 6, and
Anselm, *Cur Deus Homo*, I. 1 *Anselmi Opera Omnia* II. 48. 16–17.

himself alone, but also for God's sake. At last he reaches the point where he loves even himself only for the sake of God.[13] What has happened is that the *cupiditas* or desire which underlies all natural appetites has been sustained and directed and subordinated by *caritas*, until all its inferior tendencies are gone and desire has become pure love.[14]

VI. MYSTICISM

William of St. Thierry's treatise *On Contemplating God* opens with an invitation to re-enact the story of Abraham going up to the mountain to make his sacrifice. 'Strivings, thoughts, desires, affections, and all that is within me, come, let us go up to the mountain; . . . cares, worries, anxieties, work, labours, wait for me here with that ass the body, while I, with the lad, my faculties of reason and understanding, hurry up the mountain; and when we have worshipped, we shall return to you.'[1]

The height of spiritual experience to which Bernard would like to bring every faithful soul is a heaven Augustine would have recognized. It is a state in which the soul knows God with a supreme clarity of understanding, where to know and to be known become one; it is all intelligence and intelligibility.[2] At the same time it is the profoundest religious emotion, a powerful desire for God (if we may thus render *affectus*). It is a rest from labour, a sitting at the feet of Jesus in a perpetual sabbath of the people of God.[3]

These two elements, of heightened consciousness, and of rest from a laborious climb, are characteristic of a state which in the later Middle Ages we should call mysticism. There is, too, some trace in Bernard's account of such experiences of the loss of personal awareness in a vastness beyond, and of being

---

[13] *Dil.* viii. 23 – x. 27; cf. xv. 39–40, LTR III. 138–44.

[14] *Dil.* xiv. 38, LTR III. 152. 12–14. On aspects of Bernard's emotional life, see J. Leclercq, *Nouveau visage de Bernard de Clairvaux: approches psycho-historiques* (Paris, 1976).

[1] *PL* 184. 367A and Gen. 23: 1–19.

[2] See my *Augustine on Evil* (Cambridge, 1982), pp. 47–8, for a brief discussion,

[3] *Disputatio cuiusdam justi cum Deo*, printed among the Spuria of Bernard, *PL* 184. 1155. 'Requiescere a laboribus suis, et sabbatizare cum populo Dei, sedere ad pedes Jesu.' On Bernard's 'experience' of God, see U. Köpf, *Religiöse Erfahrung in der Theologie Bernards von Clairvaux* (Tübingen, 1980).

swept up uncontrollably into the mystical experience, as the later medieval mystics describe.[4] But these are not the dominant themes. Bernard's mysticism undoubtedly reaches the heights, but on the whole it does so by a clearly marked road. It is something which can be worked at and learned. Bernard drew not only upon Benedict's Rule but upon his reading of the Fathers in forming his idea of the patient climb. The *Lives of the Desert Fathers* contributed examples of the way in which it might be done. The Rule provides a way which is not the only way to salvation, and no one who has not professed it is bound by it in any way; it is imposed on no one, but the monk who embraces it of his own free will binds himself by it utterly. It becomes his only way to salvation. Thus the 'mystical' ascent is portrayed as a plodding climb, step by step, such as even the least spiritually gifted may attempt. The ascent by the Rule may be seen in terms of a progression of both a spiritual and a practical kind, of works and actions as well as of contemplation. Patient ladder-climbing will lead a man from the condition in which all his perceptions are those of his bodily senses, to the use of his reason, and finally to understanding; it will turn him from an animal into a man who has returned to the state in which Adam was created—a likeness of God. ('And God said, let us make man in our image, after our likeness.')[5]

Until he comes back in this way to the place where he began, man wanders in a *regio dissimilitudinis*, a 'realm of unlikeness'. He is an exile.[6] Something in him, however, remains for

---

[4] See William James's classic *Varieties of Religious Experience*, The Gifford Lectures (Edinburgh, 1901–2), reprinted with an introduction by A. D. Nock (London, 1960), Lectures XVI and XVII, on the negative aspects of mysticism. On one outstanding late medieval mystic of this cast, see C. F. Kelley, *Meister Eckhart on Divine Knowledge* (New York and London, 1977). See, too, C. Butler, *Western Mysticism* (London 1922, 3rd ed. London 1967) Chapter III, another classic study, which contrasts earlier and later medieval mysticism.

[5] Gen. 1: 26.

[6] F. Châtillon, 'Regio Dissimilitudinis', *Melanges E. Podéchard* (Lyons, 1945), pp. 85–102; Gilson, op. cit., p. 45; P. Courcelle, 'Tradition néo-platonicienne et traditions chrétiennes de la "région de dissemblance" ', *AHDLMA*, 24 (1957), 5–33; P. Courcelle, 'Témoins nouveaux de la région de dissemblance' *Bibliothèque d'École des Chartes*, 118 (1960), 20–36; R. Javelet, *Image et ressemblance au douzième siécle de S. Anselme à Alain de Lille* (Paris, 1967).

ever unchanged; the image of God itself is indestructible, even in the sinful soul, but the 'likeness' to God can be lost, and that is what has happened in fallen man.[7] The journey back to 'likeness' is a process of rectification—of reason by the Word of God, and of the will of man by the agency of the Holy Spirit[8]—so that God may be seen to be continuously at work through grace, refashioning fallen man in his own likeness.

The 'deification' involved here has been a matter of some controversy. Augustine speaks of a 'deification' which takes place in a time of 'rest' (*deificari in otio*),[9] when man comes close to God and begins to resemble him. But within the Hermetic tradition there was another notion of *deificatio*, a process of actually becoming God, where the creature ceases to be a creature and becomes divine. The *Asclepius* of Ps. Hermes Trismegistos[10] in which this *deificatio* is discussed was not much read in Bernard's day (except for one or two passages cited by Augustine), although it became popular in certain circles later in the twelfth century.[11] There is no reason to suppose that Bernard himself knew it or had any such process in mind. It is of the essence of his conception of the mystical experience that there remains a distinct entity which is the human soul, not lost in God, but simply in perfect accord with the will of God.[12] The difference between this union and the union of Father and Son is emphasized by Bernard in one of his Song of Songs sermons: it is a happy union (*felix unio*), but it is as nothing in comparison with the union between Father and Son,[13] where God is united with God.

The limited importance of the notion of self-loss in Bernard would seem to diminish the likelihood of his having been much influenced by the writings of Pseudo-Dionysius. These were coming to a new popularity during the middle years of the

---

[7] Gilson, op. cit., p. 51. Gilson's study evokes Bernard the mystic more fully than any other work has so far succeeded in doing.

8. On the teaching function of the Spirit, see *Sermo in Festo Pentecostes*, 1, f, LTR V. 163–4, and Hum. vii. 21, LTR III. 32–3.

[9] Augustine, Letter X. 2, ed. A. Goldbacher, *CSEL*, 34 (1895), p. 24.

[10] Ps. Hermes Trismegistos, *Asclepius*, ed. P. Thomas, in *Apulei Opera*, 3 (Leipzig, 1908).

[11] See, for example, the references in M. T. d'Alverny, *Textes inédits d'Alain de Lille* (Paris, 1965).

[12] *Dil.* x. 28, LTR III. 143.

[13] *SS* 71. iii. 9– iv. 10, LTR II. 220–2.

century, and William of St. Thierry seems to have made use of them.[14] Bernard himself borrows the term *excessus* to describe the state of rapture from Maximus the Confessor, one of the earliest commentators on Ps. Dionysius.[15] But on the whole his vision of the experience of union with the divine is a positive one; his is not a negative mysticism. It is the absence of the beloved, not his presence, which causes the *languor animi*, the *mentis hebetudo*, the *inertia spiritus*, the loss of lively consciousness; that is the state of the soul when it is not in union with God.[16] The soul united with God is intensely and individually alive.

VII. FROM BEAST TO GOD

This motif of the ascent from the beast-like state of fallen man, to true humanity, and then to God-likeness is repeated frequently in William of St. Thierry's writings on the Song of Songs (and elsewhere). William consistently picks out one strand for emphasis: that of the ascent of the soul to God. There are, he says, three *status* of the Christian soul in its love of God: the animal stage, when a man loves God in his heart, the rational stage, when he loves him in his soul, and the spiritual, when he loves him in *omnibus viribus*, with all his strength.[1] The intermediate *status* both illuminates and governs the lower, and it aspires towards the higher *status*.[2] It is in terms of these three that the whole of the *Song of Songs* is to be read. William thus places first the interpretation which makes the Song a conversation between the Soul and Christ as Bride and Bridegroom.[3] He speaks of the work as a song of love, of *amor*, *dilectio*, *caritas*.[4] Accordingly he finds four divisions within the Song, culminating in the union of Bridegroom and Bride.[5]

---

[14] See the *Liber de Natura et Dignitate Amoris*, iv. 10, *PL* 184. 386C, cf. Pseudo-Dionysius, *Mystical Theology*, i–ii, PG 3. 1014–52 and Letter V, PG 3. 1074–6, and see Déchanet, op. cit., pp. 3–4.

[15] See *Dil.* x. 28, LTR III. 143, and Maximus, *Ambigua, Patrologia Graeca* 91. 1202A–B.

[16] *SS* 51. 3, LTR II. 85–6, Cant. 2: 5.

[1] *PL* 184. 407C, cf. *Expositio altera in Cant.*, *PL* 180. 477.

[2] *PL* 184. 409B.

[3] *PL* 180. 475B.

[4] *PL* 180. 475B.

[5] *PL* 180. 475C.

William of St. Thierry's *Golden Letter* is designed to help 'form the novice's mind to prayer'.[6] He wants him to learn to live a solitary life of such intensity,[7] so independent of the opinion of others, so wholly directed towards God, that he will become a missionary unawares, attracting others to the holy life because of what they see in him.[8] He wants him to see his cell as the theatre where the great play of the *Song of Songs* is performed, not a narrow and confining place, but a wide and spacious stage upon which they may live. God's angels, he believes, regard cells as heaven and find them just such delightful places as heaven itself.[9] The player is at first a *homo animalis*, a merely animal man. His task is to learn to obey perfectly, so that he may gain control of his body. Then he progresses to the rational stage, when he begins to understand what is set before him by the teaching of faith. Then he progresses by living a life in accordance with what he has understood. The spiritual degree begins with the perfection of the rational man. To make progress as a *homo spiritualis* or *intellectualis* is to look on God's glory with an uncovered face, and to become perfect in this degree is to be transformed into the likeness of God.[10]

As the hero of the play makes his way from animal to rational to spiritual manhood, William is able to portray him in various costumes and in various scenes. The animal man may have a holy simplicity when he is truly devoted to God, but he is really a shapeless lump of matter at this stage. He begins to take form when he acquires the virtues: justice, prudence, temperance, fortitude.[11] On the border between animality and reason, he finds himself possessed of intelligence and inventiveness and skill, and we see man the artist, the poet, the architect, the scientist, the orator, the man of business.[12] A little further on, man learns to look on his body

---

[6] *The Golden Letter*, Prefatory letter, 9. ed. R. Thomas, *Pain de Cîteaux*, 33–4 (Chamberand, 1968). (The section-numbers are taken from the translation in Cistercian Fathers, vol. 12 and from this edition.)

[7] Ibid., I. i. 3.

[8] Ibid., I. vii. 21.

[9] Ibid., I. x. 32.

[10] Ibid., I. xiv. 45.

[11] Ibid., I. xiv. 50.

[12] Ibid., I. xv. 59.

as a sick person entrusted to his care.[13] His cell is the infirmary. He must learn to consult his doctor the confessor and show him his ulcers without shame, and to insist upon the surgeon's knife if the physician is too gentle with him.[14]

Writing this time not so much of the practical living of life as of the spiritual life of the monk, William again distinguishes three degrees of knowledge in his *Enigma of Faith*, which correspond with the three *status* of man, the beast, the rational man, the god. At the first level, a man relies upon authority and holds what he is sure of, not by knowledge, but by faith. In the second, he makes use of his reason so as to understand how he is to speak of what he believes, how he is to express it to himself. (Here he uses, not human reason, that is, not the reasonings of dialecticians, but that *ratio* which is the God-given faculty he shares with the angels.) Finally, he comes to the experience of things which is to be had in thinking of the Lord with a simple heart. There, authority and reason become superfluous: he sees by the light of an illumining and beautifying grace.[15]

VIII. SPECULATIO

This approach to understanding how we may know God had its counterpart in academic circles, in the treatment of the question in a textbook which was newly popular in the schools, and upon which Thierry of Chartres and Gilbert of Poitiers had written commentaries, and lectured. Boethius' *De Trinitate* opens with a discussion of the steps or stages of human knowledge, which places at the bottom the knowledge of the natural or physical world, with mathematical knowledge in between and theological knowledge highest of all. Boethius distinguishes them in terms of their subject-matter: physics deals with what is concrete and in motion, the mutable bodies of the created world; theology deals with the unchanging and incorporeal divine being. Mathematics, falling between the two, treats the corporeal as though it were

---

[13] Ibid., I. xviii. 72.
[14] Ibid., I. xxvi. 97.
[15] Enigma of Faith, 36–7, *PL* 180. 397–440. cf. Origen, *The Song of Songs Commentary and Homilies, Ancient Christian Writers*, 26 (London, 1957), pp. 8–9.

incorporeal, the changing as though it were changeless, and, as it were, 'abstracts' from the concrete.[1] Boethius gives a corresponding division of modes of knowledge. In physics we must think *rationabiliter*, reasonably. In mathematics we proceed *disciplinaliter*, by rule. In theology we think *intellectualiter*, intellectually.[2]

The corresponding division in Bernard and William of St. Thierry is not of subject-matter but of the mode of knowledge. Their teaching, in common with that of a number of twelfth-century contemporaries, is that the highest mode of knowledge, that which is proper to the attempt to know God, is not only rational, but also spiritual, indeed that true rationality, the rationality implanted by God in man at his creation, is indistinguishable from spirituality.[3]

Bernard formulated his scheme fully only at the end of his life, when he wrote Book V of the *De Consideratione*. The four preceding books, he reminds his readers, have had to do with *actio*, or at least with matters which require 'consideration' to lead to *actio*: *dum res aliquas non considerandas tantum, sed agendas docent vel movent.*[4] This last book is concerned solely with *consideratio*. Bernard has invited Pope Eugenius to look at himself, at what is below him, and what is about him. Now he is to consider what is above him. Such consideration requires not *actus*, but *inspectus*.[5] There is indeed no way in which it is possible to 'act' upon those things which exist always in one way and externally. What we are to consider, then, is the subject-matter of theology much as Boethius defines it, and we are to do so with our intellectual powers, not with the senses: *Invisibilia Dei per ea qua facta sunt, intellecta conspiciuntur.*[6]

There is an underlying epistemological system here which Augustine derived from the neoplatonists of his day, and transmitted. Augustine, and Bernard too, believed that we

---

[1] Boethius, *Theological Tractates*, ed. H. Stewart, E. K. Rand and S. J. Tester (London, 1973), p. 8.

[2] Ibid.

[3] See E. Bertola, *San Bernardo e la teologia speculativa* (Padua, 1959), especially pp. 53–4.

[4] *Csi*, V. i. 1, LTR III. 467. 4.

[5] LTR III. 467. 6–7.

[6] Romans 1: 20.

cannot see God clearly now because we are limited by our senses, our minds trapped in our bodies.[7] We are exiles from heaven, who need a ladder to climb up if we are to perceive something higher than the subject-matter proper to sense-perception: *hac scala cives non egent, sed exsules.*[8] The citizens of the kingdom of heaven see God directly, because they are purely spiritual, or have learned to perceive as though they were pure spirit: their reason sees clearly.[9]

Bernard goes on to give an account of the three kinds of *consideratio* by which we ascend, which corresponds exactly to the Boethian scheme of *physica, mathematica, theologia.* The practical man uses the senses as if they were the wealth of the citizens of heaven, employing them for his own salvation and that of others. The scientist employs the senses as a means of making his ascent towards the invisible higher truth. The speculative man scorns the use of any such aid, and soars in his understanding in contemplation of the sublime. He does not climb up, by gradual and patient steps; he is snatched up by raptures or sudden ecstasies. These three stages or modes of knowing God may be called: *dispensativa, aestimativa, speculativa.*[10] The practical man works steadily towards an understanding of God by making a good use of the natural world for the benefit of his fellow-men. In contrast to this epistemological Martha stands the epistemological Mary, who with God's help concentrates her powers directly upon God in an attempt to know him as he is. In between, the thinking man, the academic, prudently and diligently peers into things and weighs the evidence in his attempt to learn about God: *prudens ac diligenter quaeque scrutans et ponderans ad vestigandum Deum.*[11]

When Bernard turns to the object of this threefold enquiry, the divine being, he, like Gilbert of Poitiers, acknowledges the difficulty, if not the impossibility, of finding words adequate to express what he is, but Bernard does not attempt to run the difficulty to earth, to identify it as a philosophical problem. He

[7] *Csi*, V. i. 2, LTR III. 468.
[8] LTR III. 467. 15–16.
[9] LTR III. 467–8.
[10] LTR III. 469. 10–12.
[11] LTR III. 469. 13–17.

points out that God is simply ineffable; we know him as he is revealed by the Spirit, not by finding a form of words for him: *non verbo docentur, sed Spiritu revelantur.*[12] Man truly meets God only on a common ground of spirit.[13]

Yet he sees the Boethian ascent of understanding in terms far closer to those Anselm uses in the *Monologion* than to those of the masters of his own day. In his first chapter Anselm invites his readers to look at the innumerable good things of life, both those which they experience with their senses, and those which they perceive with their rational minds. Then he shows them how it is possible to arrange these 'goods' in a hierarchical order, so that they ascend in their thinking towards the supreme good, which is God himself, progressing light, for example, the goods he needs for bodily life to those things which seem good to the reason, and so upwards.[14] Bernard has a not dissimilar passage in his *De Diligendo Deo*, where he leads the reader on from the thought of God's goodness in giving him the things his senses perceive, food and light, for example, the goods he needs for bodily life to those higher gifts of mind and soul which God gives as good things for the soul's needs. These are dignity, the freedom of choice which makes man superior to the animal creation; knowledge, that is the power by which a man recognizes that he possesses freedom of choice; and virtue, the gift which makes a man ardently seek the God who gave him these good things.[15] The emphasis here is upon a 'speculative' spirituality, in which the mystery and height of God is always before the mind, and 'theory' never becomes mere casuistry. Peter Abelard's theoretical approach to God seemed to Bernard to lack precisely this spiritual dimension. See how 'theoretically' our theologian looks on the invisible things of God! he mocks in Letter 190: *videamus quam theorice noster Theologus invisibilia Dei contempletur.*[16] Abelard has argued himself into a position where he must say that omnipotence properly belongs to the Father alone.[17] He has reduced the mystery of the Incarnation

[12] LTR III. 470. 7.
[13] LTR III. 470. 13–15.
[14] *Anselmi Opera Omnia*, I. 14. 5–9.
[15] *Dil.* II. 2. LTR III. 121. 6–19.
[16] Letter 190. iii. 6, LTR VIII. 22. 20–1.
[17] LTR VIII. 22. 21.

to the point where he can give only one reason why God became man: to give man a rule of life by his example and by his teaching, and even by his suffering on the Cross. 'Incomparable doctor, who opens up for himself even the deep things of God, and makes them clear and easy to everyone': *Incomparabilis doctor, qui etiam profunda Dei sibi aperiens, et ea quibus vult lucida et pervia faciens.*[18] Abelard has tried to reduce mysteries of a theological kind, which can be understood only dimly even by the spiritual faculties of man, to a compass appropriate to the reason in its operations at the 'mathematical' level; he has made *aestimativa* of the *speculativa*.

IX. THE MOUNTAIN OF HUMILITY

Bernard, then, saw the daily living of the monastic life—indeed the Christian life in general—as the climbing of a ladder. The first book he wrote, a study of the *Steps of Humility* written before 1125 out of a sermon he had given, took the form of a ladder, as did the *De Diligendo Deo* and the *De Praecepto et Dispensatione*.[1] There was nothing new in this. Benedict's Rule (Chapter VII) describes the twelve degrees of humility; to keep the fear of God constantly before one's eyes, to do God's will, not one's own, to obey one's superior in all things, to be patient and persevere when such wholehearted obedience becomes difficult, to confess wicked thoughts and secret sins to one's abbot, to be content with the meanest and worst of everything, to declare oneself to be lowlier and less important than others, and to believe it, to do nothing but what is commanded by the Rule and one's superiors, to restrain one's tongue, not to laugh too readily, to speak gently and seriously and in a low voice, and as little as possible, and to behave humbly. Anselm of Canterbury began to explore the steps of humility, too, in talks which have been preserved for us by one of his monks. He distinguished seven steps up the ladder:

---

[18] Letter 190. vii. 17, LTR VIII. 32. 2–3.

[1] Cf. *PL* 184. 461. R. W. Southern, *The Making of the Middle Ages* (London, 1953) p. 214, contrasts Bernard's ladder with that of Anselm. Anselm's ladder follows a logical sequence of steps. Bernard's ladder of humility is less a progression than 'varying manifestations of a fundamental attitude'. Both, however, begin with *self*-knowledge, and Bernard certainly has the idea of 'climbing' in mind.

cognitio sui, knowing oneself so well that one is aware of one's inferiority; *dolor*, feeling one's sinfulness sincerely and deeply; *confessio*, confessing what one has learnt; *persuasio*, convincing oneself that the sins confessed are really one's own; *concessio*, accepting not only one's own judgement of one's shortcomings, but also that of others; *patientia*, bearing everything that comes as though it were the most welcome thing in the world; *amor*, ceasing to complain, because one is burning with love.[2]

Bernard's steps of humility are also steps of understanding, a progression towards the knowledge of God. From the point where he comes to know himself, by that virtue which may be defined as 'the power by which a man sees clearly how vile he is': *virtus, qua homo verissima sui cognitione sibi ipse vilescit*,[3] a man ascends to the *caritas* which stands at the top of the ladder.[4] In the process he seeks the truth in himself, in his neighbour, in his nature. In himself he seeks the truth so that he may judge himself; in his neighbours he seeks it so as to suffer their ills with them; he seeks the truth *in sui natura* by gazing on God with a pure heart (*mundo corde contemplando*). Truth can be seen only with a pure heart: *pura veritas non nisi puro corde videtur*.[5] The humble man has now progressed beyond the animal stage, because he has gained control of himself, to the rational stage, where he is able to understand the troubles of others, to the spiritual stage where his intellectual powers are sharpened. The peak of the mountain of humility is a vantage-point from which one may see the truth, where *speculatio* is possible: *in quo velut in Sion, id est in speculatione positi, veritatem prospiciant*.[6] The rest at the end of the climb infinitesimal in this life, although it is to be enjoyed without end in the next. The arrival may be only momentary, the embrace or *amplexus* of spiritual union with the beloved may be so brief that it is not really an arrival at all, but only, as it were, an observation of something happening, to

---

[2] *Memorials of St. Anselm*, ed. R. W. Southern and F. S. Schmitt (London, 1969), p. 110.
[3] *Hum*. i. 2. LTR III. 17. 21–2.
[4] *Hum*. ii. 3. LTR III. 18. 10–28.
[5] *Hum*. iii. 6. LTR III. 20. 12–3.
[6] *Hum*. i. 2. LTR III. 17. 21–5.

which the soul may return in memory afterwards so as to reflect upon it.[7] The effort, then, is great, and the reward perhaps brief.

Bernard's encounter with the Song of Songs enlarged him spiritually and intellectually. It made him think. Above all, it made him subtle in his thinking, a maker of fine distinctions; it taught him to perceive connections and contrasts. It threw into high relief for him ideas which were perhaps implicit in his response to his monastic vocation from the first, but which he could not have brought out so far without William of St. Thierry's stimulus and the vividness of the Song itself to excite him.

We shall see more of William of St. Thierry's influence on the development of Bernard's thinking.

5. *Mary*

There is one further area in which Bernard's preaching proved so memorable that he evoked his subject with an entirely new force and liveliness in the minds of his listeners. When Bernard spoke of the Virgin Mary, he struck a chord which echoed far beyond the circle of those who heard him.

He was not introducing a novel subject. The Feasts which celebrate Mary had been introduced into the West in the seventh century. A liturgical pattern was familiar to Bernard's monastic listeners, as were the titles and honours used in the Eastern liturgies.[1] Anselm of Canterbury composed a series of three prayers to Mary, to be used by the individual when he was depressed, when he was anxious and fearful, and when he felt in special need of the love of Mary and Jesus,[2] and once again he furnishes us with an illuminating and necessary comparison.

The central idea of Anselm's prayers, as of Bernard's sermons, is that Mary is the *theotokos*, the Mother of God.[3] The

---

[7] *SS* 74. i. 4. LTR II. 241–2.

[1] A. Wilmart, *Auteurs spirituels et textes dévots du moyen âge latin* (Paris, 1971), p. 331 on the earliest collection of the Miracles of the Virgin, and p. 324 on ancient prayers to Mary. See, too, *The Prayers and Meditations of St. Anselm*, tr. B. Ward (London, 1973), p. 33.

[2] *Orationes* 5, 6, 7.

[3] *Oratio* 5, S III. 13. 8–9.

theme lends itself to development in three directions. Mary, says Anselm, is the highest Being under God[4]; nothing but God is greater than Mary, because God who made all things made himself of Mary, and thus he made again everything he had made.[5] The theme of Mary's loftiness runs through *Oratio* 7: there is a pun on the grammatical progression 'great', 'greater', 'greatest' (Great Mary, greater than the blessed Marys, greatest of women).[6] We have: *valde magna; altrix; exaltata*. Mary is described as she through whom the elements are renewed, Hell is remedied, demons are trodden underfoot, men are saved, angels brought together again.[7]

Secondly, Mary is the gateway of divine mercy. 'I am sure that since through the Son I was able to receive grace, I can receive it again through the merits of the mother', says Anselm.[8] Mary is a gateway of life (*porta vitae*), door of salvation (*ianua salutis*), way of recovery (*aditus recuperationis*).[9]

Thirdly, she is the protector, the mediatrix, who can communicate man's needs to her Son, and whom man does not fear to approach at times when he is so conscious of his unworthiness that he does not feel able to come to her Son himself. She is 'spring and source of mercy' (*fons et ortus misericordiae*),[10] gentle and kind.[11]

Anselm's variations on these three ideas run through his prayers to Mary in counterpoint with his own sense of sin, in a paradox which it gives him endless wonder to contemplate: Mary is infinitely far above him, and yet utterly accessible.

These devotional responses to the idea of Mary are not without their theological difficulties. Mary is represented not only as a gateway but as a source (*fons et ortus*) of divine mercy. And it appears that something is lacking in the reconciling work of God made man if a mediator other than

---

[4]   *Oratio* 7, S III. 21. 93–5.
[5]   *Oratio* 7, S III. 22. 99–100.
[6]   *Oratio* 7, S III. 18. 4–5.
[7]   *Oratio* 7, S III. 20. 82–4.
[8]   *Oratio* 7, S III. 19. 45–6.
[9]   *Oratio* 7, S III. 20. 47–52.
[10]   *Oratio* 5, S III. 14. 38. See Wilmart, op. cit., pp. 323, 331, 343, 356 ff. on Mary as mediatrix.
[11]   *Oratio* 5, S III. 14. 46–7.

Christ himself is needed. Yet, paradoxically again, Anselm's prayer to Christ suggests the very opposite. It has an air of intimacy and freedom of speech which makes Anselm's words to the Virgin, loving though they are, seem more formal by comparison. Anselm's prayer to Christ was written in a period of dullness when he could not make the effort he wanted to make to love Christ as he ought. There are no effusions to match those of the Mary prayers, merely a straightforward beginning: 'My Redeemer, my Mercy, my Salvation'.[12]

The difference lies perhaps in the effort Anselm makes in this prayer—as he cannot in the prayers to Mary—to bring before his mind's eye with lively directness the actual events of Christ's life and suffering and death. For Mary's life there are few such recorded incidents in Scripture for him to dwell on. Anselm is sorrowful because he was not able to see Christ when he was a man 'humbled to talk with men',[13] when his side was pierced with a lance and his feet with nails.[14] He wishes he had been able to share the Virgin's sorrow and help Joseph of Arimathea take down the Lord from the Cross.[15] He asks Christ to give him a clear picture and experience of these things now, since he was not able to be present.[16] He weeps for his sins and his inability to see and understand. He longs to know Christ closely as a friend.[17]

Christ is very real indeed to Anselm. He is God, and Anselm feels at home with the idea of his divinity. It was intellectually congenial to him to dwell in the heights in this way in his thinking about God. Christ is also man to him, a man with human experiences which again Anselm can understand and envisage. Christ is close enough to Anselm in his humanity for him to find it entirely natural to turn to him as mediator. The role Mary plays is an additional means of access to God; she is the greatest of the friends a man may have in heaven amongst human beings who have died.

As to her being the ultimate source of the grace and mercy which flows from her; here there can be no doubt of the

---

[12] *Oratio* 2, S III. 6. 4.
[13] *Oratio* 2, S III. 7. 38–40.
[14] *Oratio* 2, S III. 7. 42–5.
[15] *Oratio* 2, S III. 8. 46–62.
[16] *Oratio* 2, S III. 8. 63–71.
[17] *Oratio* 5, S III. 9.

orthodoxy of Anselm's position. He holds God to be First Cause in a neoplatonic way which rules out the possibility on philosophical as well as theological grounds. But Mary remains for Anselm an embodiment of her qualities of mercy, purity, gentleness, with a fullness not found in the rest of the human race. She is a creature apparently not creaturely in her behaviour or nature. Something of the same paradoxical view of Mary is to be found in Bernard's writings and he tries hard to make her both real and extraordinary for his audience.

Bernard left no prayers. His talk of the Virgin and her relationship with her Son took place in his sermons, especially in his liturgical sermons. In the round of the year Bernard would preach for Advent, Nativity and Epiphany, for the Annunciation, the Purification of the Virgin, and the Assumption, often on one of the canticles (Vigil of the Nativity, V; Purification I, for example) or the procession of the day and its significance. In addition, he composed four homilies *In Laudibus Virginis Mariae* in the early 1120s in which he explored the text of Luke 1: 26–7 describing the coming of the Angel Gabriel to Mary.[18]

The characteristic tone of the liturgical sermons is their immediacy. Bernard wants his listeners to understand the significance of the feast day, to see it as today's Feast, with a topical importance and interest. 'Today the Virgin Mother brings the Temple of the Lord into the Temple of the Lord',[19] he says in the first of his sermons for the Purification of the Virgin. He plunges into his exploration of the theme in search 'among many new and wonderful things' of some particular *novitas* for his listeners.[20] He shows how, although her door was locked and no man could get in through solid walls, the Angel Gabriel was able to appear before Mary, for walls do not stand in the way of angelic spirits.[21] He compares the ways in which Stephen was full of grace (Acts 6: 8) and the Apostles were full of the Holy Spirit (Acts 2: 4) with the way in which

---

[18] LTR IV. 3.
[19] LTR IV. 334. 1–2.
[20] *In Laud. V. Mar.* II. 9. LTR IV. 27. 1–3.
[21] *In Laud. V. Mar.* III. i, LTR IV. 36. On Bernard's view that Mary knew what was to happen before the angels, cf. Letter 77, LTR IV. 198. 1–5.

Mary was 'full of grace'.[22] If we think about the words: 'The Lord is with you', we shall see that in Mary's case they refer not only to a *consensio* of her will with that of God, but a *consensio* of her whole flesh.[23] Sometimes his energetic tone seems a little forced, but the need to maintain a level of enthusiasm and a sense of newness in the routine of the religious life was always in the forefront of his mind.

With the same purpose in mind Bernard makes his listeners think hard about the text before them. We are told that the Virgin was betrothed to Joseph. Surely this was no matter of chance? What reason commends is not a matter of chance, and there was indeed a most *utilis* and *necessaria ratio* here. It was the custom of the Jews to hand over the bride into the groom's charge from the day of betrothal. Thus Joseph became a reliable witness to Mary's purity.[24] Out of the points given in Luke, the name of the angel, the fact that the message came from God, to Mary, a virgin espoused to a man called Joseph, and that the city was Nazareth and the region Galilee, Bernard draws detail after detail. The Angel Gabriel was not one of the least among the angels; he was often sent to earth and his name means Strength (*fortitudo*). The news came directly from God to Mary. She was the first to hear.[25] Gabriel's name is not inappropriate because he came to announce the power (*virtus*) of Christ.[26] Nazareth means 'flower'; Christ is the fruit of that flower.[27] Mary is the only example in the world of a mother who is also a virgin; the wonder of this paradox cannot be overemphasized.[28] The significance of Christ's circumcision is this: the members of the body are full of concupiscence, immoderate and inordinate. An infant cannot bear to have a part of his body cut off because of the weakness of his tender years. So divine disposition provides a means by which desire may be chastised, in that part of the body where it is agreed to be most fierce. The circumcision is carried out on the eighth

---

22 *In Laud. V. Mar.* III. iii, LTR IV. 37. 27–37.1.
23 *In Laud. V. Mar.* III. iv, LTR IV. 38 17–26.
24 *In Laud. V. Mar.* II. 12, LTR IV. 29. 9–10.
25 *In Laud. V. Mar.* I. 2, LTR IV. 14. 23–15. 5.
26 *In Laud. V. Mar.* I. 2, LTR IV. 15. 5–10.
27 *In Laud. V. Mar.* I. 3, LTR IV. 16. 3–5.
28 *In Laud. V. Mar.* I. 7, LTR IV. 18. 25–6.

day because that brings things round in a circle and makes a
crown—just as a Feast comes to an end on the eighth day
which repeats the first, and in the eight Beatitudes the last is
linked with the first.[29] It is not by coincidence that Christ was
born at night and in winter. Other infants cannot choose when
they are born, but he wanted to come quietly and unobtrusive-
ly and to leave the announcement of his birth to the angels.[30]

The purpose of all Bernard's preaching on the Virgin and her
Son is to make the reader alive to the detailed implications of
the Nativity story for his own spiritual and active life. He
emphasizes the Virgin's attractiveness of mind and body: it is
easy to see that the King of Heaven might desire her, says
Bernard, in a conscious echo of the Song of Songs.[31] She is
attractive to us, too. He has a strong sense of the fittingness of
what happened. It befits God to be born of no one but a Virgin;
it was fitting that the Virgin should bear no one but God.[32] As
children of Adam and Eve we can rejoice and be comforted.[33] A
woman replaces the woman who fell, a wise woman replaces a
foolish one, a humble woman a proud one.[34] Bernard reminds
us constantly of the human impact of these enormous events
with their heavenly dimension and their implications for the
unfolding of God's purpose in history. In the sermon for the
Feast of the Circumcision, Bernard reminds us of the list of
Christ's names in Isaiah (Isaiah 9: 6): Wonderful, Counsellor,
Mighty God, Everlasting Father, Prince of Peace, and then sets
beside it 'the name above all names', from the Song of Songs
1: 2: *Oleum effusum nomen tuum.*[35] Christ's title as 'oil'
poured out for man is his highest name. Sermon IV for the
Nativity is on the abjectness and humility of Christ's Nativity.
Bernard looks at Christ's flesh and its weaknesses. Because he
is man we can perceive him whom we cannot see spiritually in
our fleshly state.[36] But he differs from us, grieving not out of

---

[29] *In Circumcisione,* LTR IV. 274. 15–17.
[30] *In Nativ.* III. 2, LTR IV. 258. 1–21.
[31] *In Laud. V. Mar.* II. ii, LTR IV. 22. 9–13.
[32] *In Laud. V. Mar.* II. i, LTR IV. 21. 19–21.
[33] *In Laud. V. Mar.* II. iii, LTR IV. 22, 22–4.
[34] *In Laud. V. Mar.* II. iii. LTR IV. 23. 10–12.
[35] *In Circumcisione* 4, LTR IV. 275. 16–22.
[36] *In Nativ.* III. 3, LTR IV. 259. 19–20.

passion, as we do, but out of compassion.[37] Thus we see something we can understand translated for us into a higher form, in its divine perfection.

For the devotional writers of the twelfth century and beyond, Mary was to become a high centre of love and admiration.[38] Bernard met a need, with superlative skill. If we must leave his preaching with a single verdict, it is that it did precisely that wherever he preached, whoever his audience, whatever his subject. He had a rare sensitivity to the mood of his listeners, an ability to adapt himself. He saw clearly as he spoke how he could best benefit those before him. It was an intellectual power, but also an emotional one which made him outstanding as a preacher.

Bernard was a live performer rather than a master of the considered statement. The ideas he puts forward and develops in his sermons were already formed in his mind in their essentials, but with a live audience before him he became a virtuoso, playing many variations on his theme. So brilliant was the colouring he gave to what he said that it conveys gesture and intonation, the experience of listening to Bernard in person, even on the page. No other preacher of the twelfth century can match Bernard there.

---

[37] *In Nativ.* III. 3, LTR IV. 260. 6.

[38] Bernard was aware that his language about Mary sometimes went 'beyond the Fathers', as he puts it in his eightieth sermon on the Song of Songs. But his enthusiasm was tempered by a strong hostility to anything which smacked of abuse of devotion to Mary, as the selling of relics (Cant. x. 3).

Chapter III

Theology and Controversy

I. THE DEFENDER OF THE FAITH

About 1143 Everwin of Steinfeld wrote to tell Bernard of a recent unpleasantness at Cologne involving heretics, which had left him upset and troubled.[1] The heretics claim to be the sole true Church, following in the footsteps of Christ, imitating the true apostolic life. They live in poverty. They are vegetarians. They consecrate their food and drink at meals as Christ consecrated the bread and wine at the Last Supper. They baptize not only with water, but also with fire and with the Holy Ghost, claiming that all believers who have been baptized and are among the elect have power to baptize others. They oppose the established practices of the Church in administering the sacrament, condemning baptism and marriage as usually understood. Another group of heretics is found in the Rhineland too, who disagree with the first. Their position is altogether more radically opposed to orthodoxy. They deny that priests have the power of consecrating bread and wine because, they say, the Pope is no longer Peter's true successor; he is corrupted by his engagement in worldly affairs, and all his priests with him. The Church has lost the power of consecration. They condemn infant baptism, saying that Christ alone baptizes the believer, when he is of age. All the other sacraments they hold invalid.

The first group had been brought to trial. Two of them, one calling himself their bishop, had defended their heresy before the Archbishop of Cologne and certain magnates. They claimed that they were true followers of Christ; they declared themselves willing to belong to the orthodox Church if their arguments could be worsted in debate with the Church's apologists, but if not, they said that they were prepared to die for their faith. The mob took them and burned them, and they

---

[1] Letter 472, *PL* 182. 676–80, and see J. Leclercq, 'S. Bernard Docteur', *Coll. Cist.*, 16 (1954), 284–6.

went to their death, says Everwin, not only with patience, but with joy. He is disturbed by these events, because he cannot understand why these men, obviously in error, showed a spirit and a piety which is not to be found even in good Christians as a rule.[2] He describes the teaching of the heretics in outline, and also mentions another sect in the area, whose teaching is different.[3] He begs Bernard to write him a defence of the faith. There can be nothing more important, he presses; Bernard cannot say he is too busy, and if he says that the 'tower of David' is already sufficiently fortified, Everwin answers that its fortifications are not obvious to simple and slow-witted men such as himself (*nos simpliciores et tardiores*). There is a need for a plain man's guide to heresy, which will enable such honest Christians to make themselves prepared, and ready to resist the arguments the heretics may put to them.[4]

At the time when Everwin's letter arrived, Bernard had been preaching on the meaning of the 'little foxes' of the Song of Songs (Cant. 2: 15) in the sixty-fourth of his series of sermons on the Song of Songs. He had already explained that the *vulpes parvulae* could be interpreted either as temptations[5] or as heretics.[6] Now he continued, extending his reflections, considering how heretics should be dealt with by faithful Christians. Heretics, he explains, should be captured, not by force of arms, but by arguments to refute their errors (*non armis, sed argumentis, quibus refellantur errores eorum*)[7] Every effort should be made to reconcile them to the Church, for God's will is that all men should be saved.[8] Bernard felt strongly about the inexcusable ignorance of those who are too lazy to learn divine truth.[9] The man who, trained and learned (*exercitatus et doctus*), takes issue with a heretic, should have the intention of converting him clearly before his mind. He has done his work well when he overcomes his resistance and convinces him, confutes his heresy, distinguishes clearly between the

---

[2] *PL* 182. 676–7 (1–2).
[3] *PL* 182. 677–8 (3–4).
[4] *PL* 182. 679C–D.
[5] *SS* 64. i. 1 – ii. 7, LTR II. 166–70.
[6] *SS* 64. iii. 8, LTR II. 170.
[7] *SS* 64. iii. 8, LTR II. 170. 13–15.
[8] I Tim. 2: 4.
[9] LTR VII. 187–8.

truth and what merely appears to be true (*verisimilia a vero
clare aperteque distinxit*), and makes it obvious how wicked
his teaching is.[10] In Sermon 65, he apologizes to his listeners
for preaching yet a third sermon on the foxes, and then
explores the deceitfulness of heretics, their subtlety, their
vanity. He shows the good Christian how to see through them.

Sermon 66 begins with another apology: *Ecce ego ad vulpes
istas*: 'Here again I am talking about those foxes!' Now Bernard
examines the beliefs of the heretics Everwin has described to
him, their teaching on marriage, on the baptism of infants, on
purgatory, on prayers for the dead, on the invocation of
saints.[11] His method of meeting Everwin's request to simplify
his teaching for simple men is to sharpen and compress his
arguments until they are little more than indignant statements
of the absurdity of such claims; he wants to produce a strong,
clear impression in their minds of the kind of thing the
heretics are saying, so that they may recognize heresy when
they meet it. He has allowed his talks about the foxes to go on
so long with the end in view of painting a picture in bold
colours which his listeners will remember.

Bernard was to be involved in two memorable trials, at
which leading academics of the day were brought to account
for teaching which was thought to be leading the faithful
astray. Geoffrey of Auxerre gives an account of the two trials,
of Peter Abelard and of Gilbert of Poitiers, in a single chapter of
the *Vita Prima*. He sees both as aspects of Bernard's work
against the schismatics. He emphasizes Bernard's unwilling-
ness to become involved,[12] and describes how he was won
round and persuaded that it was his duty to go into battle
against these heretics. Bernard was reluctant because he
doubted whether this was the kind of task for which he was
best fitted (*suum hoc non esse renuntians*).[13] He had to devise
a method for conducting a case of this sort, rather as Anselm of
Canterbury, another reluctant polemicist, had had to do before
him.

When, a decade before the end of the eleventh century,

---

[10] *SS* 64. iii. 9, LTR II. 170. 28–9.
[11] *SS* 66. i. 1, LTR II. 178. 9–10.
[12] *VP* III. v. 12–4, *PL* 185. 310–11.
[13] *PL* 185. 311C.

Anselm of Canterbury heard that Roscelin of Compiègne was saying that he taught an unorthodox doctrine of the Trinity, he took up his pen in his own defence. He wrote an open letter to all faithful people, with an apology. Yet when he contemplates himself in the act of trying to strengthen and confirm the faith, he sees himself as a ridiculous figure, laden with ropes and tackle, working earnestly round the base of Mount Olympus, lashing it and pegging it so as to prevent its falling down.[14] He has made the attempt, but not because he believes the faith to be in need of his efforts; he has written to defend himself.[15]

But faith is one thing and the minds of the faithful another. Abelard's teaching seemed to William of St. Thierry and St. Bernard to pose no merely superficial threat to the security of orthodox faith in the minds of the faithful, but to strike at its very foundations with both subtlety and force.[16]

II. BERNARD THE THEOLOGIAN

Bernard was often asked for his advice on theological problems which had arisen in the course of the study of the Bible or which had presented themselves in some other way. Long before events obliged him to turn polemicist he had established a reputation as a reliable authority in such matters. Hugh of St. Victor wrote to him when he was composing his *De Sacramentis Ecclesiae* to ask his opinion on baptism, and incorporated much of what he said without acknowledgement in the finished work.[1] Bernard was not by inclination an academic theologian. That is to say, he was not strongly drawn to the philosophical problems raised for many of his contemporaries by the application of grammar and logic to the study of the Bible and to the discussion of Christian doctrine. He himself had no intellectual difficulties and he regarded such free-ranging intellectual curiosity as dangerous to the faith of ordinary believers. The guiding principle of all his theological problem-solving was the desire to protect and preserve orthodox belief in the minds of simple men.

---

[14] *Anselmi Opera Omnia* I. 281. 7–13.
[15] Ibid. I. 282. 1.
[16] LTR VIII. 17. 9:10.
[1] See LTR VII. 184 n.1 for the literature.

But we have seen that he was far from being a bigoted opponent of the use of secular studies, grammar, logic or any other technical assistance which might prove illuminating. He takes a sensible moderate view of several of the vexed questions of the day concerning their use. What is the place of scholarly learning in the Christian life? It is a talent to be used, says Bernard. He writes to Bruno, archbishop elect of Cologne, who had written to ask whether he should accept the bishopric. 'You are afraid, and with justification, for I fear it myself, that you might do wrong if you did not put the talent of knowledge which has been committed to you to use.'[2] What is the place of the study of the classics and other secular writings in a Christian's reading? To Gilbert the Universal, bishop of London from 1128 to 1135, Bernard says, 'Undoubtedly you are a wise man, taking your pleasure in all the books and studies of the wise men of the world, and studying the divine Scriptures so as to give life to their meaning and apply it to the present day.'[3] What is the proper use of the writings of the Fathers? They should always be cited if possible in preference to a modern opinion. Bernard had been asked why the Maccabees 'alone of all the righteous men of the old Law' have a place in the calendar and a feast-day like the Christian martyrs. Bernard delayed his answer for some time, while he looked for something in the Fathers which would provide an authoritative answer, and it was only with reluctance, he says, that he sat down to write an account of the matter afresh in his own words.[4]

These views have the ring of something settled. They are not newly struck from the mint, but rather the opinions of someone who has arrived at a position which seems right and natural to him, and from which he will not wish to depart. In a similar way Bernard sets about resolving the problems with which his correspondents present him, by asking himself what principles are involved. The principles are ready in his mind. He has only to apply them. An ethical difficulty arose for Guy, abbot of Trois-Fontaines, who had been greatly upset by a

---

[2] Letter 8, 1, LTR VII. 47. 14–6, SJ 9, 1.
[3] Letter 24, 1, LTR VII. 77. 3–5, SJ 25, 1.
[4] Letter 98, 1–2, LTR VII. 248–50, SJ 988, 1.

mistake which had resulted in there being no wine in the chalice when he came to consecrate it at Mass. 'You should, I think, consider your own intention rather than the dignity of the sacred matter', Bernard advises, 'because the motive not the matter, the intention and not the results of the action, constitute its moral character'. Bernard has talked the matter over with his own prior, and they can see no greater fault on Guy's part than ignorance; the servers are guilty of careless-ness; but there has certainly been no malice involved. Bernard offers Guy a second principle to set beside the first:'You surely know that as there is no good but what springs from the will, so there can be no great evil in a matter which is clearly involuntary.'[5]

In very much this way, when a problem arose to be dealt with in one of his sermons, Bernard applied his principles in the light of Scripture and the Fathers. Someone had asked him a question which Anselm of Canterbury had considered:[6] why could God not repair the damage done to his creation by Adam's sin without going to such lengths as to send his Son to die? He could (*valuit*), says Bernard, but he preferred (*maluit*) to follow the course he did.[7] Like Anselm, although he gives different reasons, Bernard is concerned to emphasize the hugeness of Adam's offence. He draws a most graphic contrast between the six days in which God created the whole world and everything in it, and the thirty years during which 'he worked your salvation upon the earth'.[8] He has in mind throughout the importance of sin, the hugeness of Adam's offence; this simple but powerful governing principle informs everything he says. In one of the sermons for Advent further aspects of the theology of incarnation and redemption are discussed (again, questions raised by Anselm of Canterbury and, again, with Bernard's own distinctive answers). Why did the Son become man and not the Father or the Holy Spirit? If we think about the cause of our exile, Bernard suggests, we can see, at least in part, how appropriate it was that the Son should

---

[5] Letter 69, 1, LTR VII. 169–71, SJ 72, 1.
[6] *Cur Deus Homo* I: v, S 1. 52. 12–24.
[7] *SS* 11, 7, LTR I. 58. 27–9.
[8] LTR I. 59. 12–13.

be our principal Liberator. The offence was a lie, for Satan thought himself equal with God and seduced man into a pride like his own. The Son is Truth, and so he was able to counterbalance the lie. Once more a principle is implicit in Bernard's argument, this time the notion of appropriateness or fittingness.[9]

A good deal of scholarly expertise in the academic devices of division and definition makes itself felt in Bernard's writings when he approaches a difficulty, again with an air of familiar use. For example, in another of the Song of Songs sermons Bernard distinguishes between the unity of Father and Son in the Godhead and the unity of God and man by grace. The unity is not the same in both cases. Father and Son are one in an ineffable way, consubstantial and *consensibiles*. God and man are one in a bond of love only. 'Do you not see the difference?' Bernard asks.[10] The consent between the Father and the Son arises out of their unity in essence and will. The consent between man and God involves the operation of two distinct wills, not of a single will.[11] In the treatise *On Precept and Dispensation*, too, there are distinctions. Two acts of homicide are shown to be of unequal gravity, one committed out of greed for gain and the other committed out of necessity and in self-defence.[12] We are taught to distinguish between the giver of the precept and the precept, and within precepts, between those of greater and lesser importance.

There are little scholarly jokes—a reference to 'our Master's view' (*Magistri nostri sententia*), an expression which was common in the schools; but Bernard is speaking of the monk's master Benedict, not of some contemporary teaching master.[13] He introduces a lightly ironic schoolmasterly note in such comments as: 'To return now to the little question we set out to resolve.'[14]

But over and above this evidence that Bernard was at home with the talk of the schools and had no objection to its use in

[9] Sermon I, 2, for Advent, LTR IV. 162. 10–15.
[10] *SS* 71. iii. 7, LTR II. 218. 16–220. 9. *SS* 71. iv. 10.
[11] LTR II. 220. 27–221. 10.
[12] *Pre* VII. 13, LTR III. 262. 233–263. 16.
[13] *Pre* VII. 16. LTR III. 264. 10–11.
[14] LTR III. 281.8.

the proper place, there remain substantial examples of his theological problem-solving which set the characteristic tone of his work as a speculative theologian: a blend of traditional and contemporary approaches in which the traditional is predominant. Bernard proves himself a judicious and balanced thinker. He never forgets the needs of the simple and the importance of keeping the truths of faith clear for them.

One major difficulty, which Anselm of Canterbury refers to as the 'most famous question' of the relationship between human free will and the foreknowledge, predestination, and grace of God, was taken up by Peter Abelard, in his commentary on Aristotle's *De Interpretatione*. Abelard describes unorthodox belief on this matter as the 'worst of all heresies' (*pessima omnium haeresum*) and an abomination to the natural reason of the philosophers (*verum et philosophorum naturali rationi abominatio*).[15] He states the problem in exactly the terms in which it was presented to Bernard, which we may take was the way in which it was usually raised at this time. Those who say that no future event is contingent, but that all that is to come will necessarily happen because God foresees everything and his providence cannot fail, deny that man can, by his own efforts, deserve any credit for behaving well.[16] Bernard wrote about this difficulty at length in his *De Gratia et Libero Arbitrio* of the 1120s,[17] which was sent to William of St. Thierry with the request that William read it and give his opinion before copies were made.[18] William comments on the subtlety of the argument it contains: (*quam fideliter, tam subtiliter disputavit*).[19] It will be recalled that Bernard began the work because of a challenging question put to him by one of his listeners when he had been speaking about

[15] Peter Abelard, Commentary on *Perihermenias*, *Beiträge*, 3 (1927), 427. 1.

[16] Ibid., p. 425. 25–37. There had been a shift of emphasis here since Carolingian times, when the controversy raised by Godescalc of Orbais had been concerned with the pointlessness of human effort in the face of an all-compelling divine grace. The new interest in necessity and futurity reflects the rise of logic. See Anselm, *De Concordia* I. ii, *Anselmi Opera Omnia* II. 249–50, and on Godescalc, *Les Oeuvres de Godescalc d'Orbais*, ed. C. Lambot.

[17] On the date of this treatise, see LTR III. 137–8. See *Disputatio*, pp. 86–96 for further discussion.

[18] LTR III. 165. 5–14.

[19] *VP* III. viii. 29, *PL* 185. 320.

the way in which he felt the grace of God working in him. 'What is your part; what reward do you hope for, if God does it all?' asked the listener.[20] The questioner wanted to understand exactly what was the relationship between human freedom of choice and the grace of God.[21]

Bernard's reply was, as we might expect, a practical one. He wanted to encourage effort on the part of the devout Christian. Nevertheless, he gave some thought to the speculative aspects of the difficulty his questioner had raised, and he did so in a manner remarkably independent of Augustine's treatise of the same title[22] and Augustine's teaching on the subject in general. Bernard does not go so far as the later Augustine in maintaining that grace alone can bring a man to salvation or raise many of the difficulties posed by the Pelagian controversy. Bernard's leading idea, as we have seen, is that the interaction of human free will with divine grace is one of *cooperatio*. If we take away free choice, he says, there is nothing to be saved (*tolle liberum arbitrium: non erit quod salvetur*). If we take away grace there is no means by which salvation can take place (*tolle gratiam: non erit unde salvetur*).[23] Both are needed: God is the author of salvation, and the free will of man has the capacity to be saved. To run over the argument again: the free will is said to co-operate with grace when it consents.[24] To co-operate is to be saved. To consent is to be saved.

This consent is voluntary; it is not the same thing as natural appetite, which we share with animals. Bernard here gives a series of definitions to make the difference quite clear, separating *sensus, a vitalis motus* of the body which observes the outer world, from the natural appetite which moves an animal to desire something, and the consent of the will, given freely, which is a *habitus animi*.[25] Now Bernard is able to show that the will is a *motus rationalis*, a movement of the reason, and dominant over sense and appetite.[26] The reason

---

[20] LTR III. 165. 17–19.
[21] LTR III. 165. 19–21.
[22] But cf. Augustine *De Gratia et Libero Arbitrio* I. i and 19. viii for some parallels.
[23] *Gra* 1. 2, LTR III. 166. 20–1.
[24] LTR III. 167. 1.
[25] LTR III. 167. 25–30.
[26] LTR III. 168. 2–3.

does not act to compel the will, for where there is necessity there is no will. Reason merely instructs the will.[27] Will cannot dissent from itself, nor consent except by its own willing, for it is free. It is compelled by no necessity.[28] That is why it is clear that grace does not force the will.

Throughout this sequence of demonstration and definition, Bernard has kept to plain reasoning, with very little use of Scriptural support. He has handled technically difficult matters with a clarity and elegance and simplicity which argues, not a failure to understand the technical problem, but a mastery sufficient to enable him to present an uncluttered case. Nevertheless, it is clear that Bernard was not a speculative theologian of the order of Anselm of Canterbury. He did not take a delight in these reasonings for their own sake. They are a means to a practical end: the resolution of a difficulty which is preventing some of his monks from striving with all their might to live a better life. Anselm used very similar technical skills in the art of argument as a method of setting out clearly truths whose reasonableness seemed to him beautiful.[29] Bernard engaged in speculative theology when it was necessary, Anselm because it brought him to that clear sight of divine truth which Bernard believed to be best approached by way of the *gradus humilitatis*.

III. PETER ABELARD

Bernard's gift, then, was for simplifying difficulties and making abstruse matters plain; and this was where he came to believe that his task lay. Everwin was not the only contemporary to turn to Bernard for his expert help as a theologian, however, and others required of him a display of knowledge and skill altogether more technical. Hugh of St. Victor wrote to Bernard more than a decade earlier, in 1127 or 1128,[1] to ask his advice about certain teachings of Peter Abelard, the 'dialectician turned theologian' who had already been condemned once for

---

[27] LTR III. 168. 10–17.
[28] LTR III. 170. 5.
[29] *Cur Deus Homo* I. i. *Anselmi Opera Omnia* II. 48. 8–9: 'rationis pulchritudo'.
[1] Letter 77. LTR VII. 184–200, and see D. Van den Eynde, *Essai sur la succession et la date des écrits de Hughes de Saint-Victor* (Rome, 1960).

his opinions at Soissons in 1121. Bernard wrote Hugh a long letter in reply, containing his views on baptism, the foreknowledge of Christ, unintentional sin, and a statement of his own attitude to the handling of such questions in general. Hugh incorporated some of Bernard's suggestions into his *De Sacramentis*.[2]

William of St. Thierry, too, thought he saw grave dangers in the teaching of Peter Abelard, and it was he more than any other correspondent of Bernard's who awoke a similar fear in the abbot of Clairvaux. He believed that Abelard was attacking, not small points of orthodoxy, but the very foundations of the faith. He was frightened by Abelard's persistence in such opinions after he had once been condemned. He saw his ideas crossing the sea and travelling over the Alps and awakening interest everywhere, so that they were more and more widely discussed. He feared that this would be only the beginning, and that worse was to follow if Abelard was not checked.[3] He wrote to Geoffrey, Bishop of Chartres and Bernard to tell them that he had been reading Abelard's *Theologia*, of which he had two versions. Some of the statements he had found had shocked him, and he enclosed a list of points, with his reasons for finding them disquieting, and copies of the books themselves.[4] William explains that the death of the great masters of theology (*magistri doctrinae ecclesiasticae*) has left a gap.[5] Abelard has been able to rush in unimpeded. He is like the demons who come in even greater numbers to the soul of a man possessed when the devil which first possessed him is driven out and his 'house' is swept and garnished.[6] Abelard has invaded the empty territory of the masters of theology, bringing with him his novelties of expression. He believes that he can improve theology. He is a critic of the faith, not a disciple.[7]

William judged his appeal well. He called upon Bernard in terms which he knew would win his passionate support. Otto

---

[2] *De Sacramentis* I. x. 6–7, *PL* 176. 335–41.

[3] Letter 326, ed. J. Leclercq, *R. Bén.*, 79 (1969), 376–8.

[4] Letter 326. 2.

[5] William was perhaps referring to William of Champeaux and Anselm of Laon.

[6] Letter 326. 2 and Luke 11: 25; Matthew 12: 44.

[7] Ibid.

of Freising comments that Bernard was so zealous for Christian truth that he was sometimes remarkably simple and credulous.[8] It would not be true to say that William treated him as though he were to be won over solely by an appeal to the heart. He provided him with an exact account of the grounds for his own anxiety, so that Bernard could judge for himself whether it was justified. But he captured him for the cause by appealing to the crusader in him. Bernard was the right man to tackle the problems posed by Peter Abelard's teaching not only because he had a power of seizing the essentials and explaining them to the ordinary believer, but also because he could be relied upon, once he had taken up a cause, to give it all his considerable energies.

Bernard's immediate response was to write to William to say that he thought his indignation was amply justified. The list of points would, he believed, prove to be invaluable, when he had had time to reflect upon them and see how they were to be used. It was now the middle of Lent, and Bernard proposed that he and William should meet after Easter to discuss the matter, and, for the moment, give themselves up to prayer.[9] No doubt Bernard was concerned about the season, and genuinely was anxious not to be distracted until the end of Lent by what promised to be a demanding campaign, but he was perhaps a little bewildered too. He tells William frankly that most of his questions, not to say all, are quite new to him: *cum horum plurima, et paene omnia, hucusque nescierim.*[10] Whatever he had heard of Abelard's work, from Hugh of St. Victor and elsewhere, he had clearly not read him, and it may be that the exact offence to orthodoxy implied in the points William had singled out was not yet obvious to him in every case. In general, he could see that William was right; he wanted a little time to make up his mind about the particularities of Abelard's teaching, so as to judge how to deal with him. In the event, it seems likely that he did not read systematically through Abelard's writings for himself to see whether William had

[8] Otto of Freising, *Gesta Friderici*, ed. F. J. Schmalc (Darmstadt, 1965), I. 47 (49).
[9] LTR VIII. 263. 6–16.
[10] LTR VIII. 263. 13–14.

judged him justly, or even to look for more errors. He would, perhaps, have seen no need. His chief concern was with the threat Abelard posed to the faith of simple men.

Despite his insistence that it was merely by chance that he had read Abelard's *Theologia*, William's claim that he had copies of two versions, one longer than the other[11] would suggest that he had gone to some trouble to find out what Abelard was teaching, and although he turned to Bernard with the plea that the Church desperately needed his help because no living theologian could meet Abelard in argument, he himself had already set about doing so in the *Disputatio adversus Petrum Abaelardum ad Gaufridum Carnotensem et Bernardum;*[12] there he greatly amplified the points he made in his covering letter, and, as he promised, gave his reasons for objecting to certain of Abelard's teachings.

There is every likelihood that William had known of Abelard since his own student days. He was certainly not coming new to Abelard's teaching. It has been suggested that William's *De Sacramento Altaris* is an attempt to try out the method of Abelard's *Sic et Non,*[13] but even if he made no such thoroughgoing attempt to match Abelard there was enough of the man of the schools in William to give him a good deal of common ground with Abelard in approach and method. William's attitude to Abelard was a complex one, compounded of admiration and a certain resentment that he should use so fine a mind with what seemed to William so little sense. Not only was William closer to Abelard in his cast of mind than Bernard, but he also perhaps felt some rivalry with him.

During the preceding few years he had himself been writing a commentary on Romans.[14] He found it a difficult book, and one which raised many questions: *multis et variis et difficilli-*

---

[11] Letter 326. 1. Dr C. Mews is preparing an edition of the *Theologia Christiana* for *CCCM* in which he intends to review the evidence for the circulation of the *Theologia* in more than one version and William's claim to possess two versions.

[12] *PL* 180. 249–82.

[13] Déchanet, op. cit. On the possibility that William and Abelard had once been friends, see D. Luscombe, *The School of Peter Abelard* (Cambridge, 1969), p. 50 and notes.

[14] On the dating of William's writings and for a recent bibliography see T. M. Tomasic, 'William of St. Thierry against Peter Abelard: a dispute on the meaning of being a person', *An. Cist.*, 28 (1972), 3–76.

mus quaestionibus involutam suscepimus. He read the Fathers carefully as he tried to answer these questions;[15] it may be that he had obtained a copy of Abelard's commentary on Romans in the hope that it would help him,[16] and was sufficiently alarmed by what he found to seek out more of Abelard's works.

When he had had time to collect his forces, Bernard took action. He wrote a series of letters warning his friends, those in authority, especially in Rome itself (where William had suggested that Abelard had sympathizers)[17] and Abelard's former pupils, that they must be on their guard against his teachings. He exhorted Master Guido of Castello, who had been a pupil of Abelard, not to allow his love for his old master to blind him to his errors. Abelard is putting forward many blasphemous novelties, he says, novelties both of terms and of sense; he disputes about the faith in a manner which weighs against the faith; he attacks the law in the very words of the law. He believes that he sees nothing through a glass darkly, but beholds all things face to face. When he speaks of the Trinity, he sounds like Arius. When he speaks of grace he sounds like Pelagius. When he speaks of the Person of Christ, he sounds like Nestorius.[18] He wrote to Cardinal Ivo to warn him that Abelard is crossing the boundaries the Fathers had marked out, and teaching heresy in his discussions and writings about the faith, about the sacraments, about the Trinity.[19]

His most substantial arguments were put forward in a letter to Pope Innocent II.[20] Here he shows how successfully he had mastered the new ideas William had given him. Although he relies heavily on William's account for the identification and even for the analysis of Abelard's errors, he has been able to simplify and to throw into prominence those aspects of Abelard's teaching which seem to him to threaten the faith

[15] *PL* 180. 547A–B.
[16] See Peter Abelard, *Commentary on Romans*, ed. M. Buytaert *CCCM*, 11 (1969), 27–37, on the date of the commentary.
[17] Letter 326. 1, and see Luscombe, op. cit., ch. II.
[18] Letter 192, LTR VIII. 43–4.
[19] Letter 193, LTR VIII. 44–5.
[20] Letter 190, LTR VIII. 17–40.

most. He has replaced William's technical terminology with
expressions in common usage. He has placed the emphasis
where he himself thought it should lie, that is, upon Abelard's
teaching on redemption, rather than on Trinitarian problems.
He has, in short, made very sensible use of the aid William of
St. Thierry had given him, in framing his own case against
Peter Abelard, without necessarily having done much further
research on his own account. Bernard was consistent; as
theologian and polemicist, he concentrated not upon what
were technically or philosophically the central issues, but
upon what were the most prominent and notable matters,
those most likely to be discussed among the faithful.

We can best understand his approach, perhaps, by looking
first at the substance of what he has to say about redemption,
and then at his view of Abelard's misuse of reasoning. While
there is no doubt that William was profoundly influential in
forming Bernard's mind, in this matter as in others, the
essential Bernard shows through persistently in his approach
and in his reasoning.

IV. REDEMPTION, WILL, AND NECESSITY

Between 1128 and 1136, Bernard wrote a treatise for the
Knights Templar, which takes the form of a tour of the Holy
Places. At each one he stops and gives a short talk. After the
Temple, Bethlehem, Nazareth, Mount Olivet and the Vale of
Joshaphat, Jordan and Calvary, the pilgrims arrive at the Holy
Sepulchre. Among the Holy Places, this one holds pride of
place. It is hard to know, says Bernard, whether we ought to
feel more deeply when we contemplate the place where Jesus
lay in death, or when we think of his life.[1] Both his life and his
death were necessary for the good of man, and equally
necessary.[2] By living, Christ taught us to live, and by dying, he
made it safe for us to die.[3] More, by wiping out the effect of the
original sin which prevented us from living as we should, he
made it possible for us to follow his example of life.[4] Bernard

---

[1] LTR III. 229. 17–20. For a fuller discussion of this treatise, see pp. 24–30.
[2] LTR III. 230. 8.
[3] LTR III. 230. 8–9.
[4] LTR III. 230. 12.

thus sets side by side, equal in importance, the two reasons for God's becoming man which were being debated in the schools of the day. His life sets us an example for living; his death redeems us from death.[5]

Bernard's discussion of the question: *cur Deus Homo?* in his sermons and treatises adds up to a treatment of Incarnation and Redemption more comprehensive, if less fully worked out, than that of Anselm in the *Cur Deus Homo*. It reflects a detailed knowledge of the contemporary literature. It is not, except in certain points of emphasis, an original view, but it makes a considerable contribution in its attempt to reconcile views which seemed to many contemporaries contradictory, or, at best, alternatives. Above all, for our immediate purposes, it enables us to compare, outside the arena of the trial itself, the theological ground on which Bernard and Abelard stood when they met at Sens in 1140.

Why did God become man, living a human life on earth, and dying like any mortal? Since Anselm of Laon and his brother Ralph had explored the problem in their lectures and Anselm of Canterbury wrote his *Cur Deus Homo* in the 1090s, the topic had been attracting a new interest. A number of ideas had gained currency, and one question in particular had been hotly debated. When Adam and Eve consented to sin, they did so at the instigation of the Serpent. They gave themselves up into his hands. Did it therefore follow that the Devil had rights over man for which he was entitled to compensation if he lost them? To say that he did made it easy to explain why God became man. It would be unjust of God simply to take back man for himself from the Devil who was rightly his master, but if he paid the Devil a ransom he could justly make man his own again. This hypothesis removed the difficulty of explaining why an omnipotent God did not simply put right what had gone wrong by an act of will and make all as it had been before.[6]

Anselm of Canterbury found this explanation unsatisfactory because he could not accept that the Devil could be rightful

[5] LTR III. 229. 22–230. 1. Ailred of Rievaulx on *Jesus as a Boy*.
[6] See R. W. Southern, *St. Anselm and his Biographer* (Cambridge, 1963), pp. 85–7, 93–7, 358–61.

lord over those whom he had tricked into his service. He was a thief, and a thief has no right to the property he has stolen.[7] The litigants in this case are not as Hugh of St. Victor thought, God, man, and the Devil,[8] but only God and man. An offence has been committed against God by man, and the debt to be paid is due from man alone, and to God alone. God cannot simply forget the offence to his honour, or he would remain dishonoured, a thing unthinkable with God. Man cannot repay the debt himself; he is too weak and sinful. God cannot send an angel to repay, for two reasons. He would be man's saviour, and would therefore deserve man's grateful service for ever; that service must be restored to God, but he would in any case not be able to pay the debt because he has no part in human nature. He would not, in effect, 'stand for' man. Only God himself can pay the debt if man is to become his grateful servant. Only man himself can pay the debt if it is to be duly wiped out. The only solution which presents itself is the one which was in fact adopted. God became man and was able to pay the debt on behalf of the debtor.[9]

This explanation is elegant, but it gives a single, narrow reason for the Incarnation. It does not touch on the birth of Christ as an infant, his growing up in the world, his life and ministry. Although he had certainly read the *Cur Deus Homo*, Bernard saw this example of a perfect human life which Christ set, as of sufficient importance to be put beside his redemptive death as a reason for the Incarnation.

Peter Abelard seems to have been the chief advocate of the more extreme view that the example Christ set was to be regarded, not only as of equal importance with the act of redemption, but as constituting the real reason why God became man instead of redeeming man by a direct exercise of naked power. This view was set out in one of the 'sentences' or *quaestiones* with which Abelard's *Commentary on Romans* is interspersed.[10] Abelard is discussing Romans 3: 25. What does

[7] *Cur Deus Homo* I. vii, *Anselmi Opera Omnia*, II. 55–9.
[8] Hugh of St. Victor *De Sacramentis* I, viii, *PL* 176. 307–9.
[9] *Cur Deus Homo*, II. vi, *Anselmi Opera*, II. 101.
[10] See B. Smalley, *The Study of the Bible in the Middle Ages* (Oxford, 1952), pp. 66–82, on the beginning of the *quaestio*, and R. E. Weingart, *The Logic of Divine Love* (Oxford, 1970) on Abelard's development of the example theory.

the Apostle Paul mean by saying that we are justified by Christ's blood? 'First we must ask by what necessity God became man so as to redeem us by dying in the flesh, and from whom he redeemed us, who it was, in other words, who held us captive by right and by his power (*iustitia vel potestate*), and by what right he freed us from his power (*et qua iustitia nos ab eius potestate liberavit*).'[11] These were the parts of the question in its contemporary form.

Abelard works his way systematically through all the points of view that have been advanced in the debate on the subject. Firstly, it is said by some that Christ redeemed us from the power of the Devil, who has had rights over us since Adam sinned, and obeyed him of his own free will. No lord can take another's servant legitimately without his lord's consent. There can be no Devil's rights in the matter. Man sinned against God when he disobeyed him.[12] Thus far Abelard is with Anselm.

Abelard now insists that God could simply have forgiven man's sin, as he forgave many individual men before the crucifixion. He cites a number of Scriptural texts to demonstrate that this is so.[13] The only reason Abelard can conceive why God became man and suffered as he did was to show man how to live as he ought. If he had come solely to be crucified, surely God would have had a greater reason to be angry with man for ever because he had so brutally crucified his Son, than because he had eaten a single apple while he was in paradise?[14] We are made more righteous (*iustiores*) by Christ's death than we were before, because of the example Christ set us, kindling in us by his grace and generosity a zeal to imitate him.[15]

When William of St. Thierry drew Bernard's attention to Abelard's arguments he was stirred to anger. In Letter 190 to Innocent II he says that he has searched Abelard's 'book of sentences'[16] and his *Commentary on Romans*, and found him

---

[11] Peter Abelard, *Commentary on Romans*, ed. M. Buytaert, *CCCM*, 11 (1969), 113. 129–14. 134.

[12] *CCCM* XI. 114. 135–15. 175.

[13] Ibid., p. 115. 179–91.

[14] Ibid., p. 116. 210–14.

[15] Ibid., p. 117–18.

[16] Letter 190. v. 11, LTR VIII. 26. 10–4.

thus attacking the mystery of our Redemption. He recounts Abelard's teaching, and points to what he regards as the principal offence there: Abelard is saying that it was not to free man that God became man, but for some other reason. Bernard rails against him. He tries reason: if we agree that the world is the Devil's 'house' (John 14: 30; Luke 11: 21), and man his 'goods' (Matthew 12: 29), we cannot, surely, say that the Devil has no power over man? The Devil may have usurped his power, but God permitted him to keep it.[17] Man was lawfully delivered up to the Devil, and mercifully set free, in such a way that justice was manifested even in his liberation.[18]

In Letter 190 and in the treatise he wrote for the Templars, Bernard goes on to explore the question of the Redemption in terms which show how close his concerns were to St. Anselm's in the *Cur Deus Homo*, except for this significant difference over the Devil's rights. It was fitting, he says, for man's recovery to be brought about by an act of mercy on the part of his liberator, and for justice rather than power to be exerted against man's enemy. This emphasis on *convenientia* and *decentia* is to be found throughout the *Cur Deus Homo*. Anselm's ultimate test of the soundness of his arguments is their fittingness.[19] It is only the fittingness of the things which makes it intelligible that God should use so laborious a method, when a word from him or a single act of his will would have sufficed.[20]

Bernard had been reading Anselm. He borrows Anselm's image at the beginning of the *Cur Deus Homo* of a picture which has not been painted upon a solid base, but upon the air,[21] although he uses it for a different purpose: to emphasize the difference between an empty, listless following of Christ, and a process of purposeful following, until the Christian is embraced with solemn joy and then fed in a bliss of fullness of life. He speaks, as Anselm does, of the fact that the angels cannot be restored: *sciebat enim nullam angelis patere redeundi viam.*[22]

---

[17] Letter 190 v. 12–14.
[18] Letter 190. vi. 15.
[19] *Anselmi Opera*, II. 59. 8.
[20] Letter 190. viii. 19.
[21] Letter 190. ix. 25, and cf. *Anselmi Opera*, II. 51. 20–1.
[22] LTR IV. 164. 20–1, *Sermo Primus in Adventu Domini* I. v.

Bernard has something of his own to add, an almost dramatized picture of the events of the Redemption, in which he encourages his listener to put himself in God's place. In his first Sermon for Advent, he describes the scene for us. Adam and Eve offended specifically against the Son in their disobedience (*quod Filii Dei est . . . surripere tentant*). God the Father took the offence seriously because he loved the Son, and he punished man severely. This is a view quite different from that of Anselm, who thought the offence to God's honour was certainly not the Son in particular, but to the Godhead as one. 'What', asks Bernard, 'does the Son do', seeing the Father's zeal for him and how he is refusing to spare the offenders, and indeed the whole of creation is being affected? 'See', he says, 'the Father is casting off his creatures for my sake.' It was out of love for the Father that the Son entered upon his work of redemption. 'On my account he has lost many angels and all mankind', the Son continues, as he resolves, for love of the Father, to put things right.

What Bernard was trying to achieve in this singular reconstruction of events, was to present the facts in a way which would enable his simpler listeners to understand the force of the Son's desire to redeem the world. In a similar way, he paints a picture of the scene at the heavenly Council where the method of redemption was decided upon. 'A Council was assembled in the secret places of heaven, for the restoration of lost man.' To the Council came Mercy and Truth, to meet each other, for if mercy cannot meet truth it is not mercy but misery, and if truth does not come to meet mercy it is not truth but severity. As a result of their discussion, justice embraces peace, and the plan is made.[23]

Bernard wanted to drive home as forcefully as possible the hugeness of what was done, and the great need in which man stood. 'Who can doubt that there was some great cause that such majesty should deign to descend from so far, and into so lowly a place?' he asks. 'It was out of necessity', is his answer. The theme of 'necessity' is repeated.[24] This was no empty

---

[23] *Sententiae* III. 23, LTR VI^2. 80.
[24] *Sermo in Adv.* 7. 2, LTR IV. p. 196. 9–10. 'Necessarius proinde salvatoris adventus, necessaria sic praeoccupatis hominibus praesentia Christi.'

nativity, or fruitless demeaning of himself on God's part.[25]
Three things in particular compelled the Lord Jesus Christ, he
says, to undergo the Cross and the ignominy of death; a pure
filial obedience, a *compassibilis et communis miseria*, and the
certain victory over the Devil.[26] Where Anselm thought in
terms of God's having raised the humanity in Christ to one
with his divinity, Bernard was speaking for his own contemporaries in talking of the 'descent' and humiliation involved.
He insists that so startling an act, so extreme a departure from
immutability into mutability, as God's becoming man, could
only be accounted for by a compelling necessity. The discussions Christians and Jews had been holding in recent decades
had perhaps brought more sharply into focus the astonishing
nature of what had been done in order to save mankind. It was
a great stumbling-block to Jewish converts that they were
obliged to accept that God descended from his height above
creation and became man. Gilbert Crispin's Jew of Mainz made
much of the matter.[27]

Anselm of Canterbury placed the 'necessity' involved in the
overriding importance of bringing the universe back to its right
order (*rectus orde*). Only when God's honour was restored and
man was made again a being fit for heaven, could God's plan be
carried out. Abelard, says Bernard, answers the question 'Why
did God redeem the world by so laborious a method, when a
word from him, or an act of his will would have done?' by
distinguishing between 'need', 'necessity' and 'reason'. The
'need' was man's and the angels', too, and also God's. The
angels needed perfected men to make up their depleted ranks
and fill the spaces left by the fallen angels. God himself needed
to take action to fulfil the purpose of his will. The 'necessity',
however, is man's not God's. It is we men, not God himself,
who were sitting in darkness. The 'Reason' for the Incarnation
was simply the pleasure of the good doer of the deed.[28] Exactly
this question of necessity is raised by Anselm in the *Cur Deus
Homo* where he examines how God can be said to have been

---

[25] LTR IV. 198. 13, *In Vigil Nativ.* 1.2.
[26] LTR VI². 24, Sent. II. 4.
[27] *Serm. in Adv.* I. 7, LTR IV, 166. 16–17.
[28] *Serm. in Adv.* I. 8, LTR IV. 167. 5–7.

under necessity on man's account, without himself being compelled.[29]

In the treatise for the Templars, Bernard speaks of the willingness of God to redeem the world, and of the operation of his will in general. How do we know that Christ can forgive sins or remit them (*possit peccata dimittere*)? We know that God exists, and that he can do whatever he wills (*quidquid vult potest*). This is apparent from the miracles he performs (works which no one else can do) and from what the Prophets tell us. We know, too, that it is God against whom our sins are committed, for we pray daily: 'Against thee alone have I sinned' (Job 19: 27). Who can better remit our sins than he against whom they are committed? God is certainly able to forgive, for he can do everything, and therefore we may be sure that Christ can do so. We are left with the further question: does he wish to do so? Here again, the facts speak for themselves. Christ took our flesh and submitted himself voluntarily to death. Therefore we can agree that he could, in his deity, forgive sins, and that he did, in his humanity, actually do so.[30] In this straightforward manner, Bernard encompasses the philosophical problems Anselm raises about will and necessity at a simple level, and explains their part in the work of redemption.

He has more to say on the subject in the discussion of human free choice and the 'necessity' of divine foreknowledge, predestination and grace, at which we have already glanced in the *De Gratia et Libero Arbitrio*. Bernard approaches the problem by first examining *libertas* and then asking in what sense it may be constricted or overruled by necessity. He distinguishes three *libertates* possible to man: freedom from sin, freedom from wretchedness, freedom from necessity. The first is possible in the natural state of man; the second is possible since man was restored by grace in redemption. The third will be realized only in heaven.[31] Bernard explores the

---

[29] *In Vigil. Nativ.* 1. 2, LTR IV. 198. 13.

[30] The most famous of these was Gilbert Crispin's *Disputatio Judei cum Christiano*, ed. B. Blumenkranz (Antwerp, 1956) 'Quod ergo ex deitate constat illum potuisse, ex humanitate innotuit et voluisse.'

[31] Blumenkrantz, p. 43.

difference between these freedoms of nature, grace, and glory, so as to make their character clear.

Then he turns to a passage in John's Gospel: *Si vos Filius liberavit, vere liberi estis* (John 8: 36). If man possesses *liberum arbitrium* how can he be said to need a *liberator*? How can the Son make 'truly free' what is free already? Bernard suggests that the Son frees the will, in the sense of freeing it from wretchedness (*miseria*), and that that wretchedness is something it had run into freely and voluntarily (*tam libere quam voluntarie corruerat*), by sinning. This *miseria*, a penalty of sin, is borne unwillingly by man. Man's *liberator* bears it willingly in becoming man himself, and therefore he puts himself voluntarily under the law of wretchedness, not, like man, involuntarily. So he is *liber inter miseros*, free among the wretched.[32] We can begin to see how Bernard's distinction helps him to make a difference between will and necessity, so that he is never obliged to admit the will itself to be compelled, but can nevertheless encompass necessity within his system.

The implications of his arguments become clearer as we look at his discussion of the *libertas a necessitate* man will enjoy in heaven. He poses the problem in the form of a *quaestio*: what is to be proved is that freedom from wretchedness and freedom from necessity are equally present in perfected souls in heaven and in the angels, just as they are in God and in Christ. Bernard wants to show that 'freedom from necessity' is in all rational creatures and is neither lost nor diminished by sin or wretchedness, that it is not greater in the righteous than in the sinner, nor fuller in the angel than in the man. It will not be fully realized this side of heaven, because of the clouding effects of wretchedness, but the freedom of the will from necessity is already present, intact, in every man. Bernard points out that the angel or man who chooses evil does so freely, by an act of will, and cannot be said to be compelled to sin by any force outside himself: *sua utique voluntate ductum, non aliunde coactum ut malus sit*. He persists in evil by his own will, not *alieno impulsu*, not driven to it by another, and so freedom of choice remains even where there is captivity of the mind in the bonds of sin (*captivitas mentis*).[33]

---

[32] Letter 190. viii. 19.
[33] *Cur Deus Homo* I. ix, *Anselmi Opera* II. 64.

Again, Bernard is trying to resolve an apparent paradox, as he had done in the case of the Gospel statement that man, already free in his will, is truly freed only by the redeeming work of Christ the liberator. Again, he makes the attempt by scrutinizing closely what is really meant by liberty. Men complain, he says, that they want to do good and cannot, and that it seems to them that they are compelled by some 'necessity' to choose evil. What they are really saying, Bernard asserts, is that they lack the first *libertas* (*a peccato*); because they cannot get free of sin they think they have no freedom at all, but they are willing something good in wanting to do good; it is clear that they are free to will good. They have merely lost the power to put their will to right use in action.[34] If for the moment man is not free of the wretchedness of sin, nevertheless in the meantime his *libertas arbitrii* remains *plena* and *integra*, full and whole.[35] After further demonstration, Bernard declares 'I think this is clearly shown (*aperte monstratum*), that this very liberty is retained throughout captivity in some way: *quod haec ipsa tamen libertas tamdiu quodammodo captiva tenetur.*[36] The work of redemption is to bring man a stage nearer his full liberty by saving him from sin and wretchedness.

Since the redemption of the world, divine grace has been at work in men co-operating with the free will of man to enable him to will the good more fully and effectively. Bernard describes this process most graphically in his *De Conversione*. At the time of the Council of Sens, when Bernard was in Paris, he gave a talk which seems to have taken the form of a public lecture. His future biographer Geoffrey heard him, and Peter Lombard, both of them at the time pupils of Hugh of St. Victor. The audience was a large and eager one (*tam avide concursio occurrit*).[37] Bernard addressed himself to these scholars by appealing to them in pictures. God converts the heart, he says, by illuminating it, laying the book of conscience before the mind's eye with the page open and a spotlight upon it. The man can see for himself how wicked he is, how wrapped up

---

[34] LTR III. 231–2.
[35] *Gra* III. 6, LTR III. 170. 13–35.
[36] *Gra* III. 8, LTR III. 172. 1–7.
[37] *Gra* IV. 9, LTR III. 172. 13–26.

in the pleasures of his senses. God's grace does not compel. It merely makes plain to the reason how the will ought to respond.[38] He describes the stages by which, once man begins to co-operate willingly with grace, God is able to bring him to the state he intends for him, and complete his redemption, and make him free of necessity at last.

Bernard's teaching on Incarnation and Redemption, piecemeal though it is, is both consistent and comprehensive. He had ample opportunity to hear reports of what was being taught in the schools, through his correspondence with Hugh of St. Victor, and with William of St. Thierry, who had been reading Abelard, and through his travels in northern France, preaching in Paris and elsewhere and talking to students and masters. No doubt Geoffrey of Auxerre, who became his secretary in 1145, was able to help him with an account of more recent work, but Bernard was not dependent on their assistance. Already in his earliest treatise, the *De Gradibus Humilitatis*, he was writing about the example Christ had set by his death, of the necessity which brought it about, of the example of a perfect human life he had given as a model.[39]

Bernard did not attempt to compose a treatise on the theology of the Redemption. Characteristically, he preferred to diffuse his views in his preaching, trying to bring his listeners to a vivid apprehension of certain aspects of the matter. He showed them the importance of what was at stake, the greatness of what had been done, the divine generosity which combined so many benefits in a single act of redemptive love, but his own grasp of the principles and his own view of the points of current controversy was exact. He had thought out his position fully, on the basis of a thorough knowledge of contemporary discussion.

V. THE ABUSE OF REASON

Bernard's principal accusation against Abelard himself is that he is nothing more than a dialectician turned theologian, that he allows his imagination as free a rein in interpreting Holy Scripture as he once did in devising logical difficulties and

---

[38] *Gra* IV. 10, LTR III. 173. 5–6.
[39] LTR III. 21–2.

resolving them. He is trying to reawaken false opinions long ago condemned by the Church and silenced. Some of these are his own views, novel heresies, which he is adding to the catalogue of ancient heresies. He thinks himself entitled to apply his mind to anything, in heaven or on earth and try to give a reason for it.[1]

In the *De Gradibus Humilitatis* Bernard gives almost as much space to *curiositas*, the pursuit of knowledge which does not lie on the road to salvation, as he does to the other eleven degrees of pride together. Whether or not that reflects the importance it had in Bernard's mind, there can be no doubt that he felt it dangerous. Abelard, Bernard complains, thinks it right and possible for him to make every mystery intelligible;[2] he thinks that every point of doctrine is open to reason,[3] and so he seeks to understand in a spirit of *curiositas* what it is only necessary for the faithful soul to believe.

His ways of doing this were not necessarily misconceived in themselves, but they had the disadvantage of allowing room for *curiositas*. Like Anselm, he laid himself open to attack by using analogies which his enemies were able to show to be unorthodox in their implications if they were pressed too far. In the analogy which gave rise to the controversy surrounding the *De Incarnatione Verbi*, Anselm had compared the Trinity to a man of whom it may be said that he is 'white' and 'just' and 'literate' without the listener believing that there are three men.[4] He had meant the image to serve that purpose and no more. He had not meant to imply that the Persons were in fact one in that way, but merely to show how we use language in ordinary circumstances to speak of 'many' (*plures*) when we mean 'one'.[5] Abelard had tried to throw light upon the relationship between the Father and the Son by saying that the Son was to the Father rather as a *species* is to a *genus* ('man' to 'animal', for example) or as a seal made of brass is to the brass

---

[1] Letter 190. i. 1.

[2] Letter 190. i. 2.

[3] In Anselm, however, there is always a concomitant and balancing awareness of the mystery and inaccessibility of God. *Anselmi Opera Omnia* I. 98. 1–15.

[4] Ibid. I. 282. 14–15.

[5] Ibid. I. 283. 5–6.

from which it is made. He was trying to understand what is implied by saying that the Son is begotten of the Father, in what respects that might mean that the Father was the ultimate source of whatever is found in the son.

Bernard seizes upon this analogy. Abelard is trying to 'grade' the Persons of the Trinity, saying that the Father is full power, the Son some power, the Holy Spirit no power at all.[6] He rages. This is worse than Arius. Who can endure it? Who will not close his ears to such sacrilegious words? Whose hackles will not rise at such profane novelties of both word and sense?[7] Bernard is attacking not only the particular novelty of the analogy of the brazen seal, which is 'horrifying'[8] enough, but the whole of Abelard's theological method with it, his attitudes and assumptions, his lack of decent modesty in the face of divine mysteries.

Bernard's technique as a polemicist had its positive and its negative aspects. He ridicules Abelard for failing to construct an argument which will stand up to scrutiny even in his own technical terms; and he puts forward positive alternatives to Abelard's views, so as to throw him into confusion by the contrast. These are exactly Anselm's devices and he employs them both in the *De Incarnatione Verbi*. He shows that Roscelin's argument is nonsense by outwitting him on his own ground of dialectic,[9] and he proposes a series of fresh arguments of his own to explain several points of doctrine concerning the Trinity. Bernard does not display Anselm's consummate skill as a dialectician when he tries to do the same, but he makes a fair attempt to put his finger on the weakness in Abelard's argument by using ridicule. Abelard is saying, for example, that the Holy Spirit proceeds from the Father and the Son, but not from the substance of the Father and the Son. What are the alternatives? Bernard asks. Does the Holy Spirit come from nothing, like created things? But even they are from God (Romans 11: 36). Does he come from God, then, but in the manner of a created thing? Can Abelard

---

[6] Letter 190. 1. 2. LTR VIII. 18. 20–1.

[7] LTR VIII. 18. 24–5.

[8] M. Buytaert discusses the *Capitula Haeresum* of Peter Abelard in his edition, *CCCM* XII. 466.

[9] *Anselmi Opera Omnia* II. 6. 5–10. 17 on the *dialectici haeretici*.

produce an alternative mode of the Holy Spirit's proceeding, other than the orthodox view that he proceeds from the substance of the Father and the Son?[10] He faces Abelard with a choice. He must either confess the consubstantiality of the Holy Spirit with the Father and the Son, or he must concede that he is an Arian, deny the consubstantiality of the Spirit, and say that he is created. Triumphant in his certainty that he has put Abelard into a corner by his reasoning, Bernard adds support to his case by appealing to the Fathers, in case it may seem that he himself is relying upon human reason alone.[11] Bernard regarded the questions Abelard was raising as 'battles of words' (*pugnae verborum*), full of innovations of expression (*novitates . . . vocum*); he himself proposes to keep to the *sententiae Patrum*, setting their opinions side by side and employing their words rather than his own. 'For we are not wiser than our Fathers', he says.[12]

Bernard had nothing to say against reason in itself. He held that reason was the highest faculty God had given man; the respect in which he resembles the angels and God himself is in being a rational creature. Bernard taught that a rational creature ought to 'love itself' in the sense that it seeks to be blessed, and that it ought to love God because it sees that it is through God alone that it could be blessed. Because it is rational it will understand the reasonableness of Christ's summary of the commandments, and its purpose.[13] William of St. Thierry has a good deal to say about this right use of reason in his Golden Epistle to the brothers of Mont-Dieu. He defines reason as Augustine does in his *De Immortalitate Animae*, as a gazing of the spirit, by which it looks upon the truth, not with bodily eyes, but by means of truth itself, contemplating the truth, as it were, in the truth.[14] The process of reasoning is that by which the reason conducts its search, directing its gaze through all the things available for it to look upon.[15] Thus reasoning is the seeker and reason the finder; reason is both the

---

[10] Letter 190. 1. 2. LTR VIII. 18–9.
[11] Letter 190. 1. 3, LTR VIII. 20. 7.
[12] LTR VII. 184. 17–20.
[13] *Sent.* II.1, LTR VI². 23.
[14] Golden Epistle, II. iv. 203, cf. Augustine, *De Immortalitate Animae* 6. 10.
[15] Golden Epistle. II. iv. 204, cf. Augustine, *De Quantitate Animae* 27.53.

instrument of the search and what is found. Right reason, then, is directed towards divine truth in an act of contemplation. Peter Abelard's reason is directed, as it should be, to the search for truth, but his reasoning has somehow become merely human and lost contact with the divine.

This miscarriage of reasoning has not taken place as a direct result of Abelard's concentration upon the technical skills of the liberal arts. In one of the sermons on the Song of Songs Bernard discussed ignorance, and the ways in which the study of various arts can help to repair it. Not all arts are directly helpful to salvation. The practical arts of the carpenter or mason, useful as they are in this world, are not skills which must be mastered if there is to be no impediment to salvation, Bernard promises. Even without the knowledge of the liberal arts men have been saved. This *etiam absque*, arch though it is, shows that Bernard thought the liberal arts more important than the practical ones.[16] Indeed, he is anxious to reassure his listeners that he is not intending to undervalue the study of letters or to prohibit it: *Videar forsitan nimius in suggillatione scientiae, et quasi reprehendere doctos, ac prohibere studia litterarum. Absit*, he cries, 'perish the thought'. He knows well enough how they have aided and benefited the Church, those *literati* who have mastered the arts of language, and used them either in the defence of the faith, or in the instruction of simple men.[17] Bernard takes the view that knowledge is like food: it is good for those who make sensible use of it. The key to salutary study is to concentrate upon that which is *maturius ad salutem*, to be zealous for that which kindles the love of God, and to study not for vainglory or out of curiosity but for the edification of the student and his neighbour.[18] Abelard's error has been to allow his curiosity to get the better of him, to seek glory and fame as a dialectician and, worse, as a theologian. He has abused his reason and he has abused his technical skills.

VI. TWO VIEWS OF BERNARD'S LEARNING

At the Council of Sens where he was brought at last to give account of himself, Abelard's defiance gave way to a faltering

---

[16] *SS* 36. i. 1, LTR II. 3. 22–3.
[17] *SS* 36. i. 2, LTR II. 4. 14–17
[18] *SS* 36. i. 3, LTR II. 5. 21.

defence, and he was condemned. He declared that he would make an appeal to Rome, and set out for Italy, where Bernard's letters to Innocent had preceded him. Peter the Venerable received him at Cluny on his journey and was able to persuade him to stay and become a monk there. He was successful, too, in convincing Abelard that he should retract anything in his teaching in which he was in error or had gone too far. Abelard and Bernard met and amicable relations were established. Abelard died at Cluny after a short period of what is reported to have been exemplary monastic life. He was not perhaps a broken man—there was evidently still fire in him after Sens—but he had, at least for a time, lost his fighting spirit. That had happened before and he had recovered it, but now he was ageing and ill, and he did not live long enough to consider his position afresh and perhaps return to the world.[1]

Some of his followers and former pupils were deeply upset by his apparent collapse, and it would have been surprising if none of them had spoken out, and accused Bernard and his party of foul practice.

Abelard had a most vociferous defender in Berengar of Poitiers, one of his younger pupils, who maintained that he spoke: *Catholica mente*, and that in his arguments he put forward the faith with ardour: *Christiana disputatione arden-ter et impigre declarabit.*[2] He himself had been made the victim of ill-treatment by Bernard's supporters, he claims, because he had spoken on behalf of Abelard. In a letter written to the bishop of Mende, he begs him to correct his flock, who bleat at Berengar as though he were a threat to them. 'I am not a marauding wolf', he complains, 'but a dog protecting the sheep.'[3] Berengar's accusers say that he is a 'beast' and ought not to touch the 'holy mountain' who is St. Bernard, and that he is no fit opponent for such a theologian: *non a te theologum*

---

[1] On the condemnation of Sens and the date of the Council, see J. G. Sikes, *Peter Abailard* (Cambridge, 1932), pp. 229–31, and D. E. Luscombe, *The School of Peter Abelard* (Cambridge, 1969, repr. 1970), pp. 103–42.

[2] *PL* 178. 1862D, On Berengar, see E. Gilson, *The Mystical Theology of St. Bernard*, tr. A. H. C. Downes (London, 1940), pp. 167–9, and D. Luscombe, *The School of Peter Abelard*, pp. 29–48.

[3] *PL* 178. 1871C.

talem argui oportebat.[4] Berengar defends himself; he has shown, not more effrontery than Bernard, but rather less:

Audet in litteris, audeo et ego.
Audet in theologicis, audeo et ego.
Audet in fide, audeo et ego.
Audet in sanctitate, hic non audeo.[5]

'I have bitten, I say, not the contemplative but the philosopher, not the confessor (of the faith), but the writer; not the mind but the tongue.'

Berengar said that it was as though Bernard had put his hands about Abelard's throat and throttled him before his voice could be heard (*vocem eius sine audientia strangulaverat*).[6] Berengar wrote an *Apologeticus*, denouncing Bernard and his fellow-bishops and abbots. In it he depicted Abelard's accusers as drunken fools, tossing about patristic quotations as though they were *bons mots* to be enjoyed after a good dinner.[7]

Berengar later found his book an embarrassment, and wrote a confused retraction, half apologetic, half defensive,[8] but he was, nevertheless, the only eye-witness to perceive clearly the contrasting methods of the two antagonists and describe them for us. In his satire he mocks a mode of disputation which he recognizes to be perfectly acceptable in the right circumstances, and in which he would have expected Bernard to show himself a master. His point is that Bernard has failed to live up to his reputation. His approach to Bernard's conduct of the trial suggests that Bernard's contemporaries regarded him as an educated man of a particular sort, not a dialectician but a man of letters.

The *Apologeticus* belongs to a genre of contemporary writing which became popular as controversies began to arise out of the more advanced study of grammar and dialectic in the schools. The expert is attacked for his incompetence in his own field of expertise, just as Anselm of Canterbury, for example, had pointed out technical errors of dialectic in the arguments of Roscelin of Compiègne.[9] Berengar addresses

---

[4] *PL* 178. 1872B.
[5] *PL* 178. 1872A.
[6] *PL* 178. 1872B.
[7] *PL* 178. 1858.
[8] *PL* 178. 1871–4.
[9] *Anselmi Opera Omnia*, II. 6–10

himself to Bernard's failings in the skill for which he is most renowned: that of composition. It would be fruitless to accuse Bernard of dialectical *faux pas* in making his case against Abelard, when he was not arguing as a dialectician. Berengar attacks Bernard's inadequacies as an advocate who relies upon the elegance of his language to win the goodwill of his listeners, rather than upon the validity of his argument.

It is, he says, the more to be wondered at that Bernard should prove so inadequate in this respect, since he is known to have composed little ribald songs (*cantiunculas mimicas et urbanos modulos*) from his earliest youth.[10] 'No doubt it has also slipped your memory', jeers Berengar, speaking directly to Bernard, 'that you always strove to outdo your brothers in a rhythmic contest (*rhythmico certamine*), and in versatility of witty invention (*acutaeque inventionis versutia*).' Berengar's satire, and his attack upon Bernard as a whole, depends for its effectiveness upon this story's being known to many of his listeners.

Berengar examines Bernard's literary faults in detail. In his *Apologeticus* he says that he has been reading the *Sermons* on the Song of Songs which Bernard has been publishing. He is struck by two things: the modesty and lowliness of Bernard's style (*utitur sane mediocri et temperato genere dicendi*) when the book on which he is writing demands something much finer,[11] and Bernard's arrogance in adding to the existing series of commentaries. 'If secrets were revealed to you which escaped [previous commentators]', he says, 'I would heartily applaud your work, but when I turn over their expositions with your commentary in my hands, I find you have said nothing new. Your *explanatio* seems to me, therefore, to be utterly empty (*supervacua*).'[12] Bernard had done nothing but 'plough' his way earnestly along in the furrow made by his betters, looking for anything they may have missed.[13] Thus Bernard's achievement falls short at the two points most noticeable to a grammarian or a rhetorician. His exposition lacks inventiveness and it is stylistically unworthy.

[10] *PL* 178. 1857A.
[11] *PL* 178. 1863B.
[12] *PL* 178. 1863B.
[13] *PL* 178. 1863D.

Bernard has failed, too, to take acount of the structure of the whole and the need to ensure homogeneity; he has not paid attention to the unities. Berengar singles out a sermon in which Bernard breaks off the sequence of his exposition to speak about one of his monks who has recently died. He 'brings his dead to the wedding', and thus introduces a wholly inappropriate note into the writing: *tragoedia risum procerit nuptiarum*.[14] 'We laugh at pictures which begin with a man and end in an ass', says Berengar, quoting the opening of Horace's *Ars Poetica*, a favourite quotation of contemporary authors, with its depiction of a centaur, an image of a man joined to a horse.[15] 'The whole *Ars Poetica* is up in arms against you', cries Berengar.[16] He elaborates the point at length, showing in how many ways Bernard has offended against the canons of fine writing, how he has failed to distinguish the genres of composition clearly,[17] and in every way shown himself inept in the art of composition for which he was once so famous. Berengar believes that the skills of the grammarian-poet are applicable in writing of every kind, secular or spiritual. Bernard has offended, not in failing to write as he should for his monks but in failing to write as he should as an author with a classical education.

Berengar's point is that Bernard has shown himself nothing but a charlatan, a vain and empty pretender to skills he does not possess.[18] Bernard's technical skills were undoubtedly modest in comparison with those of Abelard himself, especially in dialectic, but it is clear from what has gone before that even had he been equipped by natural ability and training to match himself closely with Abelard, Bernard would have used dialectic with restraint. It was only too easy to be led by reasoning into a potentially controversial position. In one of his Prayers William of St. Thierry puts forward the view that God provides something for the mind to fix upon so that contemplation will not fail, but have an object. He does not see at once what this object can be, and where he is to look for it. If

[14] *PL* 178. 1863–4.
[15] *PL* 178. 1864A.
[16] Ibid.
[17] *PL* 178. 1865A.
[18] *PL* 178. 1858.

it is God himself, there seems to be no 'place' to which he can direct his gaze in contemplation. If he looks for God on earth he gazes in the wrong direction. If he looks for him in heaven and tries to visualize him 'beautiful indeed, and yet corporeal' he makes the same mistake as if he looked for him on earth, because he is attempting to make him 'local'. To look for God 'in' a place is absurd, but even to look for him 'outside' a place is unsatisfactory, because that is, in effect, to exclude him from a place, when he is everywhere. William's dilemma may be summed up in his own words: 'If I envisage any form at all for you, my God, or anything which has a form, I turn myself into an idolater.' William's solution is to remember Jesus's state-ment that he 'dwells in' the Father. Here is a 'location' of the Son in the Father.[19] From this, William is able to deduce that the 'place' of God is his consubstantiality, and thus to provide himself with a focal point for his contemplation. Had Abelard suggested that the consubstantiality of the Trinity is a 'location' William would have looked on the statement with suspicion, perhaps; but he arrives at it himself by a process of close reasoning based on Scriptural texts, and he finds nothing in it to trouble him.

Again, in the *Aenigma Fidei*, William takes up a knotty question and finds a solution which is by no means uncon-troversial. He is trying to understand how God may be three and one. If he is three, 'three what?' (*quid tres?*). He suggests that the Persons may be seen as a 'sort-of-something', rather like the *quasi aliquid* of Anselm's solution of the problem of evil in the *De Casu Diaboli*.[20] *Etsi res sicut est non diceretur, non omnino tamen taceretur.*[21] 'Even if the reality cannot be spoken of, yet let something be said'. William is suggesting that we must, for practical purposes, say something of the Trinity which is not strictly accurate.

Over against Berengar's hostile account of Bernard's prowess as a scholar we must set the assessment of another opponent, Peter the Venerable, Abbot of Cluny, who was a man of most

[19] William of St. Thierry *Prayer*.
[20] *Anselmi Opera Omnia* I. 248–9
[21] *PL* 180. 413A, and see O. Brooke, 'The Speculative Development of the Trinitarian Theology of William of St. Thierry in the *Aenigma Fidei*', *Recherches de théologie ancienne et médiévale*, 28 (1961), 36.

judicious mind, and later a friend of Bernard's. About 1127 Peter wrote his open letter to Bernard, in which he defended his own monks against a number of accusations made by the Cistercians: that they permitted themselves a luxury and laxity of life which was quite foreign to the spirit of the Rule. Peter writes in no acrimonious spirit, but as one anxious to clear up misunderstandings with a fair-minded opponent whose cultivated judgement he can rely upon.[22] Bernard is, he says, a man of learning, not only in the secular field (*eruditio saecularium*) but also, and equally (*pariter*) in the *scientia divinarum litterarum* which is so much more profitable (*longe utilius*). He has left behind the 'Egypt' of secular scholarship, but he has carried off its spoils, and he is so laden with these treasures, and with the wealth of the Hebrews, too, that he is able like a rich man to supply the needs of the poor.[23] Peter's compliment is conventional, but he clearly felt that Bernard could hold his own as an educated man in any company. Certainly Bernard's letters and personal interventions in succeeding decades show that he could make use of technical principles of law.[24] The library at Clairvaux had a number of manuscripts of canon law in the twelfth century, including Ivo of Chartres's *Panormia* and an early twelfth-century copy of Justinian's *Digest* and the little-known *Summa Codicis*.[25] It is not impossible that these were collected at Bernard's request, perhaps as a result of conversations he had with jurists of Pisa and Bologna about 1135 when he first began to move in the circles of higher European politics. Again, the practical side of Bernard's thinking shows itself. He liked his learning to be useful.

Berengar's satire suggests that it was well understood where Bernard's strength lay. To a natural capacity for eloquence, a natural fluency of expression, his early education had added a stock of classical allusions, a rich vocabulary, and a facility in

---

[22] Letter 28, Constable, I. 52–101 and II. 270–4.
[23] Constable. I. 53.
[24] *Hum.* iv. 14, *Csi* iv. 14; *Mal.* viii. 17, *Dil.* xiii. 36; *Epp.* 307, 102, 409, 390, and see B. Jacqueline, 'Bernard et le droit romain', *BC*, pp. 429–33.
[25] Jacqueline, op. cit., and on the *Summa Codicis*, see E. H. Fitting; *Summa Codicis des Irnerius* (Berlin, 1894) and H. Kantorowicz, *Studies on the glossators of the Roman Law* (Cambridge, 1938), who attributes it to Rogerius.

putting forward a clear argument. Bernard was a man with a classical education; without hesitation, he took the best of what it had to offer him into his work as a preacher and a Christian apologist. He himself declared his position, and we might give him the last word. He contrasts the experience of God which is the monk's learning, with the learning of the schools: *sub umbris arborum senseris quale numquam didicisses in scholis.* 'You may experience under the shade of the trees what you never learned at school.'[26]

VII. GILBERT OF POITIERS

Otto of Freising contrasts the trial of Peter Abelard at Sens in 1140 with that of Gilbert of Poitiers at Rheims in 1148: *Nec eadem causa nec similis erat materia.*[1] He compares not only the issues, but also the two great masters against whom Bernard fought, as he believed, for the security of the souls of faithful Christians who were in danger of being led astray.[2] Bernard was not successful at Rheims, as he had been at Sens, in carrying all before him so that opinion turned decisively against the accused.[3] Pope Eugenius accepted Gilbert's recantation gladly, and sent him back to his diocese with honour (*honoris plenitudine*)[4] 'Whether the abbot of Clairvaux was deceived like a mere man, out of the frailty of human weakness, or the bishop escaped the proposed judgement of the Church by cunning concealment . . . it is not for us to discuss or to judge', comments Otto.[5]

At Sens, Bernard had been guided in putting together his case by the list of *capitula* provided by his friend and admirer William of St. Thierry,[6] who pointed out to him where Abelard was in error, and provided a commentary upon his main points

---

[26] *PL* 195. 501–2. Letter to Aelred, and see E. Gilson, 'Sub umbris arborum', *Mediaeval Studies*, 14 (1952), 149–51.

[1] Otto of Freising, *Gesta Friderici*, I, 53, ed. F. J. Schmalc (Darmstadt, 1965), p. 236. 15–16.

[2] Ibid., I. 53; p. 235.

[3] Ibid., I. 53; pp. 236–8.

[4] Ibid., I. 56.

[5] Ibid., I. 57.

[6] *PL* 184. 249–82.

so that Bernard would understand their implications fully.[7]
When Bernard was preparing for the trial of Gilbert of Poitiers
he was helped by the Premonstratensian abbot, Godescalc of
St. Martin, who drew up a list of four points for him, and
searched out patristic quotations which would support his
case. The importance of Godescalc's contribution in providing
a framework for the trial has often been overlooked. His
capitula remained the principal points under discussion
throughout the trial and afterwards; he put his finger upon
several major questions raised by Gilbert's complex and often
obscure teaching.

Among the accounts of the trial, those of Bernard's new
secretary Geoffrey of Auxerre, John of Salisbury, who was at
that time in the service of Theobald, archbishop of Canterbury,
and Otto of Freising, a former Cistercian, present events from
different points of view. Geoffrey's sympathies are entirely
with Bernard. Otto, too, presents Gilbert as a heretic and a
villain, but with the aid of a technically detailed account of the
issues in which he displays his own capacities as a scholar.
John is more judicious. He finds it hard to believe that the
master whose lectures he had himself heard, and the bishop of
whose piety he had come to think highly, could be working
actively against the faith and trying to undermine sound
doctrine.[8] It is Geoffrey who tells us of Godescalc's part in the
affair, and shows us how it appeared to Bernard himself. It is,
therefore, from his account that we can perhaps best approach
Bernard's own thinking.

Geoffrey made his first journey with Bernard (as his
secretary) in 1145. They went to Toulouse, passing through
Poitiers, where they met Gilbert, and perhaps his two

[7] It was upon William's list that Bernard based his letters to churchmen
pointing out the dangers of Abelard's teaching: Letters 187, 188, 189, 190, 192,
193, etc.

[8] John of Salisbury, *Historia Pontificalis*, ed. M. Chibnall, NMT (London,
1956), p. 27. On John's career at this time, see *The Letters of John of Salisbury*,
ed. C. N. L. Brooke, NMT (London, 1955), and A. Saltman *Theobald,
Archbishop of Canterbury, University of London*, 2 (London, 1956). On
Godescalc, see, too, N. Backmund, *Die mittelalterlichen Geschichtsschreiber
des Prämonstratenserordens, Bibl. analectorum Praemonstratensium*, 10
(Averbode, 1972). On the Council of Rheims, see H. C. van Elswijk, *Gilbert
Porreta, Spicilegium Sacrum Lovaniense*, 33 (1966), pp. 77–124 and on
Godescalc, pp. 42 and 110.

archdeacons, Calo and Master Arnald who was known for his humourlessness and bore the name Qui-non-Ridet.[9] In 1146, Gilbert held a synod at Poitiers. During a sermon preached at this time, he made some remarks on the Trinity to which Arnald made public objection. The circumstances brought the conflict in the cathedral Chapter at Poitiers to public notice.

Geoffrey describes the way in which the unsmiling archdeacon Arnald brought about Gilbert's trial, in a letter written many years later to Cardinal Albinus of Albano, when Geoffrey himself was in extreme old age. (Albinus knew that Geoffrey had been a student in Paris at the time of Abelard's trial and that he had been an eyewitness of the trial of Gilbert, and he approached him as the best living witness to be had of the events of the 1140s.)[10] Geoffrey reports that archdeacon Arnald appealed to Rome for a judgement on Gilbert's teaching. Eugenius suggested that they both submit themselves to him for arbitration at Viterbo.[11] When he had heard them debate their differences before him, he was unable to reach a decision, so he ordered them to present themselves again in Paris at Easter, 1147. On this occasion, Bernard was present.[12]

An 'inquisition' was to be made upon Gilbert's exposition of the theological treatises of Boethius. These short works had long been neglected because they appeared obscure and difficult. Their author himself says that he has deliberately made one of them, the *De Hebdomadibus*, difficult to understand, so that only those worthy to do so should penetrate to the truth it contained.[13] The *opuscula* became more popular as texts to be lectured on in the schools as the advances of the early twelfth century in the study of dialectic made them more intelligible. Thierry of Chartres commented upon them at the same time as Gilbert, but in a relatively straightforward manner, with the intention of helping his

[9] *PL* 185, 313B, *VP* III. vi. 17.

[10] The letter appears to have been written in the 1090s. See N. M. Häring's edition of Geoffrey of Auxerre's writings against Gilbert of Poitiers, *An. Cist.*, 22 (1966), 13.

[11] Ibid., p. 4 and cf. Otto of Freising, op. cit., I. 49; pp. 22–4.

[12] *Epistola ad Albinum*, 2, 4–5, and cf. *Libellus* III, 10; *PL* 185. 587C–D.

[13] Boethius, *Theological Tractates*, ed. H. F. Stewart, E. K. Rand and S. J. Tester (London, 1973), p. 38.

students to understand them.[14] For Gilbert they were a
starting-point for philosophical reflection, but it was said by
unkind critics that Gilbert's gloss was 'more obscure than the
text'.[15]

Gilbert was interested above all in what Boethius had to say
about the Trinity,[16] and about the Nature and Person of
Christ,[17] because of the bearing it had upon the possibility of
talking about God at all, even in the most technically exact
language man can devise. When he was asked to produce a
copy of his commentary, Gilbert said that he had none to hand.
After some search, a portion of the commentary was found in a
copy in the possession of Gilbert's pupils (*apud scholares*).
This *particula quaedam*[18] was found to contain teaching on
the Trinity, to which Arnald was able to point as an example of
the way in which Gilbert was leading his pupils astray.

Gilbert had drawn a comparison between the way in which
we might say of a man that he is 'wisdom personified' and the
way in which such a statement might be made about God. His
intention seems to have been to show by contrast how
differently language must be used when we apply it to God. A
man is a compound being. Many different things come
together in his existence (*diversa conferunt ut sit*). Nevertheless, we sometimes say, singling out one of the qualities of a
particular man: *nihil nisi sapientia es*: 'You are nothing but
wisdom'. How much more is God said to 'be' his wisdom, his
goodness, and so on (*dicitur esse sapientia sua, bonitas sua*),
for in him different things do not come together to bring him
into existence (*cui diversa non conferunt ut sit*).[19] God is all
one. The reported account of this passage corresponds almost
exactly with that in the complete text of Gilbert's commentary
which has come down to us.[20]

This extract was placed before the gathering, and Bernard

[14] Thierry of Chartres, *Commentaries on Boethius*, ed. N. M. Häring
(Toronto, 1971).
[15] Geoffrey of Auxerre, *Libellus*, 40; *PL* 185. 609B.
[16] *Theol. Tract.*, pp. 2–31.
[17] Ibid., pp. 73–129.
[18] *PL* 185. 588B.
[19] *PL* 185. 588B.
[20] Gilbert of Poitiers, *Commentaries on Boethius*, ed. N. M. Häring
(Toronto, 1966), p. 90. 30–6.

disputed with the bishop. Gilbert's statement was, he said, a *grave verbum et enorme*. Bernard seems to have understood Gilbert's contrast as a comparison, designed to illustrate a resemblance rather than to demonstrate a difference. He calls it a *similitudo*. He insists that any such comparison is remote from the case of God: *procul a Deo*. We cannot say that God 'is' his wisdom in just the same way as a man may be said to 'be' his wisdom. In the case of a man we are speaking of a quality as though it were a substance, in a form of *emphatica locutio*. In the case of God we speak of his 'being' wisdom, or divinity, *vere et substantive*, truly and substantively, because we speak of his substance, not of quality.[21] Bernard had, it appears, understood Gilbert to be saying precisely the opposite of what he had intended to say.

In an attempt, perhaps, to make his position clear, Gilbert denied that he had taught, or ever believed, or proposed in writing, that divinity was not truly and substantially God, or that the form and essence of God were not themselves God, but qualities like human qualities, although of a higher order. He produced as his witnesses several former pupils: the bishop of Evreux; Rotrou who was later to be bishop of Rouen; Ivo of Chartres; but on the written evidence of the text, and on Bernard's interpretation of it, it was felt that there was a case to answer. Gilbert was summoned to trial at Rheims in the following year.[22]

It was at this point that Pope Eugenius turned to Godescalc, at that time Premonstratensian abbot of St. Martin, and later to be bishop of Arras from 1150. There was no question of Bernard himself preparing the case in advance. He was busy in the months before the trial in travel and negotiation. The choice of a Premonstratensian is not in itself surprising. Relations between Norbert's canons and the Cistercians had always been close, and in 1142 an act of confraternity strengthened the bond.[23] Several Premonstratensians were present at the Coun-

---

[21] *PL* 185. 588B–C.

[22] *PL* 185. 588C.

[23] J. B. Valvekens, 'Les actes de confraternité de 1142 et de 1153 entre Cîteaux et Prémontré', *Analecta Praemonstrensia*, 40 (1964), 193–205; and 'Actus confraternitatis inter Ordinem Praemonstratensium et Ordinem Cisterciensem', *Analecta Praemonstratensia*, 42 (1966), 326–30.

cil when it met at Rheims, including Milo, bishop of
Thérouanne and abbot Hugo, Norbert's successor as head of
the Order.[24] Godescalc did not make a name for himself as one
of the major scholars of the Order.[25] There can be no doubt,
however, that he had a clear mind and was well-fitted for the
task Eugenius gave him, and it is probable that Bernard himself
recommended him.

Godescalc set about his task rather as William of St. Thierry
had embarked upon his list of points of error in Abelard's
writings, noting *capitula*, and looking up quotations from the
Fathers to show that Gilbert was in error at each of the points
in question. These he brought to the Council at Rheims, and
presented them to Eugenius, together with the copy of
Gilbert's book he had been sent.[26] If there was no correspondence beforehand—and nothing is known to have survived—it
is possible that Bernard received these unseen. Godescalc did
not himself conduct the disputation against Gilbert. It may be
that he was already suffering from the illness to which Pope
Alexander refers in a letter to the archbishop of Rheims in
1162.[27] Whether as a result of a speech impediment, or because
he was not naturally eloquent (Geoffrey's term is *nimis
elinguis*)[28] Godescalc was judged unsuitable to act as advocate,
and the list of *capitula* with the *testimonia ei contraria* was
handed over to Bernard.

Otto of Freising sums up Godescalc's points like this:
Gilbert had taught that the divine essence is not God (*Quod
videlicet assereret divinam essentiam non esse Deum*); that
the properties of the Persons were not themselves the Persons
(*Quod proprietates personarum non essent ipse persone*); that
the Persons could not be predicated in any statement (*Quod
theologice persone in nulla predicarentur*); that the divine
nature was not incarnate (*Quod divina natura non esset
incarnata*).[29] Geoffrey also lists and discusses the *capitula*,

[24] *Analecta Praemonstratensia*, 43 (1967), 352–3.

[25] M. Firzthum, *Die Christologie der Prämonstratenser im 12 Jahrhundert*
(Marienbad, 1939), discusses some of the leading scholars of the day.

[26] *PL* 185. 589A.

[27] Alexander III, *Letter* III; *PL* 200. 182D.

[28] *PL* 185. 589B.

[29] Otto of Freising, op. cit., I. 53: p. 236. 29–238. 2.

with an implied compliment to Godescalc for discovering
these errors which are found in many places in Gilbert's
serpentine commentaries, although the serpent's head is
hidden: *pluribus tamen locis, sinuosis quibusdam volumini-
bus caput contegens serpentinum.*[30] The *initium malorum*,
the root of the trouble, lies, says Geoffrey, in Gilbert's
imputing a *forma* to God, 'by which' God is, but which is not
itself God; as if he were a man, whose *forma* is *humanitas*, 'by
which' he is a man, but which is not itself the man.[31] This is
Godescalc's first objection. Gilbert has been teaching that that
'by which' God is, his very essence, is not itself God.[32]
Geoffrey enlarges upon Godescalc's second and third points, as
they are described by Otto,[33] and his account of the fourth
capitulum coincides closely with that of Otto, but again it is
dealt with at greater length.[34]

To his *capitula* Godescalc had added a number of patristic
quotations, and the whole appears to have been arranged in a
schedula in such a way that the patristic texts formed the body
of the work, with the headings probably set out in the margin,
so as to make them subordinate to the texts.[35] Even with the
texts thrown into prominence in this way the whole collection
made up a slender body of evidence in comparison with that
which the supporters of Gilbert were able to bring. They
carried in large volumes containing complete texts of the
Fathers, as a demonstration of the substantial nature of their
case and the flimsiness of the attack. Bernard cut short their
sneers, but the impact of their arrival with their evidence
massively displayed for everyone to see was not lost on him.[36]
Nevertheless, the *schedula*, slight though it was, had to stand.
It provided a structure for the debate. Bernard could not better
it with the time and resources at his command.

We can see Bernard's views at a stage when he had begun to
put them into his own words, in one of his sermons on the

[30] *PL* 185. 595C.
[31] *PL* 185. 597D.
[32] *PL* 185. 604A.
[33] *PL* 185. 609A.
[34] *PL* 185. 613D–614A.
[35] *PL* 185. 589B; Hâring, *An. Cist.*, 22 (1966), 20–1.
[36] *PL* 185. 589D.

Song of Songs, which was preached shortly after the trial at
Rheims.

The maintenance of a delicate balance between the scholas-
tic and the monastic is nowhere more apparent than in this
Sermon 80 of the Song of Songs series. Bernard begins by wrily
admitting to his monks that for several days he has not been
preaching to them, as he usually does, with the emphasis upon
the moral sense.[37] He now proposes to return to the point he
had reached when these digressions began, and consider the
text: 'On my bed through the night I sought him whom my
soul loves', which he began to examine in Sermon 75. He has
been trying to bring to the light (*ponere in lucem*), that is the
light of Christ and the Church, the delights hidden in the dense
cloud of these allegories (*harum allegoriarum densa discussa
caligine*).[38] Now, he promises to return to the moral interpretation, 'for what benefits you cannot be wearisome to me' he
assures them.[39] That will be best achieved, he suggests, if we
now 'assign' what has been said in previous sermons to refer to
Christ and the Church, to the Word and to the Soul,[40] and
consider the implications of the passage in the light of this new
interpretation.

What follows will have disappointed those of his monks who
wanted him to bring out for them straightforward lessons on
how to live better lives. Bernard subjects them to a little
scholarly exercise. He discusses the nature of the link or
kinship (*cognatio*) between the Word and the Soul.

He suggests that the *cognatio* consists primarily in this: that
the Word is the image (*imago*) and the soul is 'in its image' (*ad
imaginem*). (Genesis 1: 27). In order to understand how the
soul may be 'like' the Word, we must first understand what the
Word is. It is truth, wisdom, justice. Its image must also be
these things, then.[41] But the soul is only 'capable' of being
truth, wisdom, justice (*capax*).[42] It is not these things by its

---

[37] *SS* 80. i. 1, LTR II. 277. 7–10.
[38] LTR. II. 277. 16–7.
[39] LTR. II. 277. 18–19.
[40] LTR. II. 277. 19–20. 18.
[41] LTR. II. 278. 1–2.
[42] LTR. II. 278. 8–9.

very nature. That is why it is accurate to describe it as *ad imaginem*, but not itself the *imago*.

There must, however, be some coming together (*convenire*) of the image and that which is in its image. Otherwise the word 'image' is meaningless (*vacuum nomen*),[43] Bernard chooses rightness (*rectitudo*) and 'greatness' (*magnitudo*)[44] as attributes to examine for the light they may throw on this connection. Here he rests his case on the elementary principle of the *Categories* of Aristotle which, together with Boethius' commentary, was one of the first textbooks studied in dialectic. The substance of things does not change while they retain their identity, but their accidents do. That is true for created things, but not for God. A good man may behave badly; a strong man may become weak with age; in God, goodness, strength, greatness, rightness are not accidents, but substantial.[45] Here is a significant respect in which greatness and rightness are one thing in the *imago*, God himself, and another in the soul which is merely *ad imaginem*, and yet at the same time they are not different. The same attributes are aspects of the divine being and, in a humbler degree, qualities which may be found in the human soul.

Again, in human experience greatness and rightness are different. Only in the supreme and uncreated nature are they one.[46] There alone is there no plurality resulting from the numerousness of things, no alteration resulting from variety.[47] Bernard recalls himself from what is threatening to become a digression with: 'How did we get here?' (*Unde venimus haec?*).[48] We were trying to understand 'image' and 'in the image' by looking at *magnitudo* and *rectitudo*.[49] We may grasp the limitations of the soul as an image of God by remembering that the greatness of the soul is not itself the soul, just as the crow's blackness is not the crow or the snow's whiteness the snow or a man's rationality the man.[50] The soul can be

---

[43] LTR. II. 278. 8–10.
[44] LTR. II. 278. 10–20.
[45] LTR. II. 278. 27–9.
[46] LTR. II. 278. 30–1.
[47] LTR. II. 281. 3–6.
[48] LTR. II. 280. 4.
[49] LTR. II. 280. 5–6.
[50] LTR. II. 280. 23–5.

separated from its greatness in principle, if not in practice.[51]
Bernard allows himself a few technical terms (*in subiecto;
subiectum*), but on the whole he keeps to the simplest
dialectical principles. He demonstrates the points of resemblance and the points of difference between the Word and the
Soul, the image and that which is in its image, with elegance
and economy.

He has been preparing the ground for a brief discussion of the
highly technical problem posed during Gilbert of Poitiers's
trial. Gilbert and his disciples, he says, teach that the greatness
by which God is great, the goodness by which God is good, the
justice by which God is just, the divinity by which he is divine,
are not God. In this they are 'innovators', and not even
innovating dialecticians, but innovating *heretici*.[52] Bernard
fastens upon the way in which this technically 'proper' way of
putting it (as Gilbert sees it)[53] will mislead the simple. He
accuses Gilbert of denying something about the divinity of
God itself, not of questioning the way in which we commonly
speak of his divinity; of asking a question about *res*, not about
verba. 'If God's divinity is not God, what is it?' asks Bernard (*si
Deus non est, quid est?*). He is happy to accept Gilbert's way of
putting things. Certainly God is 'by' his divinity, but he is also
himself that same divinity by which he is: *sed eandem
divinitatem, qua est, Deum nihilominus assero*.[54] It is perfectly proper to speak as Gilbert does (*proprie dici possit*), but it
may more correctly and fittingly (*rectius, congruentius*) be said
that God is 'greatness', 'justice', 'wisdom' than that he is
'great', 'just', 'wise'. Bernard speaks as though Gilbert had
impugned the very divinity of God, questioned whether God is
divine, cut away, in short, the very foundations of the faith.
Bernard describes in his sermon how, recently, at the Council
of Rheims, he has maintained this position against Gilbert.[55]

In his sermon Bernard deals with the underlying principle at
stake in Godescalc's first three *capitula*, as Otto states them.
He reads Gilbert's teaching as a challenge to God's very

[51] LTR. II. 280. 28–9.
[52] Bernard, *SS* 80. 6; LTR II. p. 281. 9–10.
[53] Gilbert of Poitiers, ed. cit., p. 90. 28.
[54] Song of Songs, Sermon 80, 7.
[55] Ibid., Sermon 80, 8.

existence. 'Who is He whom my soul loves?' he asks in the words of the Song of Songs. The answer is of course: 'He who is' (*qui est*), the God who identifies himself by saying 'I Am that I Am'.[56] In this statement are summed up all the attributes of God. However many attributes are listed, it is impossible to add to what is already implied in saying that God exists. When we have said that God exists we have not only said the first thing we know about him, but also all that can be known about him. There can be nothing true of God which is not itself God.

Bernard was still pursuing Godescalc's points in the last book of his *De Consideratione*, which he wrote in the last years of his life as a handbook for Pope Eugenius.[57] There, he makes use of a version of the principle which furnished Anselm with his ontological argument for the existence of God in the *Proslogion*.[58] Bernard constructs an argument of his own to show that God's divinity, 'by which' Gilbert says God has his being, is nothing but God himself; that there is in fact nothing but God in God. God is that than which nothing better can be thought: *nihil melius cogitari potest*. It is 'better', Bernard maintains, to say that divinity is nothing other than God himself, than to say that it is that 'by which' God is God: *at melius illam divinitatem, qua dicunt Deum esse, non aliud quam Deum esse fatemur*.[59] It is not only self-evidently 'better'; it must also be true, since God is, by definition, that than which nothing better can be thought. This is crude stuff in comparison with Anselm's argument, but it is in keeping with Anselm's declared intention that this *argumentum* shall serve to prove the existence of God and also everything else we can know about him.[60]

Bernard was not alone in adapting Anselm's *argumentum* in this way in the first half of the twelfth century. Gilbert Crispin, for example, had made use of the principle in his *Disputatio* between a Jew and a Christian. There, the Jew argues that if God is that than which nothing greater can be thought, it is

---

[56] Exodus 3: 14.
[57] *Csi* V. v. 13; LTR III. (1966), 477.
[58] *Anselmi Opera Omnia*, I. 101. 5–6.
[59] *Csi* V. vii. 15; LTR III. 479.
[60] *Anselmi Opera Omnia*, I. 93. 6–10.

inconceivable that he could be compelled by any necessity to make himself part of the human race, and to suffer man's ills with him.[61] The principle has undergone some modification; *maius* is accompanied by *sufficientius*. God is 'that than which nothing greater or more sufficient can be thought', but it is being used as Bernard uses it, to prove something that we wish to know about God, over and above the points Anselm demonstrates in the *Proslogion*. Gilbert Crispin is able to demolish the Jew's objection, and to show that God became man without in any way offending against his greatness.[62] Bernard certainly knew something of Gilbert. At the meeting of bishops Bernard convened before the Council of Rheims met, Gilbert Crispin's name was mentioned among the foremost theologians of recent times.[63] His reputation rested largely upon this single work.[64] Bernard had a precedent for his adoption of the Anselmian argument in another context.

It is clear from the sermon on the Song of Songs and from the *De Consideratione* that in putting a finger on Gilbert's seeming challenge to the very existence of God and his apparent denial that God's divinity is God himself, Godescalc had provided Bernard with a key to Gilbert's writings. Otto of Freising says that Bernard's zeal for the faith made him *credulus*; he was easily persuaded that those masters who placed an emphasis upon the use of reasoning which he thought disproportionate were misleading simple Christian souls.[65] Bernard saw no advantage in arguing *iuxta logicorum regulam*.[66] 'This scandal began', he says to Gilbert, 'with the assertion of many people that you believe and teach that the divine essence or nature, the divinity of God, . . . is not God, but a "form" by which God exists.'[67] Gilbert's exact meaning—for he undoubtedly had been teaching in these or similar words—remains a matter for dispute. Probably he intended

[61] Gilbert Crispin, *Disputatio Judei cum Christiano*, ed. B. Blumenkranz (Antwerp, 1956), p. 43. 19–21.

[62] Ibid., p. 43. 27–8.

[63] John of Salisbury, *Historia Pontificalis*, ed. cit., p. 19.

[64] Gilbert Crispin's works mostly survive in a single manuscript, London, British Library, MS. Add. 8166. S. xii.

[65] Otto of Freising, op. cit., I. 50.

[66] Ibid., I. 56; p. 246. 6.

[67] *PL* 185. 590A.

only to try to find a means of making statements about the divine nature which, by means of a circumlocution, enlarged the powers of expression of human language about created things, and provided a means of talking about God in a language more 'proper' for the purpose.

Gilbert was much concerned, as were many contemporaries, with this question of the special properties of theological language. He held that everything which exists has its own distinct form, which is an aggregate of the form of its substance and the forms of all its accidents. He does not accept the existence of universal or common forms, in which all members of a given species participate.[68] Those things which exist in the natural world differ from higher, 'abstract' existences, such as those of mathematical truths. In mathematics, or in discussing abstractions, forms are abstracted from specific concrete examples. We understand 'whiteness is a colour' by abstracting whiteness from specific concrete examples of white objects, much as we grasp the idea of a triangle by looking at many three-sided figures.[69] In abstracting it, we take white 'from' something (*a quo*). In theological statements, that is, statements about God, the 'form' is different again. We say that God is divine 'by divinity': *a divinitate*, and thus we explain what he is substantially by means of this 'form', but the 'form' remains a convenience for labelling only. It is not something which exists in its own right. Thus it is that Gilbert can say that the *forma dei*, the form of God, or *divinitas* is that 'by which' (*qua*) God exists, and not itself God.

When we set this beside Bernard's accusation, it is clear at once that Bernard was reading Gilbert's words in a quite different way. Bernard is talking, not about the problem of theological language, the *verba*, but about the content of what is expressed, the *res*. He believes Gilbert to be saying, not merely that the word *divinitas* or the word *essentia* is not God, but that the actual divine essence or nature is itself not God. It is as though Gilbert had said that God is not divine. 'If this is what you believe', challenged Bernard, 'declare it openly, or

[68] L. Nielsen, 'On the doctrine of logic and language of Gilbert Porreta and his Followers', *Cahiers de l'Institut du Moyen-Age Grec et Latin, Copenhague*, 17 (1976), 45.
[69] Ibid., 67.

deny it'. On trial, Gilbert dared to reply (*ausus est*, says Geoffrey), in the terms of his original statement: 'The form of God and the divinity by which God is, is not itself God.'.[70]

Bernard now had the confession he wanted. 'See', he said as Geoffrey reports it, 'We have what we were looking for. Let that confession be written down.' Pen and materials were fetched and Gilbert's words were recorded. 'Let it be written with an iron pen in ink of adamant', insisted Bernard.

The discussion which followed turned decidely upon the *res* and not the *verba*. Someone pointed out that if Gilbert's mode of expression were to be used for *sanctus*, it would amount to saying that that 'by which' God is, is at the same time that which proceeds from him.[71] Someone else, perhaps Bernard himself, was able to find exactly the parallel which was needed in Augustine's *De Trinitate*.[72] 'God is great' says Augustine, 'by that magnitude which is what he is himself. Otherwise that magnitude will be greater than God.'[73] The first *capitulum* was discussed throughout the first day. Geoffrey reports with some pride that it was he himself who pointed out to the bishop 'in the hearing of everyone' that Gilbert had totally denied he had taught or written those very words which he had now confessed within the same year in Paris, before the lord Pope and the majority of the senior persons now present, and produced witnesses to confirm that he had never believed or taught such things. If indeed the disputants had failed to understand Gilbert's intention technically speaking and were piling misunderstanding upon misunderstanding with anything of the glee Geoffrey suggests, then it is not difficult to understand Gilbert's apparently contradictory responses. At Paris he had denied that his teaching was intended to undermine orthodoxy. Nothing he had said had been meant in that way, but now, when he was pressed on the exact terms of his statements, he stuck by his formulation and asserted that those were indeed the very words in which he had expressed his views of the *divinitas* of God. 'Whatever I then said', Gilbert maintained, 'I say now.' Geoffrey

---

[70]   *PL* 195. 590A.
[71]   *PL* 185. 590.
[72]   Augustine, *De Trinitate*, V. x. 11.
[73]   *PL* 185. 580.

'sighed' and turned to the assembly, to whom, taken at its face value, Gilbert's confession looked like a volte-face.[74]

The discussion moved on to the second *capitulum*, in which it was claimed that Gilbert had been teaching that the three Persons are not one God, or indeed one anything, but that they are 'by one divinity': they are: *unum, id est uno*. Again, it was the apparent offence against orthodoxy rather than the exact underlying meaning of Gilbert's statement with which the assembly was concerned. First he had apparently said that God is not divine; now he was saying that the three Persons are not one God. That, at least, was the interpretation many readers would put upon his words. As in the case of the text of Augustine on 'greatness', so here a text was found which denied so blatant a heresy plainly; but it could not, in the nature of things, meet Gilbert on his own terms, since those were new technical terms, formulae freshly minted by Gilbert himself. Bernard and his supporters quoted 'Athanasius' (Vigilius of Thapsus), who said that the 'songs of the heavenly powers confirm that one is three and three one'.[75] If Gilbert had simply been saying that God was not three in one, the text would have served its purpose.

The trial was adjourned at this point to the next day, when Bernard and his party brought so many books to the disputation that Gilbert's supporters were dumbstruck (*obstupescerent*).[76] They could no longer claim that Bernard's party had no more than a flimsy *schedula*, while they themselves had come in scholarly readiness, but Geoffrey describes how Gilbert's supporters found a way of restoring their apparent superiority. They produced witnesses from among the Greek fathers whose words were all but incomprehensible (*verba minus intelligibilia*),[77] and mystified the opposition. Geoffrey gives the impression that Gilbert's party simply wanted to create confusion in their opponents' minds by making the discussion obscure, but it may be that more was at stake. There is no reason to suppose that Gilbert wanted to

---

[74] *PL* 185. 590C.
[75] *PL* 185. 590D.
[76] *PL* 185. 591D.
[77] *PL* 185. 591A, and see N. M. Hâring, 'The Porretani and the Greek Fathers', *Mediaeval Studies*. 24 (1962), 182 ff.

win the case in such an absurd manner. What we know of him suggests that he was a man who needed to be roused to give of his best, but, as John of Salisbury describes him, once his mind was engaged with a problem, he became fiery and passionate.[78] Geoffrey's account suggests that perhaps that is what has happened here. Gilbert stood his ground when he was challenged. He asserted his position, and the use of so empty and all but irrelevant a passage from 'Athanasius', and of the previous text from Augustine, may have angered him enough to urge him to try to explain himself properly, and with technical exactitude. In order to do so, he was obliged to use forms of words and formulae which sounded obscure to the ears of those who had not been his pupils and did not understand his technical language, and to draw upon texts in Origen and elsewhere which had helped him reach his conclusions. The root of the difficulty lay in the fact that no patristic authority could support Gilbert in the matter of formulae and technical terminology, because his language was so new. Yet Godescalc's *schedula* ensured that the debate should be conducted in these terms, by authorities, not by reasoning.

By the end of the second day of the trial, the discussion had reached the fourth *capitulum*. Here many *patristica* were ready to hand to support the case put forward by Bernard's supporters. Gregory, Augustine, Leo, and others were quoted. Perhaps it was here above all that Godescalc's list of authoritative texts proved useful.[79] After a lengthy discussion, the trial was adjourned for the judgement.

The next day archbishops and bishops and abbots and a great multitude of masters met *apud Bernardum*. They agreed to write out the *capitula*: *totidem quam expressius potuere*, together with the words of Gilbert's confession, and the objections which had been made against the *capitula*. When it had been signed, the document was taken to the Pope and the Cardinals by bishops Hugh and Milo and abbot Suger of St. Denys.[80] When Gilbert's errors were set out for all to see in

[78] John of Salisbury, *Historia Pontificalis*, ed. cit., p. 27.
[79] *PL* 185. 591B.
[80] *PL* 185. 591C–D.

this way, Geoffrey comments, even if any one had wanted to stand by him as a person, no one wanted to stand up for his teaching: *si stare visi fuerant aliqui pro persona, sed non stabant aliquatenus pro doctrina.*[81] Gilbert was summoned. Under interrogation, he freely renounced each *capitulum*, saying, 'If you believe otherwise, so do I; if you say otherwise, so do I; if you write otherwise, so do I.'[82] Then Eugenius condemned the *capitula*, giving strict orders that Gilbert's book was not to be read or copied. Gilbert himself went home, as we have seen, with honour.

The accounts of Gilbert's trial which survive are the work of partial witnesses, except that of John of Salisbury, who believed Gilbert to be no trouble-maker, but a man of peace whose teaching had been misunderstood. Geoffrey's account of the *schedula*, his *Libellus* in which he sums up the discussion, and his letter written in old age, even the chapter of the *Vita Prima* of Bernard himself in which he discusses the trial,[83] were written by a frankly prejudiced polemicist, who shared Bernard's zeal for the safety of Christian souls at risk. Godescalc's claim to have made a contribution to the condemnation rests upon Geoffrey's evidence. When we look at the way in which the evidence is presented it becomes clear that Godescalc's part is described without elaboration, and with no attempt to make more of it than it deserves. Geoffrey simply tells us that Godescalc was asked to draw up a list of headings, and that he did so, adding quotations from the Fathers, and brought the resulting *schedula* to Rheims. What happened to Godescalc's list after that was not his responsibility, and Geoffrey does not mention him again. It is for this reason, perhaps, that Godescalc is given no credit by the authors of other accounts of the trial.

Nevertheless, his contribution was of the first importance. No fresh *capitula* were added. His list proved adequate to the needs of the accusers of Gilbert, and when the bishops and abbots drew up their list after the trial they ended with a

---

[81]   *PL* 185. 592A.
[82]   *PL* 185. 592B.
[83]   *Vita Prima*, III. v. 15; *PL* 185. 312.

confession of faith which exactly mirrors Godescalc's four points:

We believe and trust that God is the simple nature of divinity, and that it cannot be denied in any catholic sense that God is divinity and divinity is God.
When we speak of the three Persons, Father, Son and Holy Spirit, we say that they are themselves one God, one substance; and, on the contrary, when we speak of one God, one divine substance, we state that that very one God, one divine substance, is three Persons.
We believe that only God, Father, Son and Holy Spirit is eternal, and that all other things, whether relations, properties, singularities, or unities, or anything of this sort which are in God and are eternal, are God.
We believe that that divinity, whether we call it divine substance or nature, was incarnate, but [only] in the Son.[84]

Bernard emerges from his conduct of the two trials with credit. He had beaten neither of his opponents on his own ground, but in each case he had succeeded in some measure in *shifting* the ground, and throughout he had spoken to some effect in favour of a theological method in which formal reasoning played only such a part as would make it possible to resolve a difficulty for the simple or make something plain.

He had shown himself to be a theologian in his own right. Were his contributions to the resolution of the problems of speculative theology which vexed his contemporaries not scattered amongst so much else that he wrote and said, and were they not deliberately expressed in simple language for the benefit of those who had not had an academic training, they would stand as a clearly visible bulwark amid the speculations of the day. As it is they seem modest and unassuming, mere incidentals to the great business of his preaching and his diplomatic activities, and Bernard the theologian makes his appearance only in glimpses. Nevertheless, theologian he was, and he himself would perhaps have seen his work in this area as at least on a level with the other aspects of his work for the security of the faithful in their faith.

---

[84]   *Libellus; PL* 185. 617–18, cf. Otto of Freising, op. cit., p. 25.

Chapter IV

On Consideration

I. BERNARD'S DOCTRINE OF THE CHURCH

Bernard loved the Church with a fierce, protective love. He saw himself as her champion, yet at the same time he thought of himself as her humblest servant. The awe he felt is often obscured by his practical concern, his almost managing air as he writes on Church business. But it is important to see his profound respect for the Church as the background and starting point of all his work on her behalf.[1]

The Apostolic See has, he says, a unique privilege, in being 'endowed with full authority' over every church in the world. He lists her powers. She can, if she thinks fit, create new bishops, make bishops into archbishops and archbishops into bishops. She can summon even the most august of churchmen from the remotest part of the world when she feels it necessary and send them home and recall them as often as she wishes. It is right that she should exercise a terrible severity.[2] Bernard's own judgements are made in submission to the authority of the Roman Church: 'To whose decision I refer everything I have said', he claims. He is prepared to modify any statement he has made if it proves to be contrary to the Church's view.[3] Bernard thus identifies the Church with the Roman See, not at every point, but sufficiently closely to condition much of his thinking on the Church and her welfare.

It was for this reason that the schism of the early 1130s seemed to him so dangerous a threat to the unity of the Church as a whole. If Pope stood against Anti-pope as claimants to be vicar of Christ on earth it was as though there were rival bridegrooms for the Bride of Christ. Once he had made up his mind that Innocent II was the rightful claimant, Bernard

---

[1] Letter 126. 10, LTR VII. 316–17, SJ 129. 10.
[2] Letter 131. 2, LTR VII. 327–8, SJ 140. 2.
[3] Letter 174. 9, LTR VII. 392. 15–29, SJ 215. 9.

worked tirelessly, travelling all over Europe to win support for his cause in the highest quarters.

Bernard's certainty about the nature of the Church's authority rests upon his conviction that behind every act of the Church is Christ. Speaking of the sacraments in a letter to William, abbot of Rievaulx, he reminds him that: 'It is Christ the Lord and Pontiff of our souls who baptizes and consecrates.' In his letter to Hugh of St. Victor about baptism, Bernard traces the institution of the sacrament back to Christ himself, and his difficulty over the question Hugh had posed for him arises out of his strong sense of the importance of the Church's role in administering sacraments. Hugh had asked whether a man who is not baptized but dies in faith and with the desire for baptism, can be saved. Bernard's judgement is that he can, but he arrives at it with many provisos as to the indispensability of baptism as a rule.[4]

Bernard is always aware of the presence of Christ the Bridegroom with his Bride the Church. 'I implore you,' he writes to Stephen King of England, 'not to give the Bridegroom of the Church any more cause to chastise you more harshly still and even destroy you utterly.'[5] He reminds Pope Innocent II that as Pope he is both the friend of the Bridegroom and the guardian of the Bride.[6] He tells the future archbishop of Bordeaux, Geoffrey of Loreto, that as a friend of the Bridegroom, a bishop must not fail the Bride when she is in need of help.[7] Can you sit idly by while your mother the Church is in trouble?' he asks.[8]

There appears on the face of it to be a confusion of images here. This defenceless Bride is the awesome figure we saw Bernard regarding as a supreme authority. Bernard complicates the image still further in a letter to Gerard of Angoulême, who had supported Innocent II's rival. He has left his holy Father Innocent, Bernard tells him, and his holy Mother the Church, and in a perversion of what is proper in marriage he has joined

---

[4] Letter 353, LTR VIII. 296. 15–16, SJ 199. 1; Letter 77. i. 5, LTR VII. 187. 26–7, and 190. 20–4.

[5] Letter 533, LTR VIII. 498. 10–11, SJ 197. 1.

[6] Letter 161, LTR VII. 370. 8–9, SJ 165. 1.

[7] Letter 125. 1, LTR VII. 308. 1–2, SJ 128. 1.

[8] Ibid., lines 2–3.

himself to this schismatic 'so that they have become two in one vanity' in a travesty of a marriage. Anacletus and Gerard thus 'support each other in seeking their own interest' and, most shocking of all, they do so 'at the expense of Christ's heritage'.[9] The Church is not only Mother and Bride, then, but also the inheritance which Christ left to his people.

These three distinct pictures of the Church show her in the light of her relationship with each Person of the Trinity in turn. As Mother she is in some sense the consort of God the Father. Bernard describes the true Christian's feelings for his mother the Church, who suckles him. 'The milk from thy breasts is better than wine, the fragrance of rare perfumes cannot match it for delight' (cf. Cant. 5: 1). 'That is what he says to his mother the Church'.[10] But when he has 'tasted and seen how sweet the Lord is', the Christian addresses him, too, in a similar way, but this time as 'a very dear Father'.[11] All Christians are sons of this mother and so they are brothers.[12] 'God has favoured you and the Roman Church has favoured you, he as a Father and she as a Mother.'[13] 'How happy the Church was to have taken to her breast so great a multitude of worthy sons, for whom she had been grieving as lost! With what a glad and serene countenance God your Father has received this sacrifice at your hands!'[14]

In contrast to this Mother Church who derives from the Father something of that authority and severity of judgement which makes Bernard stand so much in awe of her, is a picture of which he is especially fond. The Church is the Bride of the Song of Songs and Christ is her Bridegroom. She must be made fit for such a Bridegroom, pure and beautiful. This is the Church seen as the body of Christ, made one flesh with him in a true marriage. But because her body is composed (in human terms) of fallible human beings, her perfect beauty is vulnerable, her purity capable of being sullied. She needs vigilant protection if she is to become and remain fit for her Husband.

---

[9] Letter 260. 3, LTR VII. 310. 21–4, SJ 129. 3.
[10] Letter 78. 9, LTR VII. 207. 5–7, Cant. 1: 1–2, SJ 80.9.
[11] Letter 78. 9, LTR VII. 207. 8–9.
[12] Letter 78. 9, LTR VII. 207. 12–13.
[13] SJ 140. 1.
[14] SJ 134. 1.

Bernard's reference to the Church as the 'heritage' of Christ suggests that he saw the Church, too, as that which Christ left behind him on earth. Here perhaps we see an association with the Holy Spirit, Christ's supreme 'legacy' to man.

It is the Church as Christ's Bride and as his legacy to man that Bernard has in mind when he describes others as the props and stays of the Church, and speaks of his own work in supporting and strengthening it. This is the Church incarnate, the Church in man, the Church able to suffer and perish. He writes to Arnold, abbot of Morimond and crusader: 'Great support of our Order, are you not afraid that the whole structure will collapse now that you have fallen?'[15] If Arnold answers that he has not 'fallen', but made a considered decision which he is prepared to stand by, Bernard will point him to those other supports of the monastic order (like himself) who are now groaning under the extra weight they are carrying. He develops the theme, describing the results of this removal of a support. There is scandal, which is in itself a destructive force. There is a danger that 'prowling wolves' and the raging and roaring lion that goes about seeking whom it may devour (1 Peter 5: 8, Ps. 13: 4), will be able to get in and eat up the children of God as though they were so many loaves of bread.[16]

The great prop and stay of the Church as a whole is the Pope. To Pope Lucius Bernard writes as to a 'father' and 'upholder of justice, who carries alone the burden of so many great affairs', who 'protects the republic of the Church with the arms of justice, calling upon him to avenge the outrages committed upon the weak whom he ought to protect'.[17] In a similar vein of encouragement to be strong in defence of the Church, he writes to the newly-elected Eugenius III.[18] Next after the Pope come the bishops who are 'columns of the Church of God'.[19] He tries to rouse the bishops of Aquitaine to action. 'Once more the sword of the enemy seems to be threatening death to the whole body of Christ.'[20]

[15] See note 9.
[16] Letter 4. 2, LTR VII. 26. 5, SJ 4. 2.
[17] Letter 520. 1, LTR VIII. 480, SJ 204. 1.
[18] Letter 238, LTR VIII. 117. 5–6, SJ 205. 3.
[19] Letter 500, LTR VIII. 457. 14, SJ 235. 1.
[20] Letter 126, LTR VII. 309. 10–11, SJ 129. 1.

These senior churchmen who are its supports appear to constitute the decision-making body in Bernard's eyes, in human respects at least. On the election of bishop Philip to the See of Tours Bernard wrote to Innocent II: 'It seemed best to me and to the pious and wise men who were with me, bishops, abbots, and clergy, to end this long ordeal of the Church and allow no more delay and subterfuge on the part of those who were serving only their own interests and cared nothing about what was to happen to the Church.[21] He makes a list of the archbishops and bishops who accept Innocent as Pope, and the Orders of the Camaldolese, the Vallambrosians, the Carthusians, Cluniacs, and Cistercians and so on, as though they amounted collectively to the Church decisive.[22]

Conversely, if the clergy and bishops do not behave as they should, they not only do not fortify the Church; they help to demolish it. The bishop of Troyes had been trying to reform the clergy of his diocese. The clergy had made difficulties for him. Bernard writes to Innocent II on his behalf, describing how the 'insolence of the clergy is being a nuisance everywhere', and how the bishops are to blame because they do not correct the errors of their clergy.[23] Bernard often bewails the secularity of the bishops and other clergy,[24] the secularity of the times as a whole,[25] the torpor and tepidity which take the place of ardour and desire for Christ,[26] the many sellers of relics, who seem to him to differ from Judas Iscariot only in this: that he was satisfied with thirty pieces of silver, while their greed knows no bounds.[27]

The result is a Church whose shame is a public scandal; 'the Devil's victory is known all over the world'. The wicked mock her and the good lament.[28] The beauty of the Church is soiled; the purity of the faith is dirtied.[29] The misery of specific

---

[21] SJ 156. 2.
[22] SJ 129. 9.
[23] Letter 152. 1, LTR VII. 358–9, SJ 158. 1.
[24] SS 77. i. 2, LTR II. 262. 23–4.
[25] SS 14. iv. 6.
[26] SS 2. i. 1, LTR I. 8. 20–1.
[27] SS. 10. ii. 3, LTR I. 49. 28–50. 3.
[28] Letter 235. 2, LTR VIII. 109. 12–14.
[29] SJ 247. 1.

churches cries out, as does the Church of Orléans.[30] The 'intrusion' of bishop Philip of Tours into his diocese is a source of distress for the Church.[31]

It is in this context that we must set Bernard's sense of the burning importance and urgency of the needs he sees about him, and which keep him from Clairvaux[32] as he travels the world trying to put things to rights.

Bernard had grown up with war. His father had been a knight; William of St. Thierry calls him a *vir antiquae et legitimae militiae*;[33] and his brothers had been soldiers until their conversion. Living in such a society, it is not surprising that he saw war on every side, war of the spirit and war of the body. Thomas, Prior of St. Victor Paris, was murdered on a Sunday, on the bishop's breast; he died in the bishop's arms, in a piety which made his murderer the worst of wild beasts, Bernard comments.[34] Within, each man fights out the battle of the virtues and vices.[35] The Christian is engaged in no mere tournament, Bernard insists, but in an encounter with an enemy who can destroy him body and soul.

In a letter written to several bishops in 1143 about the interdict laid on the kingdom of France as a result of a dispute concerning the archbishop of Bourges, Bernard tried to drive home the seriousness of what was at stake when there was discord in the Church. As a result of the schism, certain men were swallowed up by the earth and sent down still living into Hell; in their *horrenda mors* spiritual evil resulted in physical evil.[36] He describes graphically how schism resembles a tug of war in the Church. All the members of the Church follow their own appetites (*omnes suum stomachum sequuntur*), and they

---

[30] Letter 156. 1, LTR VII. 363, SJ 162, 1.

[31] Letter 151. 1, LTR VII. 357. 11–12, SJ 157, 1.

[32] Letter 143. 2, LTR VII. 342. 18–19, SJ 144. 2.

[33] *VP* I. i. 1. *PL* 185. 227.

[34] Letters 158 and 159, LTR VII. 367. 8–11; 367. 7–15. 'in obsequio caritatis . . . in opere sancto, in sanctorum comitatu; fera pessima.'

[35] R. Stettiner, *Die illustrierten Prudentiushandschriften* (Berlin 1895) lists manuscripts which provide pictures of the battle which Prudentius describes in his *Psychomachia*. cf. Hugh of St. Victor, *Miscellanea* IV. 30, *PL* 177. 712: *movent bellum contra nos diabolus, caro et mundus*.

[36] Letter 219, LTR VIII. 81. 9–10. cf. the three-fold rope of Eccl. 4: 12.

all pull with all their might in different directions, so that the rope breaks.[37]

About 1140, he wrote to Robert, abbot of St. Aubin in Anjou. He had not met him, but Robert's reputation for personal holiness had made a strong impression on Bernard. He says that he frequently finds himself dwelling with pleasure on the thought of Robert and his goodness. He looks forward to meeting him, in this world if it can be arranged, but if not, in the next.[38] There is no more for Bernard between the two scenes of meeting than a difference of date and circumstances. For Bernard the prospect of meeting Robert in heaven is not a remote possibility, but something as real and as near as if it were to take place tomorrow in his own house. In the same way, spiritual and holy war is a struggle taking place on earth whose outcome has to do with heaven. Just as the First Crusade was spoken of at the time as a 'journey' (*iter, expeditio, peregrinatio*),[39] so the soldier of Christ is on a pilgrimage, a journey from earth to heaven, the outcome of which was vitally important.

Bernard saw the Pope's duty to conduct a warfare for the good in the same terms of action, not in this world only, but in the world to come. On the one hand, he is to be assiduous in dealing with specific acts of violence in the world. Bernard describes acts of physical violence committed against clergy in several of his letters. (Archenbald of Orléans was murdered;[40] abbot Guy of Charlieu suffered at the hands of 'a monk in habit, though a false one', who had been seizing other men's goods.)[41] If Innocent takes no action, says Bernard in the letter about the murder of Master Thomas, with which we began, he is responsible for the death of so good a man. If he, whose teeth are arms and whose tongue is a sword, is to be excused action, then the Jews are not to be blamed for the death of Christ.[42] If Innocent does nothing, he makes it more difficult for other

---

[37] Ibid. 'Totis viris funes in diversa trahentes, rumpunt.'
[38] Letter 204, LTR VIII. 63. 9.
[39] C. Erdmann *The Origin of the Idea of Crusade*, tr. M. W. Baldwin and W. Goffart (Princeton, 1977), p. xv. (First published as *Die Entstehung des Kreuzzugsgedankens*, Stuttgart, 1935).
[40] Letters 161, 162, 163.
[41] Letter 198.
[42] Letter 159, LTR VII. 366. 3–5.

men to stand against unjust exactions as Thomas tried to do, even in the face of the threat of murder.[43] Thomas was killed by his own kinsmen, who threatened him with death if he did not carry out their wishes.[44] Only by a zealous assiduity in bringing the offenders to justice can the Pope ensure that members of the nobility may safely hold ecclesiastical office without greedy and powerful relations taking advantage of their influence over him.[45]

According to Luke's Gospel, just before his arrest Jesus told his disciples to make preparations for what was to come. He told them that he who did not possess a sword would be wise to sell his cloak and buy one. They found two swords and brought them to him, saying, 'Lord, behold, here are two swords, and he said to them, 'it is enough''.' (Luke 22: 36–8). Upon this episode Bernard based a doctrine which, although it is not original to him, was to become famous as a result of his exposition.[46] The two swords are taken to represent, respectively, temporal and spiritual power in the world. To whom does God, the source of all power, give these swords? Bernard argues that both belong to the Pope, but the Pope cannot commit the acts of violence which are the work of the temporal sword, even when it is justly wielded in a just war.[47] He must entrust that work to someone else. So the soldier's sword belongs to the Pope, but, although it may be drawn from its sheath at his command, it must not be drawn by his own hand.[48] When, about 1150, Bernard wrote to Pope Eugenius III to try to stir him to action in defence of the Holy Places of the

---

[43] LTR VII. 366. 8–9.

[44] LTR VII. 366. 10–11, cf. Letter 159, LTR VII. 368. 14–15, and Letter 160, LTR VII. 369. 11.

[45] Letter 159, LTR VII. 366. 15–22.

[46] E. Kennan, 'The "De Consideratione", of St. Bernard of Clairvaux and the Papacy in the mid-twelfth century: a review of Scholarship', *Traditio*, 23 (1967), 73–115, discusses the controversy over Bernard's teaching on the subject of the two swords.

[47] Augustine speaks of the *bellum justum* which is possible only when one side has attacked without provocation and their opponents are forced to defend themselves, or stolen property which may justly be recovered. See H. A. Deane, *Political and Social Ideas of St Augustine* (New York, 1963), Chapter V. This is a rather different notion from the 'holy war' or crusade. C. Erdmann traces the development of the latter idea in *The Origin of the Idea of Crusade*, tr. M. W. Baldwin and W. Goffart (Princeton, 1977) pp. 7–13.

[48] *Csi* IV. iii. 7, LTR III. 454. 4–16.

East, which were still in the hands of the infidel after the failure of the Second Crusade, he wanted him to use the temporal sword in just this way.[49] The Pope must fight in his own person with the Word, the spiritual sword.

Bernard himself is a paradoxical figure, riding headlong into battle for the peace of Christendom. Bernard's own battles were all of words, but battles they were. He wrote to King Louis of France to warn him against oppressing the innocent and to reprove him for listening to bad advice. He is distressed at reports that violence is being done and peace broken.[50] He reproaches Louis for his failure to keep his promises: 'Truly, you neither accept the words of peace, nor keep the peace you have made.'[51] Strong words are called for. 'I speak harshly', says Bernard, 'because I fear harsher things for you.'[52] To the bishop of Soissons he writes of the duty to promote peace where he can;[53] there is to be no doing evil so that good may come.[54] There was little meekness in Bernard when he went to war for the Church's peace.

He recognized the absurdity of his position. He was not a soldier but a monk: 'Who am I to set up camp, or to march out to battle?' he asks. 'What is so remote from my profession?'[55] There was, however, one battlefield upon which it was entirely proper for him to fight in person. In one of his sermons on the Song of Songs he compares the conflict of Pharaoh's army and the army of the Lord with that holy and spiritual war which is fought between the army of the Lord and the army of Satan.[56] Pharaoh's army is led by malice, luxury, and avarice, each riding in a four-wheeled chariot. Malice's chariot-wheels are savageness, impatience, boldness, shamelessness. Luxury's chariot-wheels are gluttony, lust, fine clothes, and idleness. Avarice's chariot-wheels are pusillanimity, inhumanity, contempt of God, the oblivion of death. The Song of Songs sometimes seemed to him itself a battle-song. In his first

---

[49] Letter 256, LTR VIII. 164. 2–3.
[50] Letter 220, LTR VIII. 82. 18–19.
[51] Letter 221, LTR VIII. 85. 1–2.
[52] Letter 221, LTR VIII. 86. 9.
[53] Letter 225, LTR VIII. 94. 7–9.
[54] LTR VIII. 82. 20.
[55] LTR VIII. 165. 3–5.
[56] *SS* 39. ii. 4, LTR II. 20. 8–9.

sermon he speaks of the 'daily manoeuvres and wars, from which those who live in Christ are never free'. They come from the flesh, the world, and the Devil, and, since the life of man upon earth is a constant warfare, which he experiences within himself, Bernard recommends him to keep the battle-song of the Song of Songs always in mind.[57]

In Bernard's eyes the personal war he fought against evil was merely a small part of the great battlefield on which the Church fights; every Christian is engaged in it, but those in positions of authority in the Church have a special responsibility to help others and to see to the strategy and tactics of the war as a whole. 'I am proud of my troubles, if I may be counted worthy to suffer them for the sake of the Church', he writes to Peter the Venerable, 'but most of all I am proud of the triumph of the Church.'[58] 'It is only right,' he says to Innocent II, 'that your triumphs should invigorate the whole Church; . . . the Church has suffered with you, therefore she ought to reign with you.'[59]

The end most to be desired is the unity and peace of the Church.[60] 'The garments of Christ are being divided' when the sacraments are 'torn to shreds.' But 'the tunic of Christ remains whole for it has no seam, having been woven in one piece from the top'. The tunic of Christ is the unity of the Church. 'What has thus been woven, what the Holy Spirit has unified in this way, cannot be torn up by men.'[61] There is, in the end, no need to fear for the Church's survival. But in the immediate future there is work to be done to preserve her unity and peace. If all disputes were resolved, Bernard believes, 'the honour of God, the liberty of the Church and the salvation of souls would then prosper'. Bernard is deeply glad when any disagreement or schism is brought to an end. 'On the very octave day of Pentecost, God fulfilled our desires by giving unity to the Church and peace to the city of Rome', he writes to Godfrey, prior of Clairvaux. Utterly weary, 'scarcely able to

---

[57] *SS* 1. v. 9, LTR I. 6–7.
[58] Letter 147. 1, LTR VII. 350. 15–19, SJ 147. 1.
[59] Letter 155. 1, LTR VII. 354. 5–14, SJ 155. 1.
[60] Letter 137, LTR VII. 333. 5–22.
[61] Letter 334. 1, LTR VIII. 273. 11–15, SJ 246. 1.

return home', he made his way back to Clairvaux whenever 'heaven gave back peace to the Church'.[62]

II. LORDSHIP AND SERVICE

On the election to the Papacy of Eugenius III, in 1145, Bernard wrote an anxious letter to the Curia. 'May God forgive you. What have you done? You have called a buried man back to the world of men. You have embroiled and mingled in the crowd someone who was escaping from cares and crowds.' As a monk Eugenius was, he says, running a good race.[1] Bernard is not confident that he will be able to manage both himself and his new life, 'for he is a delicate son'. He is accustomed to quiet and leisure, not to the business of the world.[2]

In the course of the following decade, Bernard wrote Eugenius a serial letter in five books, to help him come to terms with what was expected of him as Pope, without losing sight of his monastic vocation. This work, the *De Consideratione*, was Bernard's last treatise, and it has attracted attention not only for the spiritual advice it contains but also for its political doctrine. Bernard's teaching on a number of points has been the subject of much debate not least because he frequently appears to contradict himself. Elizabeth Kennan has suggested very plausibly that Bernard is systematically making use of a technique of antithesis which is a commonplace of classical and Augustinian rhetoric, and that his apparently opposing statements are in fact intended to be paradoxical, and to stimulate the reader into seeking a middle way.[3] If we look at the *De Consideratione* in the light of Gregory the Great's *Regula Pastoralis* his purpose and his method become clearer. Like Gregory, Bernard is trying to find a practical method by which a man may rule and still remain a private man, as humble as the lowliest of his subjects. Like Gregory, Bernard finds his way to a solution by confronting the

---

[62] Letter 148. 1, LTR VII. 380. 6–7.

[1] Letter 237, LTR VIII. 113. 9. 15 'Currebat bene.'

[2] Ibid., p. 114. 21.

[3] Elizabeth Kennan, 'Antithesis and Argument in the *De Consideratione* in *Bernard of Clairvaux: Studies presented to Dom Jean Leclercq* (Washington, 1973), 91–109.

paradoxes of the situation one by one and trying to resolve them.

Bernard's first letter to Eugenius himself was as reserved and full of foreboding as his letter to the Curia. He had expected to hear from Eugenius himself, but he has received no letter. He has been obliged to write.[4] It is a letter of advice which he feels to be a pressing necessity; he writes about the frame of mind in which he wants Eugenius to approach his new task; he encourages him to think of himself as having come, not to be ministered to, but to minister.[5] This anxiety for Eugenius' inner stability, for the state of his soul, for the monk in him, burned consistently in Bernard's mind through all the vicissitudes of events. It runs as a connecting thread through everything he says in the *De Consideratione*. Every general statement is referred back to Eugenius himself. Bernard wants to encourage him to consult his soul, to 'consider' within him, before he takes any action. The *De Consideratione* is a practical manual for a single individual first and foremost, and only secondly a discussion of its various themes for the benefit of a wider readership. Bernard's first concern was that this first Cistercian pope should lead the Church well.

In view of the circumstances of Eugenius' election, Bernard's emphasis upon this inner fortification of the soul as a preliminary to outward practice is striking. In the days of Eugenius' predecessor, Pope Celestine, there had been a scandal over the election to the See of York. Bernard wrote to the Curia at the time: 'We burn fiercely, I tell you; we burn hard, so that it makes life insupportable. We see dreadful things in the house of God.'[6]

In 1141, on the death of Thurston, archbishop of York, there was a dispute over the election. The King refused to consider one of the candidates, Waldef, from the Cistercian house of Kirkham. The Cathedral Chapter elected their treasurer, a nephew of the King, William Fitzherbert. The Cistercian abbots of Rievaulx and Fountains found the circumstances of

---

[4] Letter 238, LTR VIII. 115. 21. He says that he has written not: *voluntatis*, but: *necessitatis*.

[5] Letter 238, LTR VIII. 116, 21.

[6] Letter 236, LTR VIII. 111. 7–8

the election unsatisfactory and, emboldened by the rights given them by the Lateran Council in 1139 to take an active interest in the election, they wrote to Bernard to complain. The two parties, Fitzherbert's (at the suggestion of Henry of Blois, bishop of Winchester) and that of the Cistercians, led by Ailred of Rievaulx, set off for Rome to make their appeal. Ailred's delegation stayed at Clairvaux on their way, and Bernard wrote them letters of support to carry to the Pope. The case was heard in March 1142, and a decison postponed until the following year, when Fitzherbert's election was approved, provided that it could be shown that no pressure had been put upon the Chapter. Feeling in York was running high, and Bernard wrote to William, abbot of Rievaulx to ask him to be calm, and sent him Henry Murdach, a former monk of Clairvaux and now abbot of Vauclair, to advise him. Bernard himself was too ill and weary to make the journey. To Pope Celestine he wrote pressing him to take action, but Celestine died having done no more than deprive Henry of Blois of his legateship. Lucius II, his successor, was put in the picture at once and under pressure from Bernard he sent Cardinal Hincmar to England with the pallium, with instructions not to bestow it on the archbishop-elect unless he was satisfied about the election. He paused at Clairvaux on his journey, and when he returned to Rome it was without having bestowed the pallium. Pope Lucius died in 1145. Thus it was that the settlement of this matter presented Eugenius with his first test when he succeeded Lucius as Pope. Bernard urges him to action in a series of letters, praising him when he sees signs of that *zelum* which he wants him to show for the Church's welfare.[7]

Eugenius followed Bernard's advice, suspended William Fitzherbert and demanded that William St. Barbe, who was now bishop of Durham, should take an oath that the election had been a free and legitimate one. William, when he was put to it, would not perjure himself. The Chapter met at Richmond in July 1147 and chose Henry Murdac as their archbishop. It took several years for the clergy of the diocese to accept him,

---

[7] Letters 238, 239, 240, LTR VIII. 124 1 and 14.

and it is a nice irony that when Henry Murdac died the Chapter elected William Fitzherbert again. (He was eventually canonised as St. William of York.)

Eugenius was, then, plunged at once into the resolution of an old scandal, and into much other business which was likely to put a considerable strain upon his capacities as a man of 'consideration'. Perhaps the most urgent practical matter was Eugenius' own position. Innocent II had spent seven years in obtaining possession of Rome. He had consolidated his position in the end by two years' residence there, and by holding a Lateran Council, but there was persistent and deep-seated unrest in Rome. Middle-class ambition to take part in government led to revolt against the great noble families, as well as against the Pope himself. A 'Senate' was set up, on the old Roman model.

Innocent died soon after the outbreak of the revolt. His successor, Celestine, was Pope for only a few months, and had little time to bring about any improvement. Lucius II appealed for help to Conrad of Germany and to Roger II of Sicily, but neither was in a position to help him materially. Eugenius added to his own difficulties by mishandling the case of the heretic Arnold of Brescia. Arnold had been a supporter of Abelard at the time of his trial at Sens in 1140. He was a considerable demagogue, preaching a return to apostolic poverty, in terms which, had he had his way, would have abolished the existing ecclesiastical hierarchy. Eugenius gave him pardon, and made the mistake of instructing him to go to Rome, to do penance in the Holy Places. There he soon began preaching again, to rebels who found themselves in sympathy with his teaching for their own reasons.

These, then, were the unpromising circumstances in which Bernard expected his Cistercian Pope to remain a monk in his heart, and at the same time show an active zeal for the good of the Church in the world.

In the course of writing the *De Consideratione* Bernard evolved a system of spiritual and practical advice. It is not clear that he envisaged the whole at the outset. The first book was possibly intended to be complete in itself when Bernard wrote it soon after Eugenius' accession in 1145. He began the second book in the late summer of 1148, in some pain because of the failure of the Second Crusade,[8] and it was perhaps his bewilderment at the outcome of an enterprise embarked upon in such sure confidence that it had God's blessing that prompted him to attempt to take 'consideration' a little further. The last four books (Book III (1152) and Books IV–V completed in 1152 or 3) follow an overall plan set out by Bernard at the beginning of Book II. He suggests, in imitation perhaps of Augustine in the *De Doctrina Christiana*, that Eugenius should consider four things in order: himself, what is below him, what is about him, and what is above him.[9] In one sense, everything is below Eugenius, but, paradoxically, Bernard would prefer him not to think of himself as a ruler at all, but as a man with responsibilities—to correct heretics, to convert unbelievers, to check the ambitious;[10] his task is to set an example.[11] This paradox of the lowly-hearted lord of the world is one to which Bernard returns repeatedly; it becomes the theme of the treatise.

Eugenius' difficulty was Bernard's own—indeed that of every monk in public life: how to remain a monk within when every outward circumstance conspires against it. Augustine had emphasized the need for the Christian to love what is above, what he himself is, what is neighbour to him (*quod iuxta nos est*) and what is beneath him,[12] and others besides Bernard, from Rabanus Maurus[13] to Hugh of St. Victor[14] had made use of his quadripartite division. The notion that self-examination ought to be a regular part of the life of a busy man was commonplace enough, but Bernard was proposing something more thoroughgoing than that. He wanted to see the humility of the monk in the most assertive acts of the Pope's fullness of power (*plenitudo potestatis*); he wanted Eugenius to embrace both contradictories in everything he did.

---

[8] *De Consideratione*, II, i. 1–4, LTR III. 410–14. On the dating of the books of *Csi*, see LTR III. 381. On Arnald of Brescia, see R. Brooke, *The Coming of the Friars* (London, 1975), for a bibliography and R. I. Moore, *The Origins of European Dissent* (London, 1977), Chapter V.

[9] *Csi*. II. iii. 6.

[10] *Csi*, III. i. 1–2

[11] *Csi*, IV, iii. 6.

[12] Augustine, *De Doctrina Christiana* I, xxii. 23.

[13] Rabanus Maurus, *De Clericorum Institutione*, PL 107. 381.

[14] Hugh of St. Victor, *Institutiones in Decalogum*, PL 176. 17A.

Bernard's first treatise had been about humility, and he is still writing about humility in the *De Consideratione*. Like Gregory the Great in his *Regula Pastoralis*, Bernard sets out to lead his Pope from an acknowledgement of the weight of responsibility and the pressure of business under which he labours,[15] to a realization of the importance of personal humility in his handling of these affairs. In the *Regula Pastoralis* Gregory emphasizes that no one should undertake the duties of a pastor until he has thoroughly mastered all that he can learn through meditation.[16] He points out how the busy mind becomes distracted,[17] and how it loses its sense of direction in its confusion. The only defence open to those in positions of power is to withdraw into themselves, to flee, and that is an act of supreme humility.[18] Similarly in the *De Consideratione* Bernard asks Eugenius, 'Where shall I begin?' 'Let it be from your *occupationes*', he answers himself, 'for in those I especially commiserate with you.'[19] He goes on to point out the dangers of being too busy,[20] and to bring Eugenius to see the importance of withdrawal into his own mind, where he can examine himself and his activities and maintain a proper attitude of humility.

The *De Consideratione* had a forerunner as early as 1127–8, in a letter which Bernard wrote to Henry, archbishop of Sens. There we find him approaching the subject of humility in a similar way. Bernard's theme is that humility should be the most conspicuous feature of both the inward and the outward life of every Christian, however important his position. There is a nice irony—which was not lost on Bernard himself—in his writing to a bishop in this vein. 'Who am I', he says, 'to write to bishops?'[21] Bernard expresses the difficulty of the Christian who finds himself involved in public life in the words of Psalm

---

[15] Gregory the Great, *Regula Pastoralis*, I. iii. *PL* 77. 16C: 'ut quantum sit pondus regiminis monstraremus.' On humility in bishops, see Gregory *Letters*, Book V, *Letter* 18 (*PL* 77. 783–43) and 43 (*PL* 77. 771–4).

[16] *Reg. Past.* I. ii.

[17] *Reg. Past.* I. iv, *PL* 77. 17C. 'Dum confusa mente dividitur ad multa.'

[18] *Reg. Past.* I. vi, *PL* 77. 19D.

[19] LTR III. 394. 6–7

[20] LTR III. 395. 7.

[21] LTR VII. 100. 12, cf. p. 127. 22, Letter 42. 'Qui enim nos sumus, ut scribamus episcopis.'

106: 23, which describes sailors in a storm, tossed up and down upon the waves, so that they reel about on the deck of their ship like drunken men. Bernard points out that those who engage in business and are much involved in worldly affairs are bound to be disturbed and to lose their tranquillity. *Turbati* and *moti*, they reel as if drunk, and their judgement fails them. How much worse, says Bernard, are the perils of a bishop's life? He must bear, not some, but all possible temptations, without losing his balance in the storm of affairs.[22]

Bernard had heard reports which encouraged him to think that archbishop Henry was allowing himself to be led astray by bad advice. The source was reliable, and Bernard did not hesitate to act upon it.[23] Henry is to bear in mind, he says, that although God tells us to love our neighbours, and that means we must love everyone, only the wise and well-disposed are to be trusted to give advice.[24] A bishop cannot discharge his duties unless he takes advice. With the aid of good advice he can check himself from excesses and resist temptations and avoid the fate of which the Psalmist speaks. Thus he will learn to avoid extremes, and to pursue the middle way which Gregory advocates in the *Regula Pastoralis*. Bernard lists several of the contrasting excesses into which a bishop may fall, and from which he wishes to save the archbishop of Sens:[25] too much severity or remissness in correcting wrong-doers; being too quick to make promises and being slow to perform them,[26] for example. With the aid of wise counsellors, the archbishop will learn to despise fine clothes and superb horses and grand buildings, and he will be known for his personal adornments of good behaviour, his spiritual exercises, his good works.[27]

The bishop ought to be a bridge between God and man. He ought in his own person to provide a middle way. That is what his title means: he is called *pontifex* from *pons*, a bridge. By the *etymologia nominis*, the very etymology of the word, Bernard

---

[22] LTR VII. 101. 5–8.
[23] *Veredicus*; Letter 42, LTR VII. 102. 6–8.
[24] Ibid.
[25] Letter 42 i. 3; LTR VII. 103. 1–2.
[26] Letter 42 i. 3; LTR VII. 103. 13–16.
[27] Letter 42 ii. 4; LTR VII. 104. 1–3.

explains, we see how the bishop is intended to make himself a pathway between God and his neighbour.[28] The *fidelis pontifex* allows goods to pass through his hands, taking nothing for himself by way of profit, but letting the *divina beneficia* come to men and the vows of men (*hominum vota*) pass to God.[29] To be a good bridge, the bishop must forget himself altogether. He must become so humble inwardly that his own needs disappear from his mind, and all his love and desire is directed towards God and his neighbour, at either end of the bridge.

With this purpose in mind, Bernard encourages the archbishop to engage in the meditation which Gregory makes a prerequisite for every pastor. It is to be a meditation of a specific kind, introspective rather than upward-looking to God, designed to acquaint the bishop with the state of his heart.[30] Bernard argues that it is only if he knows himself that he can love his neighbour as himself, for otherwise he has no measure.[31] He sets out for him the things faith brings about: a pure heart, a good conscience, a genuine faith,[32] and humility.

Henry is to arrive at an understanding of humility by examining its opposite, pride. Bernard used the same device in the *De Gradibus Humilitatis et Superbiae*, where he ends with a challenge. 'Perhaps you are saying, brother Godfrey, that I have shown you something different from what you asked for, and what I myself promised, when I seem to have described the steps of pride instead of the steps of humility. To which I reply, "I cannot teach what I have not learned. I did not think it was fitting for me to describe steps up, when I know the descent better than the ascent." '[33] Bernard himself is learning humility by studying what he knows of its opposite, and he thinks it good practical advice to recommend others to do the same.

Accordingly, he defines pride for Henry as the desire to see oneself excel. There are two sorts of pride, blindness (*caeca*) and vainglory (*vana superbia*). Each of these may be called by other names, such as *contumacia* and *vanitas*. The first is a

---

[28] Letter 42 ii. 10; LTR VII. 108.
[29] Letter 42 iii. 11; LTR VII. 109. 1–5.
[30] Letter 42 iv. 13; LTR VII. 110. 1–5.
[31] Letter 42 iv. 13; LTR VII. 110. 8–9.
[32] Letter 42 iv. 14; LTR VII. 111. 14.
[33] LTR III, 58. 15–19. (xxi. 57).

vice which is opposed to *intelligentia*; that is, it is a vice of
ignorance. The second is a vice of the will. The opposite of
blindness, if we are thus to define by opposites, is the
knowledge by which someone knows how to think humbly of
himself (*ut quis se noverit sentire humiliter*). The opposite of
vainglory is not to consent to the opinion of others when their
view differs from the one modesty demands: *nec consentire
aliter sentientibus*.[34] Bernard is able to give the archbishop of
Sens an example from the monastic world, of abbots within his
own Order who 'break this rule of humility, and while they
wear the habit and the tonsure, they are so proud that,
although they refuse to allow the least little word of those
under their command to pass, they themselves disdain to obey
their own bishops'.[35] But the lesson, and the method of
bringing it home has a wider application, to all those who find
themselves in the position of pastor. Gregory the Great applies
the method to a long list of different types of people to whom
the pastor may find himself preaching, all arranged in pairs by
opposites so that the mean between them can be brought out.[36]

Bernard makes the parallel with Gregory's *Regula* clear in
the first paragraphs of the *De Consideratione* itself. There, he
points out to the new Pope that he has under him all the
categories of people Gregory had listed: wise and foolish, slave
and free, rich and poor, men and women, old and young, clergy
and laity, righteous and wicked.[37] This meeting of opposites
takes place within the Pope himself.[38] That is why he must
'consider', that is, study what he finds within and direct
himself in two directions, towards both the inner, contemplative life, and the outward, practical life.

Gregory insists that the preacher must make his point 'more
by actions than words' and seek to provide footprints in which
others may follow him rather than to point out to them a way
ahead which he has not yet himself travelled;[39] Bernard has
detailed advice to give on the practical aspects of his pastor's

[34] Letter 42 v. 9; LTR VII. 114. 22.
[35] Letter 42. LTR VII. 127. 25.
[36] *Regula Pastoralis* II. i, *PL* 77. 50–2.
[37] *Csi* I. v. 6, LTR III. 400. 10; cf. *PL* 77. 50–2. 'Omnes pariter participant te.'
[38] LTR III. 393. 6–7, Preface. 'Certatim illi contraria imperare contendunt.'
[39] *Reg. Past.* III. xl, *PL* 77. 124–6.

responsibilities. The Pope is to preside with care over his household,[40] to keep the clergy in order,[41] to be firm with prelates who are unwilling to submit themselves to his authority.[42] He is to choose his advisers and assistants for the right qualities.[43] He is to take special note of the difficulties presented by the behaviour of the Roman people, who have been renowned in every age for their arrogance and obstinacy.[44] Among the laity no one is likely to give him so much trouble as the ambitious advocate, anxious to press his case to the court of highest appeal, so as to make himself famous. Bernard want the Pope to have a reputation for taking note of cases where the poor and oppressed are in danger, but not to hear every appeal made to him. He is not to encourage appeals but to tolerate them.[45] Bernard adds a number of specific examples.[46]

Bernard chose the word *consideratio* to describe the reflective process by which the Pope is to make sense of his paradoxical position, no doubt because that is Gregory's word for the introspective inspection his 'pastor' is to give himself daily. The 'consideration of his own weakness' will, he is confident, keep the pastor humble and attentive to his own failings.[47]

In his chapters on the life the pastor should live Gregory emphasizes first the importance of purity of thought[48] (*cogitatio*). He speaks of the need for the pastor to bring everything which happens *apud seipsum*, before his very self, of the circumspection of mind of the good Christian.[49] Developing these ideas, Bernard tells us more explicitly what he means by *consideratio*. It is, he says, a mental activity, and its effect is

---

[40] *Csi* IV. vi. 17.
[41] *Csi* IV. ii. 2.
[42] *Csi* III. iv. 14.
[43] *Csi* IV. iv. 9.
[44] *Csi* IV. ii. 2.
[45] *Csi* III. ii. 6–9 and I. xiv.
[46] *Csi* IV. v. 13.
[47] *Regula Pastoralis* I. i, *PL* 77. 13A. J. Leclercq notices the term *consideratio* in the *Regula Pastoralis* in 'Bernard et ses modèles' *Recueil d'études sur S. Bernard et ses écrits* (Rome 1969), III. 99.
[48] *Reg. Past.* II. i–ii, *PL* 77. 26–8.
[49] *PL* 77. 123–6.

indeed to purify. It governs the feelings, directs the actions, corrects excesses, makes a man's life sound and orderly, and encourages him to behave well. It gives him knowledge of both human and divine things. It also puts things in order. It sorts out confusion, brings together random thoughts, searches out the truth, distinguishes truth from falsehood. It decides what action is to be taken, and afterwards it examines what has been done. In its vigilance it ensures that nothing remains in the mind either uncorrected or requiring correction.[50]

This catalogue of its activities is summed up in Book II, under three heads. *Consideratio* is that true and certain intuition of the mind concerning anything, or the apprehension of the truth beyond doubt. It is an intensive thinking directed towards finding something out. It is a concentration of the mind upon finding the truth.[51] It is clearly a thinking activity, narrower and humbler than true contemplation, because the objects of its enquiry are human activities and its sphere of operation a human mind.

This *consideratio* remains the subject of Bernard's treatise throughout the first four books, as he considers the Pope's relations with himself and with those beneath and around him in the world. In Book V he turns to contemplation, gazing upwards at what is beyond man's mind, so as to complete Eugenius' education as Pope.

III. FAITH AND CERTAINTY

As he looks upwards to the things above man and his world, in Book V of the *De Consideratione*, Bernard's gaze comes to rest upon the heavenly spirits. He feels it a legitimate curiosity which makes him want to know something about them. Scripture gives some indication of the names of the angelic orders (angels, archangels, cherubim, seraphim), and it is inconceivable that God should reveal these names unless he means them to be instructive.[1]

---

[50] *Csi* I. vii, LTR III. 403. 13.
[51] *Csi* II. ii. 5, LTR III. 414. 5–8. 'Verus certusque intuitus animi de quacumque re, sive apprehensio veri non dubia; intensa ad vestigandum cogitatio; intensio animi vestigantis rerum.'
[1] *Csi* I. iv. 8, LTR III. 472. 13–13.

This leads Bernard to reflect upon the various ways in which it is possible for man to learn of things higher than himself. Some of what he knows is obtained by reading, and held to be true by faith. On other matters we must be content with opinion (we do not know whether the angels have bodies of any sort, or where they come from).[2] Or again, we may know by direct understanding (where the knowledge in question is self-evident). In that way we know that the angels must possess those properties of an intellectual kind which belong to rational beings.

Clearly it is best to be certain. Opinion is unsatisfactory. Bernard believes that faith can bring men to a certainty as great as that which they find in self-evident truths. He would certainly wish to avoid any classification of matters of faith with matters of opinion. (That would make the likelihood of angels having bodies, which is a matter of opinion, seem no different from the likelihood of there being orders of cherubim and seraphim. The latter is a matter of faith, because the Bible tells us that it is so, and there should be no room for opinion about it.)

The uncertainty of matters of opinion had always been repugnant to Bernard in dealing with theological topics, where all should be secure. When he read in William of St. Thierry's list of Abelard's false teachings that Abelard had defined faith as an *aestimatio*,[3] he was instantly alert to the implications of two sorts which the word appeared to carry. First, a man's *aestimatio* is his private judgement; it is what he personally thinks. That, says Bernard, is to reduce the mysteries of the faith to a level where each person may think as he pleases about them, and describe them as he will; and it is also to imply that the mysteries of the faith remain uncertain, that opinions about them may change, when, on the contrary, they rest upon a solid and unshakable foundation of truth. If faith is subject to change, we can have no grounds for hope, and in any case, there is no reason to take so low a view of faith. Miracles and revelations from above confirm and support us in our belief; there are abundant and infallible proofs which ought to

[2] LTR III. 472. 3–6. 'Haec . . . legendo comperimus, fide tenemus.'
[3] Letter 190. iv. 9, LTR VIII. 20. 1.

make us certain. In Hebrews II: 1 faith is described as the 'substance' of things hoped for, not a shifting shadow.

Bernard returns to the subject in the fifth book of his *De Consideratione*, with a renewed anxiety to emphasize the importance of fixity and security in the definition of faith. *Confusio* is to be avoided at all costs, or faith begins to look like uncertainty and *opinio*, and that which is *firmum* and *fixum* is called into question again.[4] That is exactly the offence of which William of St. Thierry accuses Abelard: that he has reopened old questions, long since settled.[5]

Bernard came to look upon faith and opinion not merely as describing degrees of certainty, but even as opposing positions. If opinion makes an assertion it overreaches itself, he says, but if faith fails to make an assertion, it is not truly faith.[6]

Bernard sets out definitions of faith, opinion, and the *intellectus* or 'understanding' which he places between them as an intermediate stage. Faith is a voluntary and certain foretaste of a truth which has not yet been made obvious. *Intellectus* is a 'certain and clear knowledge' of what is invisible. Opinion is merely to hold something true which one does not know to be false.[7]

He brings out clearly in his discussion the way in which men err in placing their state of mind in the wrong category, thinking their 'opinion' to be 'understanding', or their 'understanding' 'opinion'. Both faith and *intellectus* can be said to involve knowledge (*notitia*), but, like the mathematical knowledge of Boethius' *De Trinitate*, intellectual knowledge lacks the penetration of divine truth which is the supreme mode and end of human knowledge. Only faith provides access by certainty to things beyond intellectual knowledge. If mere understanding tries to look on God it is an intruder (*reputatur effractor, scrutator maiestatis*). It is simply not equipped to see the *involucrum*, the mystery of the ultimate truth.[8]

---

[4] *Csi.* I. iii. 6, LTR III. 470–1.
[5] See p. 150 ff.
[6] *Csi* V. iii. 6, LTR III. 470. 25–471. 1.
[7] *Csi* V. iii. 6, LTR III. 470–1. 'Fides est voluntaria quaedam et certa prelibatio necdum propalatae veritatis. Intellectus [est] certa et manifesta notitia; opinio est quasi pro vero habere aliquid, quod falsum esse nescias.'
[8] Ibid.

In calling faith an *aestimatio* then, Abelard has not only stripped it of its certainty, but thoroughly confused the spheres of human knowledge of God. He has brought the highest mode of knowledge, faith, down to the level of the lowest, opinion.

Whether or not Bernard's reading of Abelard's intention renders the word *aestimatio* as Abelard himself would have rendered it, it shows where Bernard's own preoccupation lay: with the mystery of divine truth, and with the mystery of the faith which is able through contemplation, to penetrate confidently beyond the reach of the ordinary bounds of human thought.

Contemplation thus envisaged brings us once more to the question of Bernard's mysticism. In one of the last of his sermons on the Song of Songs he describes his own experience of the Word's sometimes coming to him and entering into him, unheralded, without Bernard's being aware of his arrival, and leaving him again in the same way. The Word, the Bridegroom, works within him at such times, so that he is aware of his presence (*intellexi praesentiam eius*). The vices are put to flight and Bernard feels himself cleansed and strengthened.[9] This is a direct experience of God within him. Nothing can be more certain, and yet nothing is more elusive. When the Word leaves him he longs for his return in an agony of desire.[10] He sets his mind upon him in contemplation and sometimes, for an instant, he knows him again in an ecstasy in which faith becomes a face to face knowledge.[11] It seems at the time that Bernard himself has become nothing, emptied out into God.[12] That is an impression only, brought about by the 'likeness' to God which is restored to him at such moments as though he were not a son of sinful Adam who lost that likeness. It is not a true losing of himself, but simply a temporary freedom from the *proprium* which he came to think of as himself, the 'self' which separates him from God. When he is stripped of his *proprium* he is joined to God, 'and to be so joined is to be

---

[9] *SS* 74. II. 5–7, LTR II. 242–4. On the place of this experience in the ladder of Bernard's mystical climbing, see C. Butler, *Western Mysticism* (London, 1922, 3rd Ed. 1967), Chapter III.

[10] *SS* 74. II. 7, LTR II. 244. 7–8.

[11] *Dil.* x. 27, LTR III. 142. 15. 'Et hoc ipsum raptim atque unius vix momenti spatio, experiri donatum est.'

[12] *Dil.* x. 27, LTR III. 142. 17: 'a temetipso exinaniri, et paene annullari.'

deified'.[13] This brief experience attained by contemplation—
and not always, but only when the Word enters into his
mind—is a foretaste of the enjoyment of God the soul is to
have perpetually in heaven. It will no longer suffer the
impediment of self, but it will remain, paradoxically, entirely
itself, a separate created substance, able consciously to enjoy
the bliss it experiences.[14] That is the end of the contemplative
exercises of this life, and that is the kind of certainty which
faith brings now, however imperfectly.

Bernard's resort to the Anselmian principle that God is that
than which nothing greater can be thought, is entirely in
accordance with this view of faith as something at once certain
and involving a mystery which cannot be resolved this side of
heaven. Anselm's definition of God says nothing about him
except that he lies at the ultimate boundary of human thought,
and yet, having said that, it says everything about him for it is
from the heights of his divinity that we must reason if we are
to learn anything about him at all. In Letter 190, Bernard applies
Anselm's principle to Abelard's teaching of the Trinity.
Abelard throws doubt upon the unity of the Trinity by his
argument that the Father is supreme power, and the Son and
Holy Spirit somehow less power. Whatever God is, he is
undoubtedly that than which nothing greater can be thought,
says Bernard; if our arguments lead us to read anything
imperfect or insufficient into the Godhead, the Trinity begins
to look like something than which a greater *can* be conceived.
Therefore we must reassess our picture of the Trinity and
remove from it the implied taint of insufficiency or imperfec-
tion. That which is a whole is surely greater than that which
consists of parts. If we think of God, as far as we are able, as a
Divine Majesty having no separation or division within him
(for these would be imperfections or deficiencies), then we are
thinking of him properly as that than which nothing greater
can be thought. Abelard's image of the Son as like a seal made
from the brass which stands for the Father implies a difference

---

[13] *Dil.* x. 28, LTR III, 143. 15. 'sic affici deificari est.'
[14] See J. Burnaby, *Amor Dei*, The Hulsean Lectures, 1938 (London, 1938),
pp. 258–63.

between Father and Son which is quite unacceptable in the light of Anselm's definition of God.[15]

This, then, is Bernard's touchstone. We must be confident, and yet humble in the face of divine truth; sure that we know and yet aware how much we cannot know; ready to give a reason for our beliefs, and yet careful not to over-rationalize. The spirit of the enquiry of faith is that in which William of St. Thierry writes in his *Enigma*. He puts together from the Fathers everything he wants to know 'concerning the Lord my God'. He is able, in simple faith, and without 'tormenting questions' and 'noisy arguments' and the subtleties of sophistry, to see to the essence of the matter. Whatever it is that the Father is, the Son is, too, and the Holy Spirit. In their being, and all that goes with it, they are one.[16] In contemplating this truth of faith he is filled with neither puzzlement nor curiosity. He says that he does not seek what cannot be known in this life. He does not attempt to bring down to the level of his understanding (*intellectus*) the way in which the Trinity can be a unity. Christ himself, and the apostles and the prophets of old taught that this is the nature of God. They did not add philosophical explanations.[17]

The Fathers were obliged to add something in the way of explanation when heresies began to arise in the Church. That is how words like 'relation' and *homoousion* were invented or applied to the Trinity. This forced 'explication' of the mystery made it necessary to review the use of language in theology.[18] The Fathers decided, says William, to allow the use of the verb in the plural in talking of God, except for the names of the individual Persons, which would take a singular verb, but they did not mean to imply that there are parts of the Trinity which make up the whole.[19] All their work in this direction was done in a reluctant way; they were concerned only to say what must be said without giving offence to the faithful.[20] The patristic vocabulary, like the divine names themselves, are simply a

---

[15] Letter 190. ii. 4, LTR VIII. ii.4.
[16] *Aenigma* 24.
[17] *Aenigma* 25.
[18] *Aenigma* 25.
[19] *Aenigma* 32.
[20] *Aenigma* 33.

means to an end. They enable men to talk about God, and just
as in the forming of a word, letters come together into
syllables, syllables into words, and words, working together
with the will of the person who puts them together, produce an
understanding of faith in the heart of the believer,[21] so we form
our idea of God with the aid of words and names, but faith
needs the minimum of assistance in this way—nothing beyond
the words of Scripture. Only in combating heresy need the
Christian go further.

[21] *Aenigma* 40.

Conclusion

'At least from now on be better-instructed, and for the time that is left, live the life of a wise man, which is a meditation upon death.'[1] Bernard ended his life in a paradox, as he had lived it. The house he had founded and which had flourished so bravely in spite of its initial difficulties was again short of money; Bernard had inevitably neglected its administration in recent years because he had been so busy in the world; his trusted secretary Nicholas had fled; many of his old friends and protectors were dead; Eugenius, the first Cistercian Pope, died in 1153; Rainard, abbot of Clairvaux, in 1150; Suger, abbot of St. Denis in 1151; Count Thibaud of Champagne in 1152. Bernard himself was tired and ill and upset by the outcome of the Second Crusade which represented the greatest failure of his life, put a positive construction upon it though he might.

Yet his last years saw the completion of the *De Consideratione* with its heavenward-directed last book, and the great series of Sermons on the Song of Songs was mounting to a climax although it remained unfinished. If these works represent Bernard's *meditatio mortis* they are rich affirmations of all that he had preached throughout his life about the larger life to come.

We have seen Bernard's duality in every department of his life: the attempt to be two men in one was not without its tensions, and they took their toll of him physically. Unlike Anselm, he did not genuinely dislike business and administration. He involved himself helter-skelter in the problems of the Church, with a nagging discomfort because such work took him away from Clairvaux; but he undoubtedly found it rewarding. We have seen how much he benefited from it intellectually. Bernard's talk was attractive and he found it easy to hold and sway an audience. The challenge of a world full of controversies gave an edge to his thought that it might otherwise have lacked.

---

[1] Rupert of Deutz, *De Meditatione Mortis*, Ch. I. *PL* 170. 357.

William of St. Thierry speaks powerfully in the *Vita Prima* of Bernard's fervent commitment from the moment of his decision to enter monastic life,[2] but Bernard himself recalls the difficulties of the early days in his fourteenth sermon on the Song of Songs. *In initio conversionis meae,* he recollects, he suffered from a coldness of heart. He was seeking to love Christ and he seemed to be incapable of feeling. There were times when the sweetness of spring swept through him and the snow and ice melted, but there were long periods of struggle in which he found himself in that intellectually and spiritually paradoxical state, an effortful apathy.[3]

Bernard came to enjoy paradoxes. He discovered them everywhere, in the writings of the Fathers, in Scripture itself, in the demands of daily life.[4] He held them up to his listeners as jewels sparkling with divine mystery. The cause of our loving God is the object of our love, he explains in the *De Diligendo Deo: Causa diligendi Deum, Deus est.* The manner in which we should love him is to love him without measuring the manner: *modus, sine modo diligere.*[5] He unravelled some of his paradoxes, so as to show that the contradiction they contained was apparent, not real. 'As to what you ask about that contrariety which seems to be present in those two sayings of Paul, where he says, on the one hand that we keep company with God in heaven and on the other that we wander in exile from the Lord as long as we are in the body'[6] he writes in his treatise the apparent contradiction lies in the impossibility of the soul being simultaneously in God's presence in heaven and wandering far from him in exile. The answer is given in Paul's own words, Bernard explains. 'We know in part and we prophesy in part.'[7]

Bernard's treatises rest upon a series of grand paradoxes, within which he explores a multitude of smaller ones. It is the

---

[2] *VP* I. vi. 28–30, *PL* 185. 242–5.

[3] *SS* 14. 6.

[4] See my article, ' "The Secure Technican": Varieties of Paradox in the Writings of St. Anselm', *Vivarium* xiii (1975) 1–21.

[5] LTR III. 119. 18.

[6] *Pre* xx. 59, LTR III. 291. 24, 'Conversatio nostra in caelis est. Philippians 3. 20 and Quamdiu sumus in corpore, peregrinamur a Domino.' 2 Cor. 5: 6.

[7] LTR III. 292. 1–2.

paradox of Benedict's Rule, he suggests in *On Precept and Dispensation*, a Rule which is put forward for everyone, but imposed on no one, that if it is closely observed it benefits a man, but if he does not observe it, it does not constitute a stumbling-block to him.[8] Bernard's first treatise, the *De Gradibus Humilitatis*, takes the form of a paradoxical jest. The full title of the work is *On the Steps of Humility and Pride* (*De Gradibus Humilitatis et Superbiae*). In fact, Bernard deals only with the *gradus* of pride, and at the point where he might be expected to turn to the steps of humility, he brings the treatise abruptly to an end. 'Perhaps you are saying, Brother Godfrey', he concludes, 'that I have done something other than you asked, and than I myself promised, when I seem to have described the steps of pride instead of the steps of humility. I reply to that "I can teach only what I have learned. I did not think it appropriate for me to describe the steps up, I who knew more of descending than of ascending".'[9] Bernard claims that he has really done what Godfrey asked after all. 'If you look closely, perhaps the path of ascent is to be found'. 'If you met a man on your way to Rome, who was coming away from there, and you asked him the way, what better way could he show you than the way he had come?' he asks.[10] The *De Gratia et Libero Arbitrio* attempts to resolve the paradox of human free will confronted with divine grace. The treatise for the Templars resolves the paradox of the soldier-monk's position. In the *Apologia* Bernard is forced to a number of paradoxical contrivances in order to carry out the wishes of William of St. Thierry, who wanted him at the same time to demonstrate that the Cistercians are not 'slandering the order of Cluny' and spreading malicious tales abroad, and 'having done just this, to turn round and condemn their excesses in food and clothing and other areas'.[11] Bernard ends the treatise with an elegant attempt to show that what he has said is not a matter of *detractio*, but of *attractio*.[12]

---

[8] LTR III. 255. 13–15, *Pre* I. 2. 'Prodest, si devote suscipitur et tenetur; non tamen, si non suscipitur, obest.'

[9] LTR III. 59. 2–3.

[10] LTR III. 59. 3–5.

[11] Letter 84 bis.

[12] LTR III. 108. 11–5, *Apo* xii. 31.

The range of types of contradiction, contrariety, antithesis and paradox here is enormous, but Bernard's response to them is consistent. They do not alarm him. He is confident in his power to use them to bring a point home to the reader with the vividness only amazement can produce. Whether he reveals a solution, so that the paradox disappears, or presents the astonishing power of the divine to make contradictories true, the result is the same. At the end of the century, the *doctor universalis*, Alan of Lille, who died a Cistercian, described the rule-breaking ways of Holy Scripture in the preface to his dictionary of theological terms. The language of the Bible, he shows, is full of defiances of the laws of grammar and dialectic and rhetoric; they are simply inadequate to convey the profundities of divine truth.[13] In a poem on the Incarnation and the Seven Liberal Arts, his refrain is: *stupet omnis regula*.[14] Even the rules are amazed.

In the same poem, Alan speaks of the Word of God, Christ himself, as the *copula* which links the disparate parts of every proposition.[15] Bernard, too, speaks of the *salubris copula*, in his *De Consideratione*.[16] He habitually looks for the mean which lies between the apparently opposing poles of the antithesis or contradiction. To keep to the mean or *modus* is a virtuous act: 'What is more characteristic of justice than the mean?' Bernard asks: *Quid tam iustitiae quam modus?* In the mean lies temperance, too.[17]

This method of tracing a middle way in resolving paradoxes depends for its effectiveness upon the assumption that the two halves of the paradox are in a harmonious balance. Bernard looks at the 'complex' of the virtues in this light in the *De Consideratione*. He describes how one imposes a check upon another (*alteram pendere ex altera*), temperance moderating justice, and so on,[18] so that the man who has all the virtues reconciles their opposing extremes in himself. This seems to Bernard a natural and proper state of things, the design of the

---

[13] *PL* 210. 687–8.
[14] *PL* 210. 577–80.
[15] Ibid.
[16] LTR III. 426. 10–12, *Csi* II. ix. 8.
[17] LTR III. 406. 15 and 22, *Csi* I. viii. 8.
[18] LTR III. 404. 10–13, viii. 9.

God who is able to make oppositions one, who has put challenging paradoxes everywhere for his faithful people to wonder at and to try to live out in their own lives. The monk's duty is to go apart *in otio*, but there is no place for such leisure, when earnest care ought to urge on every Christian to action.[19] What is expected of the individual is not a choice between the two, but an attempt to meet both imperatives. He must learn to occupy the place between.

Just as in the case of the virtues, justice does not become less just by being modified by temperance, and temperance does not become less moderate by being modified by justice, so the monk's contemplative life is not diminished by being also a life of active concern for the welfare of the Church. The Pope's high place is not brought lower by his realization that he is a mere man, naked from his mother's womb. His *plenitudo potestatis* remains a fullness of power, although he himself has no power over his own actions. Bernard's 'mean' is not simply a place between two extremes. It is a place where a man may stand in the middle of a paradox, and be himself a *copula*, linking the two halves, reconciling the irreconcilable, as Christ did in uniting God and man in himself.[20]

When Eugenius wrote to the Chapter at Clairvaux, Bernard was delighted with him, because he had sent such a good letter, expressing exactly the mean he wanted to see. 'The voice of the turtle-dove has been heard in our Chapter', he says. Eugenius' letter breathes the spirit of life. The brothers who hunger after righteousness are fed; those who hunger less are made ashamed of their inadequacy; those who do not hunger at all are thrown into confusion.[21] The zeal which it most delights Bernard to find in Eugenius is the zeal of the monk for humility, that *inclinata maiestas* and *erecta humilitas* which are so perfectly balanced in his letter.

This, then, is the sum of Bernard's achievement as a thinker. He resolved for himself the paradoxes of his chosen life as a monk and the duties which were thrust upon him as a result of his relentless activities on behalf of the Church. It is a mean without mediocrity, which he seeks, a mean in which the

---

[19] LTR III. 417. 20–1, *Csi* II. vi. 10.
[20] LTR III. 425. 21–2, *Csi* II. ix. 17.
[21] LTR III. 424. 8–10 and p. 422–3, *Csi* II. viii. 16 and II. vii. 14.

extremes remain fully distinct and as opposite as ever. Action and contemplation are to be one, and yet two different ways of life. For his readers and listeners he pointed to a mode of thought which made it possible to live in an age of expansion and intellectual curiosity and at the same time to be a monk, and an austere one.[22]

A heightened sense of danger influenced Bernard's response to the threats to the Church he perceived in contemporary events. 'Now dangerous times do not press, but thrust themselves upon us': *tempora periculosa non instant iam, sed exstant*, he insists in the *De Consideratione*.[23] *Fraus et circumventio, et violentia, invaluere super terram*. Violence and trickery are rife upon the earth. This sense that he lived in a time of extremes was perhaps necessary to Bernard, if he was to maintain the high level of passionate commitment he first brought to the monastic life. His immediate and wholehearted response to the Church's needs was all of a piece with the fierceness of his concentration upon God in contemplation. Bernard could not reconcile himself to the sensation of apathy, the chill he felt in his heart as a novice. We hear no more of that in later years.

Bernard's is not an intellectual achievement in the abstract. He lived out his paradoxes. Nevertheless, it is an achievement of mental dexterity and a considerable one. No other writer of the age achieved anything like it, for no other writer lived so intense a life of monastic commitment and was at the same time so much in the world. No Paris master faced circumstances like Bernard's. 'What have the holy Apostles taught us.' he asks. Not the art of fishing nor tent-making or anything of this kind; not how to read Plato, nor to deal in the subtleties of Aristotle, not to be always learning, and never come to the knowledge of the truth. They taught me how to live.' That is Bernard's life of the mind.

---

[22] A paradox pointed out by E. Gilson, *The Mystical Theology of St. Bernard*, tr. A. H. C. Downes (London, 1940), p. 1.

[23] LTR III. 408. 3–5, *Csi* I. x. 13.

Appendix: Peter the Venerable's Missionary Zeal

Peter the Venerable went to a good deal of trouble to find out about Muslim beliefs and teachings. He went to Spain in 1142–3 in response to an invitation from Alfonso VII of Leon-Castile.[1] There was business which both were anxious to get done: Alfonso wanted the support of the Cluniac Order for his own candidate in the disputed election to the archbishopric of Compostela; Peter wanted to collect the sum due annually to Cluny under a grant of Alfonso VI.[2] Peter could expect, too, to visit a number of Cluniac houses on his journey[3] and the idea of making a pilgrimage to Compostela would naturally suggest itself. But the most important fruit of his journey, the translation of the Koran and the collection of texts needed by Latin-speaking Christian scholars if they were to understand the exact nature of the threat posed by Islam, was perhaps an unexpected one. Whether Peter had planned this work in detail, or had only a notion of it, or perhaps hit upon the scheme as a result of his journey, is not easy to determine.[4] There can be little doubt that the journey to Spain roused Peter to a fervour he had not felt before: 'I burned as I thought about it', he says, 'I was indignant that the Latins should be ignorant of the cause of such perdition, and that that ignorance could not rouse them to resistance. For no one could reply, since no one grasped the problem.'[5]

Peter's zeal did not issue, as that of Bernard often did, in a

---

[1] 'Recueil des chartes de l'abbaye de Cluny', ed. A. Bernard and A. Bruel (Paris 1876–1903), V. 423–6.

[2] C. J. Bishko, 'Peter the Venerable's Journey to Spain', *Studia Anselmiana* xl (Rome, 1956), 163–75, p. 164. I have drawn upon this article in what immediately follows.

[3] *Visitatio locorum nostrorum*. For Peter's own account of his journeyings, see Letters 111 and 106 in Constable I, and Appendix F in Constable II, pp. 275–84.

[4] The point is discussed by Bishko, op. cit., p. 163–4. He makes the point that Peter's list of what he planned corresponds so closely with what was achieved that it seems likely to have been written in retrospect.

[5] *PL* 189. 671B–C.

multitude of letters and tirades, but in methodical plans to provide a working handbook for those who were to take up the campaign. His scheme was to inform himself and all educated Christians, to lay a solid groundwork of knowledge about the enemy and his beliefs.

He was, perhaps, to some extent at the mercy of chance in finding his translators, and in obtaining advice about the works which ought to be translated, although no doubt enquiries could be made. It seems that he stayed for a time at the first Cluniac house he would have come to on the road to Compostela, at Najera. It has been plausibly suggested that it was here that he met and discussed his plan with his team of translators: the Englishman Robert of Ketton, Hermann of Dalmatia, Master Peter of Toledo, and Mohammed, a Moor.[6] Whether they were invited to join him there, or merely happened to be passing by (from Toledo?) in their own search for texts is not clear. They probably travelled on with him for some distance after he left the monastery, perhaps beginning the translation work on the way, while it was possible to discuss it with Peter conveniently.[7] Indeed the project may have taken over Peter's time to such an extent that he never reached Compostela; there is no record of his having been there.

However Peter's team was brought together, it was a formidable one. Robert and Hermann were scholars whose primary interest lay in Arabic works of mathematics and philosophy, but their intellectual curiosity is likely to have made them ready helpers in Peter's project. Peter of Toledo may have had existing theological interests,[8] and the Moor Mohammed was on home ground. All four would have had something to contribute to the discussion. Discussion there evidently was. Peter of Poitiers[9] travelled with the abbot of

[6] Bishko, op. cit., p. 166, and see J. M. Lacarra, 'Una aparacion de ultra tumba en Estella', *Principe de Viana*, v (1944), 173–4.

[7] Bishko, p. 168.

[8] *PL* 189. 339, and see M. T. d'Alverny, 'Deux traductions latines du Coran au moyen âge', *AHDLMA*, xxii–xxiii (1947–8), and 'Pierre le Vénérable et la légende de Mahomet' in Cluny, *'Congrès scientifique'*, *Travaux du Congrès* (Dijon, 1950), 160–71. See s.v. d'Alverny, p. 233.

[9] Not the author of the *Sententiae* edited by P. S. Moore and M. Dulong (Notre Dame, Indiana, 1943).

Cluny and he worked with Peter of Toledo on his translation[10]; the Toledan knew Arabic better than Latin, and his Latin rendering was put together in an unpolished and muddled way: *impolite et confuse.*[11] Peter of Poitiers revised it, but there is every reason to suppose that all those involved talked over the work in detail as it progressed.

Peter the Venerable comments disparagingly upon the general idlenesss of contemporary Latin scholars in studying foreign languages, in terms which indicate that he did not count himself among them.[12] 'They know only their own language, in which they were born', he complains.[13] How much progress he himself made in Arabic it is hard to say, but even with the aid of his helpers, the completion of the translations was almost certainly a slow business. The Koran was finished by 1143[14] but the rest of the work required sustained effort perhaps for several years more.

Peter may have felt himself relatively new to the battle against Islam, but he was by no means new to polemic against unbelievers. His treatise against the followers of Peter of Bruys was written in the late 1130s or early 1140s,[15] and having addressed himself to the Saracens in the treatise which he based on his researches, he soon after addressed himself to the Jews, in a *Contra Judaeos* (including in it several quotations from the Islamic works he had had translated).

His tone to the Jews is rounder and more rousing than that in which he addresses the Saracens. He scolds them: 'How long, wretches, do you not believe in the truth? How long are you going to repudiate God? How long before your hearts of iron soften?'[16] The arguments of the treatise all turn on the blindness of the Jews in not perceiving what their very own

---

[10] J. Kritzeck, 'Peter the Venerable and the Toledan Collection', *Studia Anselmiana*, xl (Rome, 1956), 178.

[11] *PL* 189. 649C–D.

[12] *PL* 189. 671D, and cf. Kritzeck, 'The Toledan Collection', p. 178.

[13] Ibid., pp. 182–3.

[14] On the dating of the *Contra Petrobrusianos*, see Constable II. 285–8, Appendix G. The widest dates seem to be 1137–42, although one group of scholars favours the period before 1135.

[15] See G. Constable, 'Manuscripts of Works by Peter the Venerable', *Studia Anselmiana*, xl (Rome, 1956), 237–8.

[16] *PL* 189. 507.

Scriptures tell them: that Christ is the Son of God. 'Hear, then, Jews, and know from your Scriptures that Christ . . . is the Son of God.'[17] 'But after Christ, by the authority of your texts, has been proved the Son of God, and himself God, O Jews, perhaps you still stick to your customary dishonesty, and demand that his divinity be shown to you more clearly by other examples . . . ?'[18] Peter proceeds by eliminating alternatives—that Christ is the Son of God not merely by name (*vocaliter*), but in reality.[19] 'Read all the series of the Holy Scriptures again in order', he instructs, 'and you will scarcely find anywhere a similar usage of the name of any man. For Scripture is accustomed to say this of God alone, of the name of God alone.'[20] There is thus a use of contemporary expertise in the close analysis of grammatical usage, Scripture's *usus loquendi*, which makes Peter's account far more sophisticated than a mere marshalling of the Scriptures. The Jewish custom of concentrating upon the literal sense has a bearing here: Peter does not spend time on an appeal to the 'higher criticism' of the allegorical and tropological and moral senses; he addresses himself to the Jews on their own terms.

In attacking the Saracens, his approach is quite different. He writes a lengthy Prologue to explain how the translations came to be made, and to try to fill his Christian readers with a sense of the importance of the task of winning over the Saracens. He is writing about something unfamiliar to himself, and even more unfamiliar to the Christian party. The debate with the Jews is an old one, whose arguments are well known. The debate with Islam is unknown ground, and Peter maps it out a little uncertainly at first, feeling his way. He is sure that at least everyone must agree that it is profoundly troubling that Islam is so widespread (*valde dilatatus est*).[21] There may be some dispute as to whether its errors can strictly be called a heresy (Peter considers the word in its ancient usage and decides that it may) but in any case, whether it is a heresy or

[17] *PL* 189. 509.
[18] *PL* 189. 519.
[19] *PL* 189. 520A.
[20] *PL* 189. 535D.
[21] *PL* 189. 668D.

merely a delirium from which the Muslims are suffering, it is important that battle should be engaged against it.

The Prologue out of the way, Peter addresses himself directly to the Saracens, with the utmost gentleness, and very gingerly at first. 'It seems amazing, and perhaps it is, that I, a man far distant from you, speaking a different language, set apart by his profession . . . should write from the uttermost West to you in the East . . . and speak to those I have never seen, and perhaps never shall see. I approach you . . . not as our men tend to do, with arms, but with words, not by force, but by reason, not in hatred, but in love, such love as there ought to be between the worshippers of Christ and those turned away from Christ, such as existed between our apostles and the gentiles of the day, whom they invited to [accept] the law of Christ.'[22]

Peter is now in a difficulty. He must find common ground with the Muslims. With the Jews he has at least the Old Testament in common, but the Muslims accept only parts of the Scriptures. He appeals to that universal human duty to seek the truth in which he is sure the Muslims will be with him.[23] He tries to get them to accept not only part of the Bible, but the whole.[24] He examines their story of the loss of the original text, and the false reconstruction by Jews and Christians. What proof is there for this account, he asks?[25] For a moment his irritation shows as he confronts the absurdity of the Muslim position.[26] He apologizes smartly, with an acknowledgement of the limitations of his knowledge.[27] Then he finds his feet and begins at the beginning with the Muhammadan contention that Muhammad is a prophet. What is a prophet, he asks?[28] There follows a close definitional analysis.[29] Deprived of a solid base of agreed authority on which to argue about the interpretation of the text, Peter has turned to reasoning, not of an advanced technical kind, but

[22] *PL* 189. 669D–670B.
[23] *PL* 189. 673B–C.
[24] *PL* 189. 675–6.
[25] *PL* 189. 685A.
[26] *PL* 189. 687A–B.
[27] *PL* 189. 678.
[28] *PL* 189. 688A.
[29] *PL* 189. 701A.

such as might be expected to appeal to intelligent men who were not necessarily highly trained logicians.

Peter's approach, then, to both Jews and Muslims, is to try to find common ground for the discussion, to get on terms with them, to reassure them of his peaceful intention and his wish to do them good. Sometimes he is angry at their folly. He is holding reined in throughout a sense of indignation and a passionate desire to see them converted. This is not a meek or mild treatise, despite the tone Peter attempts to set.

On the doctrinal content of Islam, Peter provides a summary.[30] Here we can see the result of Peter's labours, and it is not unimpressive. He has brought the Muslim faith into a Christian perspective and put in order those errors which principally conflict with the Christian creed. The chief error of the Muslims is to deny the Trinity in Unity of the Deity, he says. They do so, not like the Jews, who hold to a straightforward monotheism, but by proposing a duality of the Divine Being and its Soul (*ipsam divinam essentiam et eius animam*). That, they say, is why God speaks in the first person plural at the beginning of the Koran. From this first misunderstanding much flows. The Muslims do not accept that Christ is the Son of the Father, for they say that there can be no fatherhood without conception. They regard Christ as a mere prophet. They believe that when the Jews wanted to kill him he slipped from their grasp and ascended to the stars (*ad astra*). There he lives now, in the flesh (*in carne*) in the presence of the Creator, until the coming of Antichrist. When Antichrist comes, Christ will kill him with the sword of his power (*gladio virtutis suae*) and convert the rest of the Jews to his law. The Christians, who have long lost his law and his Gospel, he will teach, and all Christians will become his disciples. Then at the sound of an archangel blowing a trumpet Christ himself will die, with all creatures, and then be resurrected and lead his own to judgement. God alone will judge. The prophets will act as intercessors and aids.[31] This amazing tale is presented *tout court* for Bernard's inspection with the letter Peter wrote to him

---

[30] This *Summula* (*PL* 189. 651–8) belongs with the letter Peter wrote to Bernard in 1143, telling him of his translation (Letter 111).
[31] *PL* 189. 651–2.

to try to persuade him to take up the campaign of preaching against Islam which Peter now feels to be so urgently necessary.[32]

When, disappointed of Bernard's help, Peter himself began the work, he produced the treatise we have been examining. He cannot have expected the Saracens themselves to read his diatribe. It is in Latin and as far as we know it was never translated. The language barrier which has prevented Christians from understanding Islam will surely work the other way, too, and prevent the Muslims from understanding Peter's arguments. The Prologue suggests that he meant to provide Christian missionaries with material and to suggest a method of approach to them by giving them a pattern in his treatise.

[32] V. Berry, 'Peter the Venerable and the Crusades', *Analecta Anselmiana* x1 (Rome, 1956), p. 145.

Select Bibliography

Sources

(With the exception of those printed in J. P. Migne, *Patrologia Latina*)

ABELARD, PETER, *Commentaria in Epistolam Pauli ad Romanos*, ed. M. Buytaert, *CCCM*, xi, 1969. *Theologia Christiana*, ed. M. Buytaert, *CCCM*, xii, 1969. *Dialogus inter Philosophum, Judaeum et Christianum*, ed. R. Thomas. Stuttgart, 1970.

AILRED OF RIEVAULX, *Opera Omnia*, ed. Hoste, *CCCM*, i, 1971.

ALANUS DE INSULIS, *Textes inédits*, ed. M. T. d'Alverny. Paris, 1965.

ALBERTUS AQUENSIS, *Historia Hierosolomytana, Recueil des historiens des Croisades; Historiens Occidentaux*, iv, Paris, 1879.

ANSELM OF CANTERBURY, *Opera Omnia*, ed. F. S. Schmitt. Rome/ Edinburgh 1938–68, 6 vols. *Memorials*, ed. R. W. Southern and F. S. Schmitt, London, 1969.

ANSELM OF HAVELBERG, *Dialogus*, ed. G. Salet. Paris, 1965.

BERNARD OF CLAIRVAUX, *Sancti Bernardi Opera*, ed. J. Leclercq, C. H. Talbot and H. Rochais. Rome, 1957–78, 8 vols.

BOETHIUS, *Theological Tractates*, ed. H. F. Stewart, E. K. Rand, and S. J. Tester. London, 1973.

CASSIODORUS, *Institutiones*, ed. R. A. B. Mynors. Oxford, 1939.

CÎTEAUX, EARLY TEXTS, 'Les plus anciens textes de Cîteaux', *Cîteaux*, ii, 1974.

EADMER, *Vita Anselmi*, ed. R. W. Southern. Oxford, 1962.

EKKEHARD, *Hierosolomyta*, ed. H. Hagenmeyer. Tübingen, 1877.

ERIUGENA, JOHANNES SCOTUS, *De Praedestinatione*, ed. G. Madec, *CCCM*, 1, 1978.

GILBERT CRISPIN, *Disputatio inter Judaeum et Christianum*, ed. B. Blumenkranz, Antwerp, 1956, and A. Abulafia. London, 1983.

GILBERT OF POITIERS, *Commentaries on Boethius*, ed. N. M. Häring. Toronto, 1966.

GUIBERT OF NOGENT, *De Vita Sua*, ed. G. Bourgin. Paris, 1905.

HEBREW CHRONICLES, *The Jews and the Crusaders: the Hebrew Chronicles of the First and Second Crusades*, ed. and tr. S. Eidelberg. Wisconsin, 1977.

HERMANNUS JUDAEUS, *De Conversione Sua*, ed. G. Niemeyer, *MGH*, 1963.

ISIDORE, *Etymologiae*, ed. W. M. Lindsay. Oxford, 1911. 2 vols.

JOHN OF SALISBURY, *Historia Pontificalis*, ed. M. Chibnall. London, 1956.

Libellus de Diversis Ordinibus, ed. G. Constable and G. Smith. Oxford, 1972.

Logica Modernorum, ed. L. M. de Rijk. Assen, 1967. 2 vols.

ODO OF DEUIL, *De Profectione Ludovici VII in Orientem*, ed. and tr. V. G. Berry. Columbia, 1948.

ORDERIC VITALIS, *Historia Ecclesiastica*, ed. M. Chibnall. Oxford, 1969–80. 6 vols.

ORIGEN, *Origenes Werke*, VI, ed. H. Baehrens, Leipzig, 1920.

OTTO OF FREISING, *Gesta Friderici*, ed. F. J. Schmalc. Darmstadt, 1965.

PETRUS VENERABILIS, *Sermones Tres*, R. *Bén.*, lxiv, 1954, 232–54. *The Letters of Peter the Venerable*, ed. G. Constable. Harvard, 1967. *Contra Petrobrusianos*, ed. J. Fearns, *CCCM*, x, 1968.

PS. HERMES TRISMEGISTOS, *Asclepius*, ed. P. Thomas, in *Apulei Opera*, iii. Leipzig, 1908.

Rhetorica ad Herennium, ed. H. Caplan. London, 1954.

ROBERT OF MELUN, *Questiones*, ed. R. Martin, *Spicilegium Sacrum Lovaniense*, xiii, 1932.

RUPERT OF DEUTZ, *Commentaria in Evangelium S. Johannis*, ed. R. Haacke, *CCCM*, 9, 1969.

Sentences of the School of Anselm of Laon, ed. O. Lottin, *Psychologie et morale aux xiie et xiiie siècles*, v. Gembloux, 1959.

SIMON OF TOURNAI, *Disputationes*, ed. J. Warichez, *Spicilegium Sacrum Lovaniense*, xii, 1932.

THIERRY OF CHARTRES, *Commentaries on Boethius*, ed. N. M. Häring. Toronto, 1971.

WILLIAM OF ST. THIERRY, *The Golden Letter*, ed. R. Thomas, *Pain de Cîteaux*, xxxiii–iv. Chamberand, 1968.

WILLIAM OF TYRE, *Recueil des Historiens des Croisades, Historiens Occidentaux*, I, i. Paris, 1844.

Secondary Literature

BACKMUND, N., *Die mittelalterlichen Geschichtsschreiber des Prämonstratenserordens, Bibl. analectorum Praemonstratensium*, 10. Averbode, 1972.

BALDWIN, J. W., *Masters, Princes and Merchants*. Princeton, 1970. 2 vols.

BARBER, M., 'The Origins of the Order of the Temple', *Studia Monastica*, xii, 1970, 219–20.

BECKER, G., *Catalogi Bibliothecarum Antiqui*. Bonn, 1885.

BERNARD, J. H., tr. *Guide-Book to Palestine, Palestine Pilgrims Text Society*, vi. London, 1894.

BERRY, V., 'Peter the Venerable and the Crusades', *Studia Anselmiana*, xl, Rome, 1956.

BERTOLA, E., *San Bernardo e la teologia speculativa*, Padua, 1959.

BESSUBRÉ, M., *Bibliographie de l'ordre des Templiers*, 1978.

BISHKO, C. J., 'Peter the Venerable's Journey to Spain', *Studia Anselmiana*, xl, Rome, 1956.

BREDERO, H., 'Études sur la Vita Prima de S. Bernard', I. *An. Cist.*, 17. 1961. 3–72; II, *An. Cist.*, 17, 1961, 215–60; III, *An. Cist.*, 18. 1962, 3–59.

—— 'The Canonisation of St. Bernard', in *St. Bernard of Clairvaux*, ed. B. Pennington, *CS*, xxviii, 1977, 63–100. Much of Bredero's work in this area is brought together in *Bernard von Clairvaux im Widerstreit der Historie.* Wiesbaden, 1966.

——'Une controverse sur Cluny au xiie siècle', *Revue d'histoire ecclésiastique,* 1981, 48–72.

BROOKE, O., 'The Speculative Development of the Trinitarian Theology of William of St. Thierry in the *Aenigma Fidei' RTAM,* xxvii, 1961.

BROOKE, R. *The Coming of the Friars.* London, 1975.

BROWNLOW, W. R. B., tr., *An Account of the Pilgrimage of Saewulf to Jerusalem and the Holy Land, in the Years 1102 and 1103, Palestine Pilgrims Text Society,* iv. London, 1872.

BRUNDAGE, J. A., 'A Transformed Angel: the Problem of the Crusading Monk', *Studies in Mediaeval Cistercian History.* Spencer, Mass., 1971.

BUTLER, C., *Western Mysticism,* 2nd ed. London, 1926.

CHÂTILLON, F., *'Regio Dissimilitudinis', Mélanges E. Podéchard* (Lyon, 1945), 85–102.

CONSTABLE, G., 'A Report of a Lost Sermon by St. Bernard on the failure of the second Crusade', *Studies in Mediaeval Cistercian History, Presented to J. F. O'Sullivan.* Spencer, Mass., 1971.

COWDREY, H. E. J., 'Abbot Pontius of Cluny', *Studi Gregoriani,* xi, 1978, 177–276.

COURCELLE, P., 'Témoins nouveaux de la région de dissemblance', *Bibliothèque d'École des Chartes,* cviii, 1960, 20–36.

CSANYI, D. A., 'Optima Pars', *Studia Monastica,* ii, 1960, 5–78.

D'ALVERNY, M. T., 'Deux traductions latins du Coran au moyen âge', *AHDLMA,* xxii–xxiii, 1947–8.

—— 'Pierre le Vénérable et la légende de Mahomet', in *Cluny: Congrès scientifique* (Dijon, 1950), 160–71.

DÉCHANET, J. M., *William of St. Thierry* (tr. R. Strachan), *CS,* xi, 1972.

DELEHAYE, P., *Les légendes hagiographiques.* Brussels, 1906.

DEREINE, C., 'Vie commune, règle de saint Augustin et chanoines réguliers au xii siècle', *Revue d'histoire ecclésiastique,* xli, 1946, 365–406.

ELSWIJK, H. C. VAN, *Gilbert Porreta, Spicilegium Sacrum Lovaniense,* xiii, 1966.

ERDMANN, C., *The Origin of the Idea of Crusade,* Stuttgart, 1935, and (tr. M. W. Baldwin and W. Goffart), Princeton, 1977.

EVANS, G. R., 'St. Anselm's Analogies', *Vivarium,* xiv, 1976, 81–93.

—— 'A Change of Mind in Some Scholars of the eleventh and early twelfth Century', *Studies in Church History,* xv, 1978, 27–38.

—— *Augustine on Evil.* Cambridge, 1982.

—— *Alan of Lille. The Frontier of Theology in the Later Twelfth Century.* Cambridge, 1983.

FARMER, D. H., 'William of Malmesbury's Commentary on Lamentations', *Studia Monastica,* iv, 1962, 309.

FITTING, E. H., *Summa Codicis des Irnerius.* Berlin, 1894.

FIRTZTHUM, M., *Die Christologie der Prämonstratenser im 12 Jahrhundert.* Marienbad, 1939.

GIBSON, M. T., *Lanfranc of Bec.* Oxford, 1978.

GILSON, E., *The Mystical Theology of St. Bernard* (tr. A. H. C. Downes). London, 1940.

—— 'Sub Umbris Arborum', *Mediaeval Studies*, xiv, 1952, 149–51.

GREEN, W. M., 'Mediaeval Recensions of St. Augustine', *Speculum*, 29, 1954, 531–4.

HALLIER, A., *The Monastic Theology of Ailred of Rievaulx* (tr. C. Heaney). Shannon, 1969.

HÄRING, N. M., 'The Porretans and the Greek Fathers', *Mediaeval Studies*, 24 (1962), 181–209.

—— 'The Writings against Gilbert of Poitiers by Geoffrey of Auxerre', *An. Cist.*, 22 (1966), 14–16.

JAMES, W., *Varieties of Religious Experience.* Edinburgh, 1901–2, repr. with an introduction by A. D. Nock, London, 1960.

KELLEY, C., *Meister Eckhart on divine knowledge.* New York and London, 1977.

KENNAN, E., 'Antithesis and Argument in the *De Consideratione*', in *Bernard of Clairvaux; Studies presented to Dom Jean Leclercq* (Washington, 1973), 91–109.

KRITZECK, P., 'Peter the Venerable and the Toledo Collection', *Studia Anselmiana*, xl, Rome, 1956.

—— *Peter the Venerable and Islam.* Princeton, 1964.

KNOWLES, D., *Great Historical Enterprises.* London, 1963.

—— *Cistercians and Cluniacs.* Oxford, 1955.

LADNER, G. B., *The Idea of Reform.* Cambridge, Mass., 1959.

LACKNER, B. K., 'The Liturgy of Early Cîteaux', *Studies in Mediaeval Cistercian History Presented to J. F. O'Sullivan*, CS, xiii, 1971.

LAMBERT, M. D., *Mediaeval Heresy.* London, 1977.

LANG, A. P., 'The Friendship between Peter the Venerable and Bernard of Clairvaux', *St. Bernard: Studies Presented to J. Leclercq.* Washington, 1973, 35–53.

LECLERCQ, J., 'Le commentaire de Gilbert de Stanford sur le Cantique des cantiques', *Studia Anselmiana*, xx, 1948, 205–30.

—— 'Études sur S. Bernard et le texte de ses écrits', *An. Cist.*, xviii, 1962.

—— 'Drogon et S. Bernard', *R. Bén.*, lxxiii, 1953, 116–31.

—— 'S. Bernard docteur', *Coll. Cist.*, xvi, 1954, 284–6.

—— 'Les sermons sur les Cantiques de S. Bernard', *R. Bén.*, lxvi, 1956, 63–91.

—— Études sur le vocabulaire monastique du moyen âge', *Studia Monastica*, xlviii, 1961.

—— 'Gebouin des Troyes et S. Bernard', *Revue des Sciences Philosophiques et théologiques*, xli, 1957, 632–40.

——*Recueil d'études sur S. Bernard.* Rome, 1962–9. 3 vols.

—— 'L'attitude spirituelle de S. Bernard devant la guerre', *Coll. Cist.*, xxxvi, 1974, 195–225.

—— 'Textes sur la vocation et la formation des moines au moyen âge', *Corona gratiarum Miscellanea . . . E. Dekkers*, II (Bruges/The Hague, 1975), 169–94.

LEFÈVRE, J. A., 'Que savons-nous du Cîteaux primitif?', *Revue d'histoire ecclésiastique*, 51, 1956.

LUBAC, H. DE, *Exégèse Médiévale*. Paris, 1959. 2 vols.

LUSCOMBE, D., *The School of Peter Abelard*. (Paris, 1967.) Cambridge, 1969.

MANSELLI, R., 'Il monacho Enrico e la sua eresia', *Bullettino dell' Istituto storico italiano per Il Medio Evo*, lxv, 1953, 1–63.

MERTON, T. et al., *Bernard de Clairvaux, Commission d'histoire de l'ordre de Cîteaux*. Paris, 1952.

MOHRMANN, C., *Études sur le latin des chrétiens*. Rome, 1961. 3 vols.

MOORE, R. I., *Origins of European Dissent*. London, 1977.

MORRIS, C., *The Discovery of the Individual*. London, 1970.

MURPHY, J. J., *Rhetoric in the Middle Ages*. California, 1974.

NIELSEN, L., 'On the doctrine of logic and language of Gilbert Porreta and his followers', *Cahiers de l'Institut du moyen-age grec et latin, Copenhague*, xvii, 1976.

NELSON, J., 'Society, Theodicy and the Origins of Heresy: towards a reassessment of the Mediaeval Evidence', *Studies in Church History*, ix, 1972.

O'BRIEN, R., 'Saint Aelred et la *lectio divina*', *Coll. Cist.*, xli, 1979, 281–93.

OHLY, F., *Hohelied-Studien*. Wiesbaden, 1958.

RICHÉ, P., 'Le Psautier, livre de lecture élémentaire', *Études mérovingiennes*, 1953.

ROCHAIS, H., 'Enquête sur les sermons divers et les sentences de S. Bernard', *An. Cist.*, xviii, 1962.

—— 'A Literary Journey: the New Edition of the Works of St. Bernard', in *Bernard of Clairvaux: Studies Presented to Dom J. Leclercq*. Washington, 1973.

RUNCIMAN, S., *The Crusades*. Cambridge, 1951–4. 3 vols.

SALTMAN, A., *Theobald, Archbishop of Canterbury*. London, 1956.

SIKES, J. G., *Peter Abailard*. Cambridge, 1932.

SMAIL, R. C., *Crusading Warfare*. Cambridge, 1956.

SMALLEY, B., *The Study of the Bible in the Middle Ages*, 2nd. ed. Oxford, 1952.

SOMMERFELDT, J. R. (ed.), *Cistercian Ideals and Reality*, CS, lx, 1978.

SOUTHERN, R. W., *St. Anselm and his Biographer*. Cambridge, 1963.

TOMASIC, T. M., 'William of St. Thierry against Peter Abelard: a dispute on the meaning of being a person', *An. Cist.*, xxviii, 1972.

VALVEKENS, J. B., 'Les actes de confraternité de 1142 et de 1153 entre Cîteaux et Prémontré', *Analecta Praemonstratensia*, xl, 1964.

VAN DEN EYNDE, D., *Essai sur la succession et la date des écrits de Hughes de Saint-Victor*. Rome, 1960.

WASSELYNCK, R., 'L'influence de l'exégèse de S. Grégoire le grand sur les commentaires bibliques médiévaux', *Recherches de théologie ancienne et médiévale*, xxxv, 1965, 183–92.

WEINGART, R. E., *The Logic of Divine Love*. Oxford, 1970.

WILMART, A., 'La legende de Ste Édith en prose et vers par le moine Goscelin', *Analecta Bollandiana*, lvi, 1938.

Index